VICTORY
THROUGH
ORGANIZATION

*Why the War for Talent Is Failing
Your Company and What You Can
Do About It*

Dave Ulrich

David Kryscynski

Wayne Brockbank

Mike Ulrich

New York   Chicago   San Francisco   Lisbon   Athens   London
Madrid   Mexico City   Milan   New Delhi   San Juan
Seoul   Singapore   Sydney   Toronto

1 2 3 4 5 6 7 8 9 0   LCR   21 20 19 18 17

ISBN: 978-1-259-83764-7
MHID: 1-259-83764-5

e-ISBN: 978-1-259-83765-4
e-MHID: 1-259-83765-3

Library of Congress Cataloging-in-Publication Data

Names: Ulrich, David, 1953- author.
Title: Victory through organization : why the war for talent is failing your
   company and what you can do about it / Dave Ulrich, David Kryscynski,
   Wayne Brockbank, and Mike Ulrich.
Description: New York : McGraw-Hill, [2017]
Identifiers: LCCN 2016055009 (print) | LCCN 2017005410 (ebook) | ISBN
   9781259837647 (alk. paper) | ISBN 1259837645 | ISBN 9781259837654 () |
   ISBN 1259837653
Subjects: LCSH: Personnel management. | Human capital—Management.
Classification: LCC HF5549 .U393 2017 (print) | LCC HF5549 (ebook) | DDC
   658.3—dc23
LC record available at https://na01.safelinks.protection.outlook.com

McGraw-Hill Education books are available at special quantity discounts to use as premiums and sales promotions or for use in corporate training programs. To contact a representative, please e-mail us at bulksales@mheducation.com.

The Human Resources Competency Study is the result of countless hours of work from many in the HR profession. We would like to dedicate this book to the sponsors and partners who made this work possible. In particular, we thank the Stephen M. Ross Executive Education Program at the University of Michigan and the RBL Group for financial sponsorship and administrative support of the study.

We also thank our 22 regional partners who diligently contributed to logic and adminis-tration of this round of the study. We are deeply indebted to them as listed below:

Partner Organization	Website
Asia Pacific Federation of Human Resource Management (APFHRM)	www.apfhrm.com
Australian Human Resources Institute (AHRI)	www.ahri.com.au
Bangladesh Society for Human Resources Management (BSHRM)	bshrmbd.com
Business Results Group (South Africa and African continent)	www.brg.co.za
Chartered Institute of Personnel Management of Nigeria	www.cipmnigeria.org
China Europe International Business School (CEIBS)	www.ceibs.edu
Conference Board of Canada (CBoC)	www.conferenceboard.ca
European Association for People Management (EAPM)	www.eapm.org
Hong Kong Institute of Human Resource Management (HKIHRM)	www.hkihrm.org
HR Norge (Norway and Scandanavia)	hrnorge.no
Human Resource Certification Institute (HRCI) (Primarily US and world wide HR certificants)	www.hric.org
Human Capital Leadership Institute (HCLI) (Primarily Asia)	www.hcli.org
IAE Business School (Argentina and all of Latin American)	www.iae.edu.ar
IPADE Business School (Mexico)	www.ipade.mx
ISE Business School (Brazil)	www.ise.org.br
Israeli Society for Human Resource Management (ISHRM)	www.ishrm.org.il
Japanese Management Association (JMA)	www.jma.or.jp
Lagos Business School (Nigeria)	www.lbs.edu.ng
National HRD Network (NHRDN) (India)	www.nationalhrd.org
Pro HR Talent Solutions (China)	www.prohr-intl.com
Sapir College (Israel)	www.sapir.ac.il
Solid Consulting Partners (Turkey)	www.solidtr.com

CONTENTS

PREFACE

We are observers, advocates, provocateurs, researchers, and agitators for the HR profession. For over 30 years, Wayne Brockbank and Dave Ulrich have studied, written about, and trained HR professionals at the Ross School at the University of Michigan and in their private consulting practice. Dave Kryscynski (DK) and Mike Ulrich have more recently received their PhDs in organization and HR science, bringing rigorous theory and research to the improvement of HR.

As seasoned and emerging HR promoters, we have come to share some assumptions about the state of HR today. The following six assumptions form much of the basis and context for this book:

1. *HR matters:* We firmly believe through personal experience and empirical data that HR matters to a business. Wayne's in-depth advisory work with leading global companies has shown that HR work today shapes business strategy and helps the business to deliver results. His current work on information and culture highlights some of the emerging ways for HR to deliver real value. Dave's recent work on leadership capital shows that quality of leadership impacts shareholder value, thus giving HR professionals a line of sight to market valuation of their work. DK and Mike's work shows the empirical impact of HR on desired firm outcomes.

2. *HR research is imperative:* We strongly believe in empirical and qualitative information. We see the recent push in HR for more analytics as a good sign as long as the analytics focus is on information that will improve the business. Too often HR analytics are about HR for HR, not HR for the business. DK and Mike bring exceptional rigor to the information that provides valid insight to how HR decisions impact business results. Academic studies on HR, human capital, and strategic HR are emerging in the HR, strategic, and organization literatures. These studies are helpful when they connect to HR phenomena and deliver insights with rigor. DK and Dave's paper on

the importance of timely and rigorous HR research won the Academy of Management Perspectives Best Article award in 2016.

3. *HR professionals are changing:* After having trained tens of thousands of HR professionals, we are coming to realize that progress is being made in quality of HR departments, professionals, and practices—albeit slower than we would hope. We continue to see the 20-60-20 distribution of HR professionals. Twenty percent are exceptional and deliver real value. We need to stay out of their way and learn from them. Twenty percent are laggards, not able or willing to use HR to drive business results. We need to not let them deter us. Sixty percent are open to learning and making progress toward more impactful HR. We are committed to these aspiring HR professionals who want to learn and make a difference.

4. *HR departments and practices are becoming more important:* We have worked on the transformation of HR departments and HR practices for many years. We have been advocates for HR structure matching the business structure and for HR practices offering integrated solutions to business problems. Just as HR departments combine individual HR professional competencies into a stronger HR function, we have also advocated that an organization's capability (or culture) is more important than the competencies of individuals.

5. *HR colleagues are incredibly gifted:* We have been privileged to work with outstanding HR colleagues in over 80 countries in the world. Some of these colleagues are among the 22 partner associations in the Human Resources Competency Study (HRCS) who have partnered with us before. Other colleagues are thought leaders whose insights continually inform us. We hope that as we absorb their work into ours, we give adequate credit and build on their insights and ideas.

6. *HR is a dynamic and innovative discipline:* We are continually amazed at the ever-changing twists in the HR profession. Over the 30 years of our research on HR competencies, we have seen many topics emerge that are now foundational parts of HR (e.g., business partner, strategic HR, HR strategy, HR transformation, HR value added). We continue to be excited about what's next for how HR adds value. We all were fortunate to participate in the HR

Certification Institute's (HRCI's) book *The Rise of HR* where thought leaders provoked and anticipated some emerging themes. We hope that we can continue to anticipate future trends and push boundaries. We often call this future focus "planting the grass" for what comes next.

With these six assumptions under our belts, we muddle forward. Some of our movement forward comes from intense consulting assignments where we are invited to solve previously unsolvable business problems through HR insights. Some of our learning comes from listening to thoughtful HR leaders wrestle with ways they can have more impact. Some of our insights come when we have to present to small and large groups on topics that stretch us to discover new insights. We try to combine these personal experiences into more rigorous research. Over the last 30 years, we have done seven rounds of the HRCS. This study has explored the competencies of HR professionals that drive individual and business performance. Doing empirical research requires asking the right questions, getting a great response rate and sample, and analyzing data to see trends.

In this seventh round, we hope we have asked some innovative questions about both competencies for HR professionals and activities for HR departments to be effective. In this present work, we have taken an important step forward from prior rounds of our research by examining both *individual* HR competencies and the practices of the HR *department* as a whole. In other words, we explore both how the individual contributes to performance as well as how the HR department as a unit contributes to performance.

We found that the organization has three to four times more impact than the individual (i.e., the whole is more than the parts). This finding leads to the primary title of this book, *Victory Through Organization*. The subtitle, *Why the War for Talent Is Failing Your Company and What You Can Do About It*, reveals our opinion that the oft-cited "war for talent" may have gone too far and may be leading HR professionals astray in the modern business environment. Having great people is critical and wonderful, but if HR departments are not organized appropriately to do something with them, then they are missing a major opportunity.

As we have analyzed the data, we already realize questions we could or should have asked. With the help of 22 regional partners, we believe we have a remarkable data set, one of the best we have seen in the HR space. Our analyses now highlight findings that may continue to shape the HR profession.

We are enormously grateful for the many sponsors and supporters of this work. The Ross School of Business Executive Education (in particular Melanie Barnett) and RBL Group (in particular Norm Smallwood) have financially sponsored this work for 30 years. None of the principal investigators have even taken a salary or stipend for this research, donating now thousands of hours to the improvement of the profession. In this round, we are particularly indebted to:

- Jacqueline Vinci—project management
- Dave Gutzman—CustomInsight

We hope you take away a strong sense of our primary mission of *Victory Through Organization*: to further establish HR as a prominent strategic partner of the business and to embrace HR's role in creating an organization that is greater—and performs greater—than the sum of its "employee" parts.

PART I

HR MATTERS

CHAPTER 1

WHY HR AND WHY NOW? 1

HR is not about HR. HR begins and ends with the business. Every business is a product of its context. Business success comes when the internal strategy anticipates or responds to external conditions.

In our quest to discover the role HR plays in business strategy and success, and to identify the role it *should* play, we have been personally involved with a wide variety of specific business challenges in recent years. These challenges (and successes) have helped us enormously to focus and apply our research.

Business Challenge and Success Models

The business situations we have looked at and investigated include (but are not limited to) the following:

- *Leaders at a consumer electronics company look to the future and see emerging trends in an aging population who will require increased healthcare. They decide to shift their business from consumer products to healthcare services.*
- *Leaders at a leading retailer recognize that technology has changed when and how consumers shop. They realize that the "box" store will be supplemented by online purchasing. As they move into the online space, they realize they have to manage a dual organization, one focused on traditional retail through stores and another focused on Internet-driven distribution.*
- *A consumer products company has had outstanding financial performance compared to competitors. Their costs are lower and innovation revenues are higher. But their stock price lags. They are trying to figure out how to increase investor confidence in their future earnings and get full market value for their economic success.*

- *The founder of a conglomerate has had enormous success, growing to become one of the largest firms in the region. The average age of his management team is in the sixties, and he realizes that he has to prepare the next generation of leaders who will manage the company after he is gone.*
- *An Asian organization has achieved remarkable success in its market. It has moved from being a regional success to a country success and now has aspirations to become the global leader in its industry. It looks to expand to North and South America, Europe, and Africa in the next few years. Leaders are wondering if this expansion should be through acquisition or organic?*
- *A retail store has grown through geographic expansion to where its footprint now reaches over 80 percent of those who live in its served market. It now needs to focus on increasing revenue per square foot rather than simply adding more square footage.*
- *A private equity fund has now become a private equity firm. As a fund, it bought, fixed, and sold businesses. Now it is holding those businesses in its portfolio for a much longer period and has to transform them before divesting them.*
- *A consumer products firm has very successful products. But many of the products are nearing the end of their life cycle. The firm does not have a good track record of reinventing its existing products or coming up with new ones, and is worried about responding to future opportunities. Small, agile competitors seem to be taking away share at some key accounts.*

What These Business Cases Mean for HR

When business leaders are asked about their most difficult challenges in responding to external challenges, they often refer to executing with discipline, deploying talent, ensuring leadership, managing change, using information, and transforming culture. These are all HR-related issues, and they are often the hardest aspects of responding to evolving business challenges.

In each of the preceding business settings, the "solution" to the business challenge was centered on wisely investing in individual talent, organization capability, and leadership. Most important, these are the outcomes of good

HR work. Business leaders increasingly recognize that much of their success ultimately comes from wise and well-directed HR efforts.

The evidence for why HR matters for business outcomes comes from many diverse sources. Over time and through our research, we have found the following:

- Only 61 of the original Fortune 500 firms still exist as independent firms.
- Successful chief executive officers (CEOs) have the same skills set as successful chief human resource officers (CHROs), in comparison to chief marketing officers (CMOs), chief information officers (CIOs), or even chief financial officers (CFOs).
- Approximately 30 to 40 percent of board of director time is spent on organization and people issues.
- Investors are increasingly aware of leadership capital as part of their investment decision making.

Bottom line: These days, business leaders care about HR because these HR issues are now business issues.

An Integral Part of Excellence

Now because HR is primarily about the business, the HR profession is undergoing major transformation. When HR leaders are asked to define their "customers," they are increasingly referring to the customers of their business, not just the employees inside their organization. HR practices are increasingly being aligned to an "outside-in" focus where staffing, training, performance management, and culture deliver value to these "real" customers.

An employee "brand" is increasingly linked to the firm brand whereby those employees focus on delivering on brand promises to outside customers. Market value is as much about intangibles and leadership as financial results. In fact, those intangibles and leadership excellence are leading indicators of those financial results; intangibles are the cause, financials are the effect. HR professionals are not only invited to the table where strategy is discussed, they are increasingly expected to add value to the discussions and to be part of intangible and leadership excellence.

An Organization Focus

The scope of HR has also expanded. For decades *human resources* has primarily referred to talent and all the ways in which people are managed, including bringing the right people into an organization, moving them through the organization, administering their benefits and other "hygiene" issues, and appropriately moving them out of the organization (Ulrich & Allen, 2014). In recent years, HR has expanded from a nearly exclusive focus on people and how individuals think, behave, and act to an additional emphasis on organization.

What does this organization focus entail? An organization focus examines work*place* as much as workforce, work *processes* as much as people, *organization capabilities* as well as individual competencies. Organization culture (as a way to describe the organization) has become a complementary outcome of good HR work, *in addition to* individual competence. This means that responses to the business challenges listed previously include getting the right talent (people, individual skills, and workforce) and the right organization capabilities (culture, work, and processes). At the end of the day, HR helps deliver both individual competence and organization capability to solve business problems.

Evolving to New Competencies

To respond to these HR expectations and opportunities, HR professionals must acquire new competencies and HR departments must focus on the right activities. *This book offers HR professionals tools to better respond to emerging opportunities. It also offers guidance for how to build more effective HR departments to deliver real value.* The ideas in this book are based on 30 years (seven rounds) of studying HR professionals, with a focus on the results of the latest (2016) round of research with over 30,000 global respondents both inside and outside HR. In addition to these research findings, we offer a number of insights, frameworks, tools, actions, and cases where HR has delivered business value.

We envision the ideas in this book being used by multiple audiences who shape the HR profession. The more than 2 million HR professionals worldwide will discover the competencies they must master to be personally effective, to serve key stakeholders, and to deliver business results. Those senior HR leaders charged with creating value-added HR functions will find unique insights on how to build a more effective HR department. Business leaders who want to respond to business challenges through HR practices will learn how to make more informed and tailored HR investments.

The Four Forces Reshaping HR Impact on Business Success

We see four reasons why HR matters more now than ever for business success: business context, pace of change, stakeholder expectations, and personal context (see Figure 1.1). For HR professionals and business leaders to fully understand the increased expectations of HR, it is useful to recognize and adapt to these four forces. We'll refer to the Four Forces throughout the book.

Force 1: Emerging Business Context: STEPED and the Content of Change

A business leader whose firm operated in more than 80 countries asked us how he could make sense of and respond to the changes happening within the countries he visited. Another colleague asked us how to organize the complex

Figure 1.1   Four forces for emergence of HR

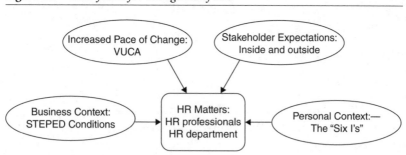

world in which we live into a relatively simple framework that might help her anticipate industry changes. While there are many frameworks capturing the relevant trends in the business context,˙ we prefer a typology of six categories (known as STEPED) that leaders can use to understand how contextual changes affect how businesses operate:

- Social (expectations, values, lifestyle, have/have-nots)
- Technological (information access and frequency)
- Environmental (public policy, social responsibility, care for the planet)
- Political (regulatory shifts)
- Economic (industry evolution, industry consolidation)
- Demographic (age, education, and background of people)

Using this framework, leaders can better diagnose geographic or industry trends. Because of trends in these six categories, HR professionals are asked to do more to help businesses position themselves to win. When our colleague would visit a country where he did business, he would ask for trends in these six areas to help him understand the context of his company's strategic choices. This STEPED framework can also be used to review industry trends. For example, an HR leader in a beverage company facilitated a team discussion about how the environment would shape her business in the future (see Table 1.1).

Table 1.1   *External content trends, strategic opportunities and threats, and HR implications*

Trend	Strategic Opportunities	Strategic Threats	HR Implications
Social	Emerging economies eager for Western products	Healthy eating trends reduce soda consumption by 25% in U.S./W. Europe	Source talent in emerging markets; Consider talent for adjacent businesses

---

˙Our work is certainly not the first to create a simplified framework for the business context. Other models such as the PEST framework and the PESTEL framework cover identical concepts in slightly different ways. We use the STEPED model because it fits conceptually with the challenges we regularly encounter in HR.

Table 1.1   *External content trends, strategic opportunities and threats, and HR implications (continued)*

Trend	Strategic Opportunities	Strategic Threats	HR Implications
Technological	Mobile computing offers new marketing opportunities	Increased threat of hackers or other corporate piracy/threat	Build a culture of information privacy and access information talent
Economic	New middle class in merging economies	Recession has impacted sales	Create a change plan to adapt to changing market conditions; move quickly
Political	Emerging economies increasingly open to trade and investment	More pressure to eliminate unhealthy drinks, e.g., NYC recent sugary beverage tax	Prepare an organization innovation strategy for new business opportunities
Environmental	Reduced cost of packaging/garbage by decreasing package size	Reaction against environmentally difficult packaging, e.g., plastic, metal cans	Ensure that corporate social responsibility is embedded into culture and key decisions
Demographic	Growth markets in LATAM, India, China, and SE Asia	Aging population in most mature markets reduces % of target customers	Build a country strategy of how to do business in emerging geographies

These six (STEPED) trends increase the relevance of HR, as responding to these factors requires high sensitivity to HR issues in the organization. You can see the HR emphasis in the last column of Table 1.1.

Force 2: Increased Pace of Change: Volatility, Uncertainty, Complexity, and Ambiguity

In addition to these business context areas, HR has grown in business importance because of the dramatically increased pace of change in business today.

As a model, we look to the VUCA model from the Cold War; during that time the U.S. military leaders recognized that military engagements were dramatically changing. They began to capture these changes with the acronym *VUCA* standing for the following:

- *Volatility:* The nature and dynamics of change, and the nature and speed of change forces and change catalysts.
- *Uncertainty:* The lack of predictability, the prospects for surprise, and the sense of awareness and understanding of issues and events.
- *Complexity:* The multiplex of forces, the confounding of issues, no cause-and-effect chain, and confusion that surround an organization.
- *Ambiguity:* The haziness of reality, the potential for misreads, and the mixed meanings of conditions; cause-and-effect confusion.

These four processes require that organizations become agile and responsive (e.g., in the military this assessment led to an emphasis on special forces who could move quickly in military assignments). HR professionals can help business teams feel less threatened by and more able to respond to external changes by facilitating structured dialogues around these external trends. Table 1.2 applies VUCA to the beverage example described earlier.

We have found in our research that under conditions of increased change, investments in HR matter more for business success. The challenges of VUCA elicit more attention to HR issues than some of the other forces we've examined. Teach your organization to deal effectively with VUCA, and you've accomplished a lot.

Force 3: Key Stakeholder Expectations

The context (STEPED) defines opportunities and threats in the business environment, the processes (VUCA) define the intensity and pace of change, and understanding stakeholder expectations defines who HR must satisfy to help the firm succeed.

Table 1.2   *External process trends: Creating organizations to respond to VUCA*

Trend/ Definition	Organization Response	Beverage Example	HR Implications for HR Practices and Culture
Volatility *Pace of change*	Respond to . . .	• We have to create an innovation cycle for new products (half-life of products is shortening). • We have to create a faster response time to market opportunities.	The following implications apply to all four elements of VUCA: • Create more agility throughout the organization. • Bring discipline and precision to the management of change. • Have decentralized execution of centralized operations. • Teach employees how to think and act, not what to think and do. • Empower people to apply ideas and innovate. • Focus less on plans and more on planning.
Uncertainty *Cannot predict the future*	Manage . . .	• We don't know which products will be successful in the future. • We don't know for sure who our competitors will be nor which countries we should compete in.	
Complexity *Chess on five levels*	Simplify . . .	• We have to manage the increasing complex global supply to commercialization process. • We have to build a matrix organization with business, geography, and function.	
Ambiguity *Unclear where future threats will come from*	Resolve . . .	• We don't know how technology and information will shape consumer choices. • We are not clear about who our future competitors might be.	

Because of contextual and intensity changes, stakeholder expectations are dramatically changing too, again increasing the relevance for HR. Figure 1.2 captures many of the stakeholders for a company and what they

Figure 1.2   Key stakeholders to HR and their needs and expectations

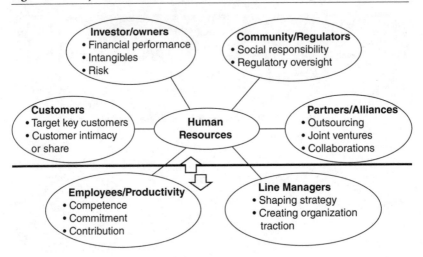

likely expect from their interactions with a company. These stakeholder expectations set the criteria for effective HR. More and more, HR stakeholders are external (above the line in Figure 1.2): customers, investors, communities/regulators, and partners. HR is increasingly being asked to help deliver customer share, investor intangibles, community reputation, and partnership cooperation. As these external stakeholder expectations increase, HR plays a significant role in delivering these outcomes. In addition, more traditional HR focuses on the excellence of internal stakeholders, including employees and leaders, helping employees become more productive and leaders become more strategic.

Force 4: The Personal Context of Today's Work

STEPED defines the playing field, VUCA defines the pace at which a game is played, and stakeholders define for whom we create value. But all these changes in external context also affect how people respond when playing the game. Their responses to workplace change—and workplace behavior itself—is in turn influenced by six societal shifts (Six I's) that put enormous pressure on shaping the emotional impact of how people live and work.

Here are the six I's:

1. *Intensity:* People often live with a reality TV mindset where intensity and insults replace insight and civility, emotional outbursts matter more than reasoned dialogue, and individuals are moted to "win" (e.g., television shows like *Survivor, Apprentice, American Idol*) generally at the expense of others. Television snippets and Internet news report and magnify the sound bites that demean and demoralize. In this world, 140-character Twitter comments are forwarded when they capture a clever phrase or insult. While most people's normal lives are not as emotionally intense as those seen in social media, people become inured to emotional outbursts and come to expect them.

2. *Individuation:* People live in a world of hyper free-agency, where individuals win by taking control of their careers, maximizing their self-interests, and eschewing long-term commitment to a community or organization. Career mobility is a given, as one Silicon Valley executive said, "My people go to lunch and come back with a job offer." Relatively few have expectations of long-term employment with one company or team. Everyone is encouraged to be authentic by taking charge of their lives and becoming their own brand.

3. *Isolation:* People act increasingly in personal cocoons that require less interaction with others. SOHO (small office, home office) is becoming a dominant organizational setting. Students are encouraged to and can get a degree through technology without ever attending a class or having the social experience of a university. Digital natives are spending up to 7.5-plus hours a day in front of a screen (i.e., TV, phone, computer). With this group, process addictions are as prevalent as substance addictions. When people have personal contact, these personal touches are frequently through Twitter, Facebook, and LinkedIn, which capture activity more than social connection. People are connected, but not connecting. It is not a surprise that feelings of anomie and isolation are increasing. And the consequences of social isolation are not good. Social isolation predicts mortality more than smoking, drinking, obesity, depression, or anxiety.

4. *Indifference:* Throughout the world, the next generation has learned to moderate expectations. For generations, a primary goal of parenting is to provide children with opportunities to live better than their parents, with each generation building on the previous. Now, this is less likely. Maturing adults get an education, but not a job and even less often a career. Increasingly voters are cynical about politicians having the voters' interest in mind. While people are busy, they are not sure they are being fulfilled.

5. *Immediacy:* A sense of time and duration has also shifted. Many seek immediate gratification without investing in long-term preparation. Long term feels like next week. Immediacy occurs when we want new products like watches, phones, computers, or clothing or when we see political expediency and deal making taking precedence over long-term, value-based decisions. Relationships are disposable. People are far less likely to get married, but move into and out of relationships.

6. *In-group (labels):* It is a world with increasing subgroups. The gap between the rich and the poor, the have's and the have-not's, has increased. With statistics, you can quickly find patterns that label people into a subgroup. Managing information from cookies reinforces these labels and becomes the focus for tailored advertising, customized products and services, and unique offerings. Cloud data is designed to create customized insights. Most people chose to live in neighborhoods with like-minded and socially similar individuals. Political polarization exists where neighborhoods have a singular political focus, resulting in increasing political extremism.

These six societal affective trends are discouraging, yet they define how individuals live and have the potential to undermine and destabilize organizations. Employees who are demoralized by these factors create organizations without capacity to respond to STEPED or VUCA conditions and without ability to serve key stakeholders. It is not a surprise the employee engagement scores on most surveys are at an all-time low. HR professionals have the challenge to shift these seemingly negative trends into positive opportunities to enable their organization to become communities of action where the following takes place:

- Employees channel intensity to create value for others.
- Individual self-interest is replaced by shared purpose.
- Isolation is overcome with personal connection.
- Indifference shifts to renewal.
- Immediacy for today's results becomes the pathway for a longer-term vision or strategy.
- Labels are replaced with valuing differences that make teams stronger than individuals.

When these six contextual trends turn positive, HR professionals help individuals replace cynicism with commitment and isolation with community. HR professionals must be aware of these trends and influences and be prepared to deal with the effects of them. It is not a surprise that studies of conscious capitalism and firms of endearment show that firms with purpose and social responsibility gain higher productivity among employees.

So Again, Why HR and Why Now? (Why Is *Victory Through Organization* Relevant?)

Businesses are shaped by the context in which they operate (STEPED), they have to respond to the velocity of the changes they face (VUCA), they have to serve external and internal stakeholders, and organizations are more successful when employees have positive personal affect. Each of these Four Forces requires new thinking and action from HR professionals to create organizations that will survive and thrive. Obviously, responding to these Four Forces is not HR acting in isolation, but through cooperation with business leaders and other staff professionals.

HR matters because it is not about HR, but about the business. Going further, that business is not about what we do today, but how we prepare for tomorrow; to prepare for tomorrow requires understanding of context, process, stakeholders, and personal affect; that by managing these forces, organizations will become competitive; and that competitive organizations are the outcomes of HR.

The ideas in this book will help shape the HR profession. In Part I (HR Matters) we have laid out societal forces that increase HR relevance (Chapter 1) and we overview the research (Chapter 2) that will help HR departments and HR professionals deliver more value.

In Part II (Organization), we discuss the importance of the organization for business success (Chapter 3) and introduce high-priority HR practices. Chapter 4 reviews how organizations can better leverage HR in the organization's overall information agenda, as well as building stronger integration among the HR practices. Chapter 5 offers insights on delivering HR practices for employees and using HR analytics for HR.

In Part III (Individual) we go into depth on the competencies that will help HR professionals be more personally effective as Credible Activists (Chapter 6), deliver value to key stakeholders as Strategic Positioners (Chapter 7), and impact business results as Paradox Navigators (Chapter 8). We also highlight enabling strategic HR competencies of Culture and Change Champion, Human Capital Curator, and Total Rewards Steward (Chapter 9) and foundation enablers of Compliance Manager, Technology and Media Integrator, and Analytics Designer and Interpreter (Chapter 10).

Finally, in Part IV we lay out and summarize the implications of these ideas for business leaders, senior HR leaders, and HR professionals (Chapter 11).

In sum, our ultimate hope in doing this research and writing *Victory Through Organization* is to make HR less about HR and more about the business.

CHAPTER 2

THE EMPIRICAL BASIS OF HR EFFECTIVENESS

2

If the expectations and opportunities are rising for HR (as defined in Chapter 1), then what does HR have to do to respond? Many thoughtful HR leaders have imparted their personal views about what HR must do to be effective. Opinions and anecdotes are easy; we realized 30 years ago that these thoughtful personal cases needed more rigorous research across organizations to establish a more robust view of what HR professionals and HR departments must be, know, and do to be effective.

To pivot from anecdotes to sustained insights, we have engaged in extensive data collection and empirical analysis. As a fair warning to you as a reader, this chapter is quite technical and presents a great deal of conceptual and analytical rigor. If you would like to deeply understand the empirical underpinnings of our arguments, then this chapter will give you many details. If, however, heavy empirical discussions are not to your liking, you may prefer to skim this chapter and move quickly to Chapter 3. We have made an intentional choice to report detailed methodology, data, and results so that you can evaluate the quality of our work and the robustness of the insights we draw from the data. We also believe that the rigorous empirical work differentiates this study from many other HR competency studies we encounter, and we want to help you appreciate the difference.

For 30 years, we have studied the competencies of HR professionals in an attempt to identify what competencies HR professionals must master to deliver value. We have also been intensely involved in the transformation of HR departments and HR practices.[1] We believe that while case studies and personal experiences offer great insights, to move the profession forward requires more comprehensive research. This chapter, in five sections, accomplishes the following: (1) highlights our previous work, (2) summarizes the state of the art on HR competencies and others' work, (3) reviews design choices for the current seventh (2016) round of the Human Resources Competency Study (HRCS), (4) reports characteristics of the sample as a view on the state of the profession, and (5) overviews high-level findings of this round of research focused on the impact of both personal HR competencies and well-functioning HR departments on various business outcomes.

Each of these five chapter goals is summarized in Sections 1 through 5, which follow.

Section 1: Highlights of Our Previous Work

Over our 30 years of doing the HR competency research, we have been able to frame many core ideas and concepts that have shaped the HR profession. We are clearly not alone in evolving HR, but we have helped shape ideas for the HR profession around several core concepts that have emerged:[2]

- *HR as business partner:* HR professionals should be business partners with the line managers.
- *HR value added:* HR exists to deliver value to key stakeholders.
- *Strategic HR:* There is a logical process and sequence starting with business environment, then on to strategy, then organization, and then finally to HR priorities.
- *HR strategy:* HR departments should have a mission to deliver talent, leadership, and organization capabilities to increase business performance.
- *HR governance structure:* HR departments should be organized to match the business organization, which in many (not all) cases requires the "three pillar" model for HR (shared services, centers of expertise, and corporate HR).

- *HR transformation:* HR transformation comes through four phases: why transform, what are the outcomes of transformation, how to transform HR work, and who is involved in HR transformation.
- *HR deliverables:* HR should focus on outcomes delivered in talent, leadership, and organization more than administrative activities or HR practices like staffing, training, and compensation. The outcomes of HR become the goals for the HR department, capabilities an organization requires to win in the marketplace, and intangibles for investors.
- *Organization capabilities:* Organizations can be defined by their capabilities, which include information, culture change, speed or agility, collaboration, innovation, customer service, or efficiency.
- *HR outside in:* HR delivers value to external customers, investors, and communities.

Much of this work revolves around building better HR professionals through competency models and building better HR departments through focusing on the right HR practices.

Section 2: State of the Art of HR Competency Models

In recent years, many HR associations, organizations, and thought leaders have worked to create HR competency models. We have synthesized this work in Table 2.1 into six domains for HR competencies.[3] For a more detailed examination of each of the competency models, the reader may benefit from connecting with the referenced HR association directly. This enormous body of work indicates the relevance of the Four Forces for the increasing attention to HR laid out in Chapter 1. This work has been used to certify, staff, develop, and reward HR professionals. Our assumptions and approach for the seven rounds of HR research and competency work indicate how we have uniquely contributed to the HR competency discussion.

Table 2.1 Integration of HR competencies into six HR domains

HR Association	Core HR Domains					
	Business	Personal	HR Tools, Practices & Processes	HR Information System & Analytics	Change	Organization and Culture
Society for Human Resource Management (SHRM)[4]	• Business acumen	• Ethical practice • Leadership and navigation	• HR expertise	• Communication • Critical evaluation	• Relationship management • Consultation	• Global and cultural effectiveness
CIPD			• Resourcing and talent planning • Learning and talent development • Performance and rewards • Employee engagement • Employee relations	• Service delivery	• Information	• Organization design • Organization development
Australian Human Resources Institute (AHRI) (model of excellence)	• Business driven • Strategic architect • Future oriented	• Ethical and credible activist • Critical thinker • Courageous • Understand and care	• Workforce designer • Expert practitioner • Solutions driven		• Change leader • Influencer • Collaborative • Resolver of issues	• Organizational capability • Culture leader

Table 2.1 Integration of HR competencies into six HR domains (*continued*)

HR Association	Core HR Domains					
	Business	Personal	HR Tools, Practices & Processes	HR Information System & Analytics	Change	Organization and Culture
National Human Resource Development (NHRD) (HR compass)	• Strategic thinking and alignment • Business knowledge • Financial perspective	• Personal credibility • Service orientation	• Functional • Recruitment • Performance management • Talent management • Compensation and benefits • HR and labor law		• Execution excellence • Change orientation • Networking management	• Managing culture and design
Asociación Mexicana en Dirección de Recursos Humanos (AMEDIRH)[5]		• Self-awareness • Synthesis • Formulation • Coaching			• Collaboration • Knowledge management	• Innovative culture
Boston Consulting Group	• HR business partner		• Managing talent • Improving leadership • Recruiting • HR processes			• Restructuring organization
Deloitte	• Commercial awareness • Business acumen	• Trusted advisor	• HR expertise • Employee relations		• Influence	

Section 3: Design Choices for HRCS Round 7 (2016)

In conducting the seventh round of the HRCS for 2016, seven key design choices illustrate our approach to defining the competencies that make effective HR professionals and the practices that make effective HR departments.

1. *Collaboration:* We have consistently collaborated with the leading HR professional associations around the world. The Ross School of Business at the University of Michigan and the RBL Group (our consulting firm) have been the primary sponsors for this 30-year research agenda. In this seventh round we have worked with 22 HR associations, which cover the entire world (see Figure 2.1). Each of these 22 global partners conducted focus groups within their respective geographies where members addressed three questions:
   a. What are the major challenges facing your industry and organization?
   b. What are implications of these challenges for talent, leadership, and organizations?
   c. What are HR professionals undertaking to address greater business value in the future than they have in the past?

   We believe that such collaboration enhances perspectives and offers scale and scope for the work.

Figure 2.1   Regional partners for HR competency study

2. *HR competencies and results:* HR competencies models generally answer the question, "What are the competencies of the HR professional?" These are descriptive statements that describe the current state of HR competencies, but not the impact of those competencies on key outcomes. Our research links HR competencies to personal individual effectiveness, key stakeholder outcomes, and business results so that competencies deliver value.

3. *Beyond self-report:* We recognize the dangers of self-reporting about one's competencies (people generally judge themselves by their intent; others judge people by their behaviors). We use a "360-degree methodology" to overcome self-bias. In this round we have about 4,000 HR professionals who responded to the study. They provided self-reported data on their individual competencies. Their data were augmented by about 28,000 HR and non-HR associates who provided additional 360-degree data. With this 360-degree data, we have a more complete image of the competencies and their impact.

4. *Global sample:* We have worked to determine common HR competencies for HR professionals worldwide and unique competencies for specific regions. Our book *Global HR Competencies* highlights these differences. In this round we worked with the 22 regional partners to identify HR participants and associate respondents from around the world. We find that while there are common domains of HR competencies, they are applied differently around the globe.

5. *State of the art and evolution of HR competencies:* From the first round (1987) of the HRCS, we have carefully ensured that the issues covered in the survey represented the present and the future of the HR field. We have done this study in waves, every 4 to 5 years. We find that the competencies vary about 25 to 33 percent each wave. In this round we had 123 competency items; about 60 percent were carried over from the 2012 study because they were high predictors of key outcomes from previous rounds.

6. *Variance and similarity of competencies:* We have worked to see how HR competencies vary by the demographics of the HR professional (gender, age,

career stage, title, time in job) and by the organization setting (industry, firm size, company culture, strategy, capabilities required to win, country). In this round, we have results by these demographic categories (not all reported in this book, but available from authors).

7. *HR competencies versus HR departments:* For the previous six research rounds, we have focused primarily on the competencies of HR professionals. In this round, we also wanted to identify the practices of HR departments and how they would impact key stakeholders and overall business performance. There is an ongoing debate about the relative impact of individuals (talent) versus culture (organization). In this round we were able to create HR department level results by asking questions about the HR department and by aggregating those scores into about 1,400 organization units.

We believe that these seven design choices allow us to integrate and build on the previous work and confidently use this research as a way to continue to better use HR to solve business challenges and to evolve the profession.

Section 4: Characteristics of the Sample and the State of the HR Profession

And now, as we forewarned, we are going to dive into the detailed data. As noted in Table 2.2, this seventh round of the HRCS has data from about 32,000 overall respondents in 1,400 businesses, with about 4,000 HR self-reporting (HR participants) and 28,000 associate reports.* This is the largest sample of the seven rounds, thanks to our exceptional regional partners.

---

* In determining the final sample size, we had to account for missing data. We received over 38,000 surveys, but unless the respondent answered 50 percent of the questions, we were not able to use the information.

Table 2.2   *Overview of participation from seven rounds of research*

	Round 1 -1987-	Round 2 -1992-	Round 3 -1997-	Round 4 -2002-	Round 5 -2007-	Round 6 -2012-	Round 7 -2016-
Total Respondents	10,291	4,556	3,229	7,082	10,063	20,023	31,868
Business Units	1,200	441	678	692	413	635	1,395
Associate Raters	8,884	3,805	2,565	5,890	8,414	17,353	27,904
HR Participants	1,407	751	664	1,192	1,671	2,638	3,964

Table 2.3 reports the demographics of the seven rounds of study. Given the size of the sample, we believe these insights capture some of the shifts in the makeup of the HR profession. There are some interesting insights from Table 2.3:

1. *Gender:* The gender has shifted dramatically in the profession over the past 30 years from 77 percent to 36 percent male, but this gender shift seems to have stabilized. This finding may indicate that the rate at which females are entering the HR profession has slowed or plateaued.

2. *Years' experience in HR:* Over the three prior studies, we found that approximately 25 percent of participants had been in HR positions less than 5 years, which we suggested could be attributed to growth in the profession or a trend of organizations moving people across functions. In the 2016 study, we see that the HR professionals with less than 5 years of experience make up only 16 percent of the survey participants. The decrease in less experienced HR professionals was offset by an increase in experienced professionals, where nearly half of the participants (47 percent) had 15 or more years in HR. While there is not a definitive explanation for this shift, one plausible explanation would be that it has become difficult in recent years to enter the HR profession.

3. *Role of HR professionals:* Since the 2012 study, we have seen resurgence in the percentage of HR professionals working in generalist positions (from 40

to 55 percent). With the exception of the HR planning, strategy, and affirmative action roles, all specialist groups experienced a slight drop in representation in the 2016 study. Generalists making up 55 percent of the survey participants is actually consistent with our pre-2012 data.

Table 2.3   *Personal characteristics of HR professionals over 30 years*

	Round 1 -1987-	Round 2 -1992-	Round 3 -1997-	Round 4 -2002-	Round 5 -2007-	Round 6 -2012-	Round 7 -2016-
Gender of HR Participant							
Male	77%	78%	70%	57%	46%	38%	36%
Female	23	22	30	43	54	62	64
Years in HR for HR Participant							
5 years or less	10	14	13	25	24	25	19
6–9 years	14	19	15	18	20	18	19
10–14 years	26	24	21	22	23	25	23
15 or more years	50	43	51	35	32	32	39
Primary Role of HR Participant							
Benefits/medical/ safety	6%	5%	5%	4%	3%	3%	2%
Compensation	5	4	4	6	6	7	6
HR planning/ strategy/ affirmative action	6	8	5	8	14	14	10
Labor relations	6	8	5	6	5	4	4
Org. development/ effectiveness/ research	2	5	3	13	7	9	5

Table 2.3   *Personal characteristics of HR professionals over 30 years (continued)*

	Round 1 -1987-	Round 2 -1992-	Round 3 -1997-	Round 4 -2002-	Round 5 -2007-	Round 6 -2012-	Round 7 -2016-
Recruiting	3	6	4	4	6	11	8
Training	7	14	6	12	9	11	10
Generalist	61	45	60	48	49	40	55

Table 2.4 shows the respondents by region. Simply stated, thanks to our regional partners, this study offers a truly global perspective of the HR profession.

Table 2.4   *2016 respondents by region*

	HR Participants per Region	Total Respondents per Region	% of Total Respondents
North America (US & Canada)	1,153	9,767	30.8
China	568	4,442	14.0
Africa	456	3,209	10.1
Turkey	323	3,112	9.8
Latin America	336	2,813	8.9
Other Countries in Asia	328	2,469	7.8
Europe	258	2,222	7.0
Australia & New Zealand	168	1,540	4.9
Japan	166	1,024	3.2
India	116	718	2.3
Middle East	73	421	1.3

Tables 2.2 to 2.4 indicate the breadth of this sample. We believe it represents the largest global comprehensive assessment of HR professionals and HR departments.[6]

Section 5: Overview of Key Findings

This research answers six questions about how HR can add value:

1. What are the competencies of HR professionals, and how do they differ by individual and organizational context?
2. What competencies do HR professionals require to be personally effective (i.e., to be invited "to the table")?
3. When engaged "at the table" (in business discussions), what competencies do individual HR professionals bring that add value to key stakeholders?
4. When engaged "at the table" (in business discussions), how do HR professionals represent the HR department's practices and policies to add value to key stakeholders?
5. What competencies are required of HR professionals to drive business results?
6. What is the relative importance of the competencies of HR professionals versus HR department practices in driving business results?

The preceding Questions 1 through 3 focus on the competencies of the individual HR professional and how those competencies affect individual outcomes that matter for the business. To address Question 1 we perform a factor analysis to see how individual competency items load together into HR competency domains and then we report average competencies by different demographic cuts.

Research and Methodological Choices

For Question 1 we performed a factor analysis that allowed the data to reveal to us the nine competency domains that make up the competency model we present in this book. Those domains are presented shortly.

To address Question 2, we examined how an individual's HR competencies relate to that individual's overall effectiveness in the eyes of the raters in the 360-degree survey design. Individual effectiveness is the general sense from others that this particular HR professional is highly effective in his or her job. An HR professional's personal effectiveness is determined by the question (Figure 2.2):

*Overall, compared with the other HR professionals whom you have known, how does (**HR PROFESSIONAL**) compare?*

Figure 2.2   *Measurement for individual performance of HR professionals*

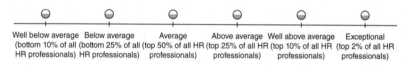

Well below average	Below average	Average	Above average	Well above average	Exceptional
(bottom 10% of all HR professionals)	(bottom 25% of all HR professionals)	(top 50% of all HR professionals)	(top 25% of all HR professionals)	(top 10% of all HR professionals)	(top 2% of all HR professionals)

The score on this question indicates the overall personal effectiveness of the individual HR professional.

Question 3 refers to the value that an individual HR professional brings once involved in business discussions. We wanted to know which personal HR competencies impacted an HR professional's ability to create value for a host of stakeholders, including external customers, investors, communities, regulators, employees, and line managers. To determine the value an HR professional brings to different stakeholders, we asked six questions, one for each stakeholder (Figure 2.3):

*Overall, compared with the other human resource professionals whom you have known, how does (**HR PROFESSIONAL**) compare in creating value for ([1] **external customers**, [2] **investors/owners**, [3] **communities**, [4] **regulators**, [5] **line managers**, [6] **employees**)?*

Figure 2.3   *Measurement for individual performance of HR professionals*

Well below average	Below average	Average	Above average	Well above average	Exceptional
(bottom 10% of all HR professionals)	(bottom 25% of all HR professionals)	(top 50% of all HR professionals)	(top 25% of all HR professionals)	(top 10% of all HR professionals)	(top 2% of all HR professionals)

The results of these survey questions help identify how personal HR competencies deliver value to different stakeholders. We have about 4,000 HR professionals in this analysis.

Questions 4, 5, and 6 shift our focus from purely individual HR competencies and individual results to the HR department and organizational level. For this work, we combine the 4,000 HR professionals into about 1,400 organization units where they work. Some of these 1,400 organization units have 1 HR professional, some might have up to 10 or more. So we have the average HR competencies for all HR professionals within that organization unit.

At the department or organization level, we wanted to know the impact of how the HR department designs and delivers HR practices that add value to key stakeholders as measured with this question:

Please indicate the extent to which you agree that your **HR department** *designs and delivers HR practices that add value to the following stakeholders of your business:*

Table 2.4 *Question wording for value created for stakeholders by HR department*

	Strongly Disagree	Disagree	Neutral	Agree	Strongly Agree
External customers					
Investors or owners					
Communities where you operate					
Government regulators					
Line managers in your organization					
Your employees					

So for 1,400 organization units, we know (1) the average competencies of all the HR professionals in that unit and (2) the extent to which the HR department's HR practices add value to key stakeholders. Assessing individual and collective (combined) HR competencies and their impact on stakeholders provides some interesting implications (see Table 2.5)

Table 2.5   *HR value for stakeholders as determined by individual HR professional or department's HR practices*

		Individual HR Professional Adds Value to Key Stakeholders	
		Low	High
HR department designs and delivers HR practices that add value to key stakeholders	High	2	4
	Low	1	3

In cells 1 and 4, the HR professionals represent themselves and the HR department HR practices in consistent ways (low or high). In cell 2, the HR professionals' personal competencies are not adding personal value to key stakeholders, but the HR department is doing so. In this case, the HR professional represents the HR department's HR practices once invited to the business dialogue. In cell 3, the individual HR professional's competencies are adding value to key stakeholders, but the HR department's HR practices are not. In this case, the HR professional represents his or her personal expertise once invited to the business dialogue.

Thus in Question 4 we explore the relationship between collective HR competencies in the HR department and the extent to which the departments' HR practices create value for a host of stakeholders, including external customers, investors, communities, regulators, line managers, and employees.

Question 5 then shifts our focus from the intangible value that the HR department creates for stakeholders to the prior business performance of the organization. Table 2.6 summarizes the differences between our prior business performance measure and our intangible value for stakeholder measures.

Exploring the business performance in the past is somewhat straightforward using well-established measures in business research. In our case we adopted a validated business performance scale that asks survey participants to rate the performance of the organization in the past 3 years to the

Table 2.6   Business performance versus stakeholder value findings

Prior Business Performance Findings	Intangible Value for Stakeholders
• Looks more backward and reports financial results of what has happened	• Looks more forward to figure out how to serve stakeholders and thereby anticipate what may happen
• Emphasizes a more internal perspective on how the firm performs	• Considers stakeholders both outside and inside the organization (HR outside in)
• Focuses on more tactical and transactional HR practices to drive results	• Focuses more on high-impact systemic HR solutions
• Captures more the legacy and historical reputation	• Moves HR into the future (information age)
• Not much variance explained	• Substantial variance explained
• Offers more answers for what HR can do to deliver business results	• Challenges HR to think much more broadly in terms of value creation

performance of competitors on the following dimensions: profitability, labor productivity, new product development, customer satisfaction, employee attraction, and regulatory compliance. This approach gives us multiple respondents to multiple performance items. Prior work shows that informed survey respondents can assess the relative performance of their organizations and provide reliable proxies for the performance of the organization in the recent past.

Projecting potential business performance is more challenging, however. Recent research suggests that one key to sustainable business performance over time is creating value for the many stakeholders of the business. Creating value for stakeholders establishes a sense of partnership with stakeholders. As long as the business consistently creates value for stakeholders, they contribute their resources and energy to support the business. One manifestation of this is customer loyalty, but employees, investors, communities, and regulators all have important implications for the effective operation of the business day to day. Thus, one way to approximate the potential business performance in the future is through measuring the intangible value the organization creates for its critical stakeholders. This may indicate the extent to which stakeholders are deeply invested in helping the organization perform into the future.

Finally, with Question 6, we compare the relative impact of individual HR competencies versus the quality of the HR department in determining both prior business and stakeholder intangible results. Figure 2.4 visually depicts these key explanatory and dependent variables for the HRCS study and highlights which tables report the relevant findings.

Below we offer a high-level overview of the findings of the study; then in subsequent chapters we provide additional details, insights, and interpretations related to these results.

Figure 2.4   *Visually depicting the key independent and dependent variables in round 7 of the HRCS*

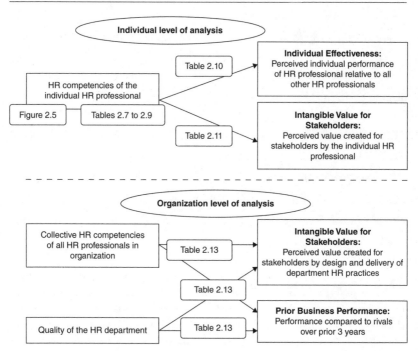

Question 1: What Are the Competencies of HR Professionals, and How Do They Differ by Individual and Organizational Context?

In the research, we examined 123 specific items (or questions) that define what HR professionals should be, know, or do. We performed factor analyses on these items to determine domains of HR competence.[†] Our research resulted in nine domains (or factors) for HR competencies (see Figure 2.5). Because of the results reported Figure 2.5, we clustered the nine domains into three general categories: core competencies, strategic enablers, and tactical support elements.

Three of these competencies were core drivers (explained further in the discussion that follows):

- *Strategic Positioner:* Able to position a business to win in its market
- *Credible Activist:* Able to build relationships of trust by having a proactive point of view
- *Paradox Navigator:* Able to manage tensions inherent in making change happen (e.g., be both long and short term, be both top down and bottom up)

We categorized three domains of HR competence as *strategic* enablers, helping position HR to deliver strategic value:

- *Culture and Change Champion:* Able to make change happen and to weave change initiatives into culture change
- *Human Capital Curator:* Able to manage the flow of talent by developing people and leaders, driving individual performance, and building technical talent
- *Total Rewards Steward:* Able to manage employee well-being through financial and nonfinancial rewards.

[†]We worked to make sure that the 123 items were accurately clustered into key domains by doing factor analysis. The choices in factor analysis were complicated (e.g., do we do analysis on 32,000 overall respondents or on the 28,000 associate respondents or the 4,000 HR participants?). We also worked to make sure that the 123 items were "cleanly" factored into a single domain. We tested the best fit of these items for 5, 6, 7, 8, 9, or 10 domains. After over 200 factor analyses, we made a judgment that nine domains best characterized the 123 items. Specific factor loadings and assumptions are available from the authors.

We categorized the final three enablers as *tactical* or *foundational* elements of HR:

- *Technology and Media Integrator:* Able to use technology and social media to drive high-performing organizations
- *Analytics Designer and Interpreter:* Able to use analytics to improve decision making
- *Compliance Manager:* Able to manage the processes related to compliance by following regulatory guidelines

Each of these nine HR competencies is important for the performance of HR professionals. We will report the overall results by rater type, gender, and region.[‡]

Figure 2.5   2016 HR competency model: round 7

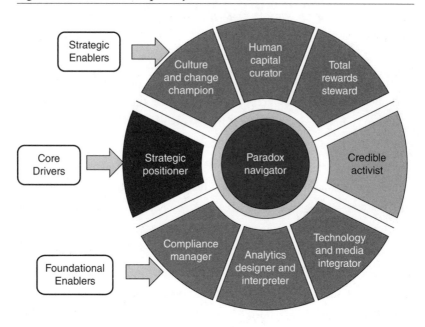

[‡]We have the results of these nine competencies by many demographic breakdowns (e.g., tenure of HR professional, size of firm, industry, role of HR professional, and so forth). These additional specific results are available from the authors.

Like the Four Forces reshaping HR impact presented in Chapter 1, these nine domains (and this chart) will be referred to throughout the book.

Table 2.7 shows the mean (1 = low to 5 = high) scores for each of the nine HR competence domains by different respondent groups. The nine competence domains represent the rows, and the five columns represent different respondent groups to the 360-degree exercise. The pattern among the nine competence domains are quite similar (see the scores in each column).

As the data show, HR professionals are seen by their raters (in Column 1) as having more competence as Credible Activists (4.33/5) and Compliance Manager (4.32/5) and less competence in Total Rewards Steward (3.88/5) and Technology and Media Integrator (3.92/5). This same pattern holds regardless of who is rating the HR professional (self-rating, Column 2; supervisor rating, Column 3; HR associate, Column 4; and non-HR associate, Column 5). These results make sense in that HR professionals have traditionally been known for their personal credibility and their compliance roles. We should note that we use 0.15 as a threshold for meaningful differences.[§]

The results by column are quite interesting. HR professionals self-assessments (Column 2) are somewhat higher than supervisor ratings (Column 3), but lower than ratings by HR associates (Column 4) and even lower than ratings by non-HR Associates (Column 5). Supervisors who observe HR professionals doing their work may expect them to live up to higher expectations. HR associates see their HR colleagues as having more skills than the HR professionals themselves, and non-HR associates have even higher ratings of HR professionals.

Perhaps HR professionals (Column 2) recognize their limitations more than those who rate them, perhaps they have limited self-confidence in their own skills versus how others see them, or perhaps associate raters assume that HR professionals can do more. We tend toward the third explanation

---

[§]We are often asked about "statistical significance" of these findings. With a sample of this size, almost all findings are "statistically" significant. We are more interested in "meaningfully significant," which implies information insights that are worthy of attention.

and see these findings as a license for HR professionals to do more in these nine competency domains. Their HR and non-HR associates already observe them as better than they rate themselves. HR professionals sometimes lament how they are perceived by their peers, but their lowered self-image and self-confidence may be a larger liability to their effectiveness.

Table 2.7   *Round 7 competency domain averages by rater type*

	1 All Raters[a]	2 Self- Ratings	3 Supervisor Ratings	4 HR Associate Ratings	5 Non-HR Associate Ratings
Number of raters	27,904	3,964	3,738	13,168	10,998
Strategic Positioner	4.13	4.05	3.94	4.13	4.21
Credible Activist	4.33	4.35	4.27	4.29	4.42
Paradox Navigator	3.99	3.87	3.86	3.98	4.08
Culture and Change Champion	4.03	3.96	3.88	4.02	4.11
Human Capital Curator	4.01	3.90	3.88	4.01	4.08
Analytics Designer and Interpreter	4.01	3.89	3.78	4.04	4.06
Total Rewards Steward	3.88	3.76	3.81	3.86	3.95
Technology and Media Integrator	3.92	3.77	3.78	3.93	3.96
Compliance Manager	4.32	4.34	4.31	4.30	4.38
Overall Averages	**4.07**	**3.99**	**3.94**	**4.06**	**4.14**

[a]Non-self ratings

Table 2.8 shows that female HR professionals generally score higher than males across the nine HR competence domains, and although the specific domain scores are only slightly different, the pattern holds. This finding is consistent with gender differences in other 360-degree surveys. As HR has become a more female profession (see Table 2.3), it may be a setting for women to demonstrate more competence than men.

Table 2.8   *Competencies by participant gender on nine domains*

	Female	Male
Strategic Positioner	4.14	4.11
Credible Activist	4.34	4.29
Paradox Navigator	4.01	3.94
Culture and Change Champion	4.04	3.99
Human Capital Curator	4.02	3.97
Analytics Designer and Interpreter	4.01	3.98
Total Rewards Steward	3.90	3.84
Technology and Media Integrator	3.94	3.85
Compliance Manager	4.34	4.29
Overall Average	**4.08**	**4.03**

Table 2.9 reports results by geography. Again, the pattern exists across regions of HR professionals being more effective as Credible Activists and Compliance Managers and less effective as Total Rewards Stewards and Technology and Media Integrators. Overall, HR professionals have higher scores in North America (4.18), Oceania (Australia and New Zealand) (4.11), and China (4.11) and lower overall scores in Japan (3.74) and Latin America (3.92). These results may reflect the maturation of the HR profession in each of the regions.

We should add a personal observation that as we have visited multiple regions, we have found competent and committed HR professionals in each of the regions. We also see emerging innovative HR practices from each region. For example, Japanese HR professionals have leading-edge practices

Table 2.9 Competencies by region on the nine domains[a]

	North America	LATAM	Oceana	Europe	Turkey	Mid-East	Africa	China	Japan	India	Asia Other
Strategic Positioner	4.25	4.00	4.16	4.06	4.11	4.12	4.18	4.09	3.85	4.07	4.06
Credible Activist	4.45	4.18	4.40	4.22	4.31	4.29	4.36	4.35	4.09	4.25	4.25
Paradox Navigator	4.11	3.87	4.02	3.91	4.04	3.98	3.93	4.01	3.58	3.96	3.91
Culture and Change Champion	4.14	3.86	4.09	3.93	4.01	4.01	4.06	4.04	3.74	4.03	3.94
Human Capital Curator	4.09	3.84	4.08	3.89	4.00	4.01	3.98	4.12	3.71	3.99	3.92
Analytics Designer and Interpreter	4.09	3.94	4.01	3.90	4.10	3.98	3.98	4.04	3.67	4.01	3.92
Total Rewards Steward	3.98	3.66	3.90	3.72	3.97	3.84	3.78	4.00	3.63	3.89	3.83
Technology and Media Integrator	4.06	3.75	3.90	3.71	4.03	3.97	3.84	4.01	3.34	3.95	3.84
Compliance Manager	4.47	4.20	4.39	4.24	4.30	4.18	4.27	4.32	4.09	4.19	4.22
Overall Average	4.18	3.92	4.11	3.95	4.10	4.04	4.04	4.11	3.74	4.04	3.99

[a]Non-self rating

39

in engaging employees in decision making, gaining credibility for senior HR leaders, and making HR decisions based on rigorous data.

Question 2: What Competencies Do HR Professionals Require to Be Personally Effective (i.e., to be invited "to the table")?

As discussed earlier, we did not want to merely describe what HR competencies exist and the extent to which they exist, but their impact on important outcomes. One outcome is the overall personal effectiveness of about 4,000 HR professionals. We assume that being seen as effective enables the HR professional to be "invited to the table" or given access to business discussions.

We analyzed the relationship between the nine HR competency domains (independent variables) to determine which HR competencies helped HR professionals be seen as more effective and get invited to business discussions.[7] Table 2.10 scales these findings to 100 percent to help illustrate the relative importance of each of the nine competencies for explaining individual effectiveness. These nine HR competency domains explain a remarkable 83 percent (overall R^2) of the individual HR effectiveness score. While all nine competence domains impact HR's personal effectiveness, Table 2.10 also reports that Credible Activist was by far the most important competency in determining HR overall personal effectiveness (19.3 percent).

These data suggest that HR professionals need to have a minimum competency in many domains, but their overall effectiveness comes mostly from their being a Credible Activist because they meet commitments, have political savvy, and take positions. In Chapter 6, we review the underlying factors of being a Credible Activist and offer specific actions for being more personally credible. It is also interesting that Total Rewards Steward and Technology and Media Integrator are negative scores, which will be discussed in Chapters 9 and 10.

Table 2.10   Independent impact of each HR competency on overall individual effectiveness[a]

	Percentage of Overall Effectiveness Explained by Each Competency Domain (adds up to 100%)
Strategic Positioner	**14.5**
Credible Activist	**19.3**
Paradox Navigator	**11.7**
Culture and Change Champion	**14.2**
Human Capital Curator	**13.1**
Analytics Designer and Interpreter	8.2
Total Rewards Steward	*(6.2)*
Technology and Media Integrator	*(4.9)*
Compliance Manager	7.9
Percentage of effectiveness R^2 explained by competencies	83.4

[a]In all tables, **bold** numbers are statistically significant at 0.05 level; scores in ( ) are negative.

Question 3: When Engaged "at the Table" (in Business Discussions), what Competencies Do Individual HR Professionals Bring That Add Value to Key Stakeholders?

As noted in Chapter 1, stakeholders have increasing and differing expectations of businesses and HR. In this research round, we measured the extent to which the HR professionals are seen as delivering value to each of six stakeholders: four outside the organization (customer, investor, community, regulator) and two inside the organization (line manager and employee).

We analyzed the relationship among each of the nine competency domains and the extent to which the individual HR professional creates value for each of the stakeholders. As in Table 2.10 earlier, we scale the results to 100 percent to show the relative importance of each of the nine HR competencies on each of these stakeholders.

Table 2.11 shows that the competencies for HR professionals should vary depending on who they personally represent when engaged in business discussions. These results show that once invited to the business discussion (because of being a Credible Activist), an individual HR professional needs to thoughtfully determine who he or she represents in those discussions. While all the nine competence domains matter, if HR professionals represent employees or line managers (internal stakeholders), they must continue to be Credible Activists. But if they represent customer and investor interests, they need to become Strategic Positioners. To represent regulators, they also need skills as Compliance Managers. It is also interesting to see that HR competencies in the Culture and Change Champion have relatively consistent and high impact for all stakeholders, while competencies in the Technology and Media Integrator and Total Rewards Steward have less impact on stakeholders.

Traditionally, HR professionals are employee advocates, but today they also serve line managers to deliver strategy and they also serve the business by representing external customers, investors, and the community. *The competencies that are required to add value on the inside are fundamentally different from those that are required to add value on the outside.* Firms don't exist to make managers and employees happy; they exist to make customers and shareholders happy. If HR wants to contribute to the purpose of the firm, the Strategic Positioner (followed by the Culture and Change Champion) competencies are mandatory. Specific actions and tools for being a Strategic Positioner will be discussed in greater detail in Chapter 7.

The purpose of Table 2.11 is to show how much of the value created for different stakeholders can be explained by each competency domain when we account for the other competency domains at the same time. These results show the percentage of variance in stakeholder value creation explained by each of the competency domains (scaled to 100 percent).

Table 2.11 Independent impact of each HR competency on the value created for stakeholders by the HR participant[a]

	External Customers	Investors/ Owners	Communities	Regulators	Line Managers	Employees
Strategic Positioner	**19.2**	**20.5**	**16.1**	**18.1**	**13.6**	**12.9**
Credible Activist	**11.7**	10.2	**12.9**	7.7	**19**	**20.3**
Paradox Navigator	**11.3**	**11.1**	**11.9**	9.6	**12**	**11.3**
Culture and Change Champion	**14.2**	**13.7**	**15.2**	9.3	**13.6**	**14.4**
Human Capital Curator	**12.5**	**13.1**	**12.5**	9.2	**14.9**	**12.2**
Analytics Designer and Interpreter	**10**	**11.4**	7.6	**12.8**	**8.4**	*(6.8)*
Total Rewards Steward	7	6.4	**10.2**	**8.8**	*(5.3)*	**8.3**
Technology and Media Integrator	**7.4**	6.6	6.5	6.2	*(4.6)*	5.3
Compliance Manager	*(6.7)*	*(7.1)*	7.2	**18.3**	**8.5**	**8.5**
Percent of R² explained by competencies	82.4	78.1	83.4	72.3	83.6	82.7

[a]Columns add to 100%

43

Question 4: When Engaged "at the Table" (in Business Discussions), How Do HR Professionals Represent the HR Department's Practices and Policies to Add Value to Key Stakeholders?

and

Question 5: What Competencies Do HR Professionals Require to Drive Business Results?

(Note we are addressing Questions 4 and 5 together.) To further determine what an HR professional should be, know, and do, we examined which HR competencies in the HR department had the strongest relationship with the organization's past and potential performance. As mentioned earlier, prior business performance was a six-item scale (profitability, labor productivity, new product development, customer satisfaction, attraction of new employees, regulatory compliance) and potential business performance was a ratings scale that determines the value created for different stakeholders (employee, organization, customer, investor, community, regulator).

Table 2.12 shows results for about 1,400 units where individual HR competence scores are combined. This table reveals interesting patterns about how HR competencies create value for key stakeholders. We recognize that this is a complicated table. For each stakeholder we show two columns. The first column under each stakeholder represents the value that an individual HR professional creates for the stakeholder, and the second column under each stakeholder represents the value the HR department creates for that stakeholder. Thus Table 2.12 allows us to see how different competencies have different stakeholder outcomes depending on the level of analysis (individual or department).

First, the Paradox Navigator competency seems to have the strongest relationship with prior business performance (Column 13) followed by the Strategic Positioner and the Technology and Media Integrator. This is a fascinating and new finding. Our explanation: Given the dramatic changes in the four external forces reviewed in Chapter 1, organizations also have to change to survive.

Creating agile organizations requires navigating paradox, which implies "and/also" thinking. For example, *paradox* means that organizations should be top-down and bottom-up; focused on customers outside and employees inside; being divergent and convergent; and encouraging freedom and control. Navigating these conflicts and tensions enables dialogue that encourages organization agility. Chapter 8 will review the ideas and tools for navigating paradox.

Second, in most cases, the relative importance of the individual HR competencies on external stakeholders matches the relative importance of the averages for all HR professionals in an organization of how HR practices impact stakeholders (the even columns). (Note that the odd columns for the six stakeholders shows the impact of the individual HR professional's competence on each stakeholder and are similar to Table 2.11.) These similar scores indicate that in most cases individual-level competencies and department-level competencies have similar effects on stakeholders. In these cases, individual HR professionals represent the HR practices of the HR department.

Third, there are a few cases where the competencies of the individual HR professional has more impact on the stakeholders than the competencies of the HR department (e.g., Strategic Positioner impact on line manager, Credible Activist on regulator, and Culture and Change Champion on external customers and regulators). In these cases, the individual HR professional has more impact than the collective HR professionals (Cell 3 of Table 2.5).

Fourth, there are a few cases where the collective HR competencies have more impact than the competencies of the individual HR professional (Analytics Designer and Implementer with employees; Technology and Media Integrator on customers, investors, and line managers; Total Rewards Steward on employees). In these cases, the HR department practices have more impact than the individual HR professional (Cell 2 of Table 2.5).

Table 2.12 *Independent impact of each HR competency on the perceived organization unit performance*[a]

	External Customers		Investors/ Owners		Communities	
	1 Individual (100)	2 Department (100)	3 Ind. (100)	4 Dept. (100)	5 Ind. (100)	6 Dept. (100)
Strategic Positioner	**19.2**	**20.4**	**20.5**	**20.5**	**16.1**	9.7
Credible Activist	**11.7**	9.5	10.2	14.0	**12.9**	7.8
Paradox Navigator	**11.3**	9.9	**11.1**	11.7	**11.9**	14.2
Culture and Change Champion	**14.2**	*(8.6)*	**13.7**	9.8	**15.2**	13.2
Human Capital Curator	**12.5**	8.1	**13.1**	8.2	**12.5**	9.1
Analytics Designer and Interpreter	**10.0**	10.2	**11.4**	7.2	7.6	7.7
Total Rewards Steward	7.0	9.6	6.4	8.8	**10.2**	**19**
Technology and Media Integrator	**7.4**	**18.7**	6.6	13.6	6.5	11.3
Compliance Manager	*(6.7)*	*(4.9)*	*(7.1)*	*(6.2)*	7.2	7.9
Percent of R² explained by competencies	82.4	19.8	78.1	12.2	83.4	17.8

[a]These results show the percentage of variance in business unit performance explained by each of the competency domains for both individual HR professionals and department HR professionals. Columns add to 100%

Regulators		Line Managers		Employees		Prior Business Performance
7 Ind. (100)	8 Dept. (100)	9 Ind. (100)	10 Dept. (100)	11 Ind. (100)	12 Dept. (100)	13 Department (100)
18.1	14.8	**13.6**	*(8.0)*	**12.9**	8.4	14.2
7.7	*(5.9)*	**19**	12.6	**20.3**	**19.7**	10.5
9.6	9.6	**12**	12.3	**11.3**	12.4	**18.9**
9.3	*(7.1)*	**13.6**	13.5	**14.4**	11.7	10.9
9.2	6.4	**14.9**	**21.4**	**12.2**	9.0	9.0
12.8	17.1	**8.4**	6.3	*(6.8)*	4.8	8.8
8.8	10.4	(5.3)	(8.3)	**8.3**	8.7	8.4
6.2	7.5	(4.6)	5.7	5.3	4.2	12.5
18.3	**21.2**	**8.5**	12	**8.5**	**21.1**	*(6.7)*
72.3	22.4	83.6	15.3	82.7	16.2	7.7

Question 6: What Is the Relative Importance of the Competencies of HR Professionals Versus the Activities of the HR Department in Driving Business Results?

One of the unique opportunities in this study is to compare the relative impact of individual HR competencies versus the activities of an HR department in predicting business results. The question of individual competence versus organization capabilities in driving business results has enormous implications on where to focus improvement efforts: on upgrading individuals or departments.

In this study, with information on about 1,400 businesses, we were able to determine whether the competencies of the HR professionals or the quality of the HR department had more impact on business performance. As indicated in Table 2.13, we found that the quality of the HR department had nearly four times (7.7 to 31 percent) the impact on business performance (Column 1 of Table 2.13) than the competencies of the HR professionals within the department. This research also found that the value created for stakeholders (employees, line managers, customers, investors, and communities) was two to five times more by the HR department than by the HR professionals. Upgrading HR professionals matters, but upgrading the HR department matters even more.

The old adage in HR has been "I like my HR professional, but I don't like the HR department or processes." These data challenge this maxim. While the competencies of HR professionals affect business performance, the quality of the HR department activities matters more. Given that much of the HR field for the past 25 years has focused on identifying the competencies for individual HR professionals, these findings are quite important and potentially game changing as we think about how to take the HR field to the next level of high impact.

These findings drive the title and focus of this book, *Victory Through Organization*, because organization matters more than individuals in creating business value. While this study focuses on individual versus organization within the HR context, the broader implications of this finding are discussed

Table 2.13   *Percentage of variance in the value the hr department creates for stakeholders explained by different variable groups*[a]

| | Business Performance | Stakeholders for HR | | | | | |
		External Customers	Investors/ Owners	Communities	Regulators	Line Managers	Employees
HR Professional Competencies	7.7	19.8	12.2	17.8	22.4	15.3	16.2
Activities of HR Departments	31	46.5	52.4	52.8	41.7	60.7	59.8
Other Variables (e.g. Strategy, Culture)	61.3	33.7	35.4	29.4	35.9	24	24
Multiple Regression R²	45.2	52.5	49.5	39.5	36.9	51.6	57.2

[a]These columns sum to 100 percent, representing the percentage of explained variance in the model that can be explained by each variable category. Columns total 100.

in Chapter 3 and the specific activities of an HR department that deliver value are reviewed in Chapters 4 and 5. We place these three "organization" chapters in Part II, ahead of the individual HR competency chapters (Part III) because of the remarkable impact of organization on key outcomes.

Conclusion and Key Findings

Chapter 1 built a case for why HR matters based on Four Forces in the socioeconomic climate. To respond to these opportunities and challenges, HR professionals and HR departments must evolve. Evolution of HR is not random but can be guided by rigorous research. In this chapter, we reviewed our historical research to position our current findings toward continuing to shape the HR profession. Table 2.14 summarizes the six questions we answer with our unique findings and insights. By building organizations to drive business results, being a Credible Activist to build reputation, acting as a Strategic Positioner to serve external stakeholders, and navigating paradox to deliver business performance, the HR profession can respond to future opportunities.

Table 2.14   Key Questions and Overall Findings

Key Question	Overall Finding	More Information
1. What are the key competencies of HR professionals and how do they differ by individual and organizational context?	• 9 overall competency domains • 3 core drivers, 3 strategic enablers, 3 foundational enablers	Chapter 9 on strategic enablers Chapter 10 on foundation enablers
2. What competencies do HR professionals require to be personally effective (i.e., to be invited "to the table")?	• Be a Credible Activist	Chapter 6 on being a Credible Activist

Table 2.14   Key Questions and Overall Findings (continued)

Key Question	Overall Finding	More Information
3. When engaged "at the table" (in business discussions) and HR professionals represent *themselves*, what competencies are required to add value to key stakeholders?	• If inside (employee, line), be a Credible Activist • If outside (customer, investor), be a Strategic Positioner	Chapter 7 on being a Strategic Positioner
4. When engaged "at the table" (in business discussions) and HR professionals represent the *HR department's practices and policies,* what competencies are required to add value to key stakeholders?	For the most part, the competencies of individual HR professionals' impact on stakeholder outcomes is the same as the collective competencies of HR professionals as they impact how HR practices influence stakeholders, with a few exceptions (culture and change and analytics).	Discussed in Chapters 6 through 10
5. What competencies do HR professionals require to drive business results?	• Navigate paradox (manage tension and divergent/convergent cycle), followed by Strategic Positioner and Technology and Media Integrator	Chapter 8 on being a Paradox Navigator
6. What is the relative importance of the competencies of HR professionals versus the activities of the HR department in driving business results?	• Recognize the importance of HR department • Build capabilities (information/external sensing, speed, culture, collaboration, efficiency, customer responsiveness)	• Chapter 3 on why organization matters • Chapter 4 on information and HR solutions • Chapter 5 on HR practices and HR analytics

PART II

ORGANIZATION

CHAPTER 3

WHY ORGANIZATION MATTERS: THE VALUE OF THE ORGANIZATION BEYOND INDIVIDUAL TALENT

3

In Chapter 2 we provided an overview of the empirical basis for the fundamental messages of our research and this book. We reviewed the legacy and current competencies that are required by HR professionals to be seen as competent by their clients and associates. We also examined those that are most closely associated with business performance and value for alternative stakeholder groups. We concluded Chapter 2 with the question, "What is the relative importance of the competencies of HR professionals versus the activities of the HR department as a whole in driving business results?" The concluding statistics of that chapter reveal that *HR-department-level activities have substantially greater impact across virtually all stakeholder categories than do the competencies of HR professionals.* This important finding suggests that HR department activities, rather than individual HR talent, have predominant impact on business performance and stakeholder value.

In the next three chapters, we provide variations on the theme of the *Victory Through Organization.* In Chapter 3 we apply organizational logic, research, and application to organizations as a whole (e.g., corporations or business units). In Chapters 4 and 5 we apply organization logic to HR departments.

In Chapter 3 we review the empirical evidence in greater detail. We discuss why organizations exist and their central role in economic results. Given the current preoccupation of HR departments with individual talent, we examine the importance of building individual excellence while focusing primarily on *organizational* capability to create competitive advantage. With this foundation, we review three categories of organizational capabilities, 11 key capabilities in all, that have been identified through the most recent

Human Resource Competency Study (HRCS). We provide a four-step process by which to create and sustain these requisite organizational capabilities. We then conclude by providing the logic for designing and conducting an organizational capability audit of your own for your organization.

Organization Matters

Let us begin with the fundamental premise of this chapter: Organization matters. In fact, it matters a lot. To stakeholders, organization matters more than individual talent. IBM's shareholders ask, "Has IBM lived up to its financial promises?" IBM's customers ask, "Has IBM done what it promised?" IBM's regulators ask, "Has IBM complied with specific regulations?" IBM's employees ask, "Has IBM treated me fairly?" The audience of the San Francisco Symphony asks, "Has the orchestra performed well?" The fans of Manchester United ask, "Has my team won?" Notice that stakeholders are interested in organizational performance—that is, *results*. Their expectations focus on the team, the organization, and to a much lesser degree, on the performance of any one individual. Individual performance is certainly expected and important. But competitive advantage resides in making the whole greater than the sum of the parts. Stakeholders recognize the importance of individual talent, but they primarily hold the organization accountable.

This logic is reinforced by the results from the most recent HRCS, as introduced in Chapter 2, which merit further exploration. (See Table 3.1—which was also presented in Chapter 2 as Table 2.13.) In our research we distinguish between two categories of outcomes: business performance and stakeholder value. Our measure of business performance focuses on the organization's performance over the last three years. Thus the business performance measure can best be interpreted as past performance. In contrast, the measure of stakeholder value serves as an indicator of the sustainable intangible value. Many have argued that intangible value created for stakeholders is a significant indicator of future performance.[1] Because of HR's mission to create and sustain organizational capability that promotes high performance, the following chapters will emphasize the influence of HR organization on stakeholder value.

Table 3.1 *Influence of individual competencies and HR department activities on overall business performance and stakeholder value creation*[a]

	Business Performance	External Customers	Investors/ Owners	Communities	Regulators	Line Managers	Employees
HR Professional Competencies	7.7	19.8	12.2	17.8	22.4	15.3	16.2
Activities of HR Departments	31	46.5	52.4	52.8	41.7	60.7	59.8
Other Variables (e.g., strategy, capability, culture)	61.3	33.7	35.4	29.4	35.9	24	24
Multiple Regression R²	45.2	52.5	49.5	39.5	36.9	51.6	57.2

[a]Columns sum to 100

57

These empirical results are striking and compelling. They show the following:

- When HR departments function as integrated organizations, they have approximately *four times* the impact on business performance as when compared to the competencies of individual HR professionals. This trend continues when we compare the organizational to individual impact on every stakeholder.
- HR as an organization creates over *twice* the value for external customers than do competent individual HR professionals.
- HR's impact on the value created for investors and owners is well over *three times* the impact of individual HR talent.
- HR as an organization has approximately *twice* the impact of individual talent on the communities and regulators.
- The value that HR organizations create for line managers is *four times* greater than that of HR individuals.

The implications of these findings are quite dramatic for HR departments, the agenda around which they are jointly unified, and how they function as integrated organizations. They challenge the long-held assumption that managers and employees like their HR professional but "hate HR." While these stakeholders may like their HR professional, real value comes from the collective efforts of the HR organization.

Importance of the Organization

Prima facie evidence suggests the importance of organization. Organizations pervade almost every aspect of life. With few exceptions, most people work directly or indirectly for organizations. Even private consultants tend to work for organizations as advisors. Sherlock Holmes employed Dr. Watson and Miss Hudson. The U.S. government is the largest employer in the world. The largest private employers in the United States are Walmart and McDonald's. We enjoy football (in all of its permutations); even individual sporting events (such as golf or tennis) are made possible by organizations. In the United States there are 1.5 million registered not-for-profit organizations.[2] According to Gallup's 2013 self-reported survey,[3] 37 percent of Americans claim to attend organized religious services of some kind.

In addition to such prima facie evidence, empirical evidence also supports the importance of organization in achieving economic and social results. Studies over the past three decades have consistently shown that organizational variables are greater predictors of firm performance[4] than contextual variables such as industry characteristics and geographical location.[5]

A survey of the literature in economics, sociology, organizational behavior, law, and psychology reveal five major reasons why organizations exist. In order to better manage and leverage the importance of organization, it is useful to understand the fundamental drivers that bring organizations into existence and to define the value they create:

- *Specialization:* Building on the work of earlier economists and philosophers, Adam Smith[6] argued that organizations exist to leverage the efficiency of labor specialization. His classic explanation is the manufacturing of pins. He suggests that one individual working alone might make 20 pins in a day. However, through the specialized division of labor in which "one man draws out the wire, another straightens it, a third cuts it, a fourth points it, a fifth grinds it," and so forth, 10 individuals working together might produce upward of 48,000 pins in a day.

- *Information cost optimization:* Nobel Prize–winners Ronald Coase and Oliver Williamson[7] suggest that organizations exist to compensate for a failure of markets to fully capture the value of goods or labor in market pricing. It is conceivable that a society might have no economic organizations. This might be the case if the value of the contribution of every worker at the end of every day could be calculated and people paid accordingly. Thus economic value would be created by each individual being an individual contributor with individual contracts to sell goods or services to customers. However, under the following conditions, the costs of determining the value of labor contributions become prohibitive. First, because the value of an employee's technical work and cultural fit might be unique to a specific firm, such bilateral contracting with individual workers becomes economically infeasible, especially if employees act opportunistically in trying to convince the payer that the value of their idiosyncratic work is greater than it is in actuality. Such is the case when the work has these characteristics: (1) when the work is best done in teams, (2) when the work is quality-based (as opposed to its being quantity-based) and its value is therefore more difficult to determine, (3) when value is created through intellectual contribution, (4) when the value of today's work might be determined only in the long run, and (5) when people doing the work are geographically dispersed. Such attributes certainly characterize today's work environment. To compensate for these dynamics, such employees are not left to their own individualized contracting decisions, rather they are hired by the firm. They are given goals and other output expectations. Supervisors and other monitoring mechanisms gather information about their performance and their value to the firm. A major value of this approach is in helping management to improve the efficiency of the firm by reducing the costs of monitoring and supervision. This can be done by creating common goals and values that mitigate the tendency toward opportunistic and free-riding behaviors while concurrently reducing the information costs of performance monitoring and supervisory oversight.

- *Complementarities:* A similar stream of thought suggests that organizations exist to coordinate work activities that are complex and differentiated on one hand but are interdependent and complementary on the other.[8] Firms such as GE optimize their performance to the extent that they integrate, coordinate, and leverage the firm's collective knowledge, capabilities, technologies, activities, structures, processes, business unit strategies, regulatory constraints, and market conditions. This is done to reduce costs as well as to optimize outcome results. Considerable research has shown that individual organizational practices tend to have weak, inconsistent, or statistically insignificant impact on business outcomes. But when collective organizational practices function as integrated systems, they have a positive impact on aggregate business performance. The implications are clear.

Organizations exist to make the whole greater than the sum of the parts. It is the work of management and HR to help ensure that these components work together technically, politically, and strategically.

- *Psychological fulfillment:* It has long since been argued that people have a fundamental drive or need to associate with other humans. While the empirical foundation of Abraham Maslow's needs hierarchy is specious at best, it continues to be used as a metaphor to explain human motivation.[9] As applied to organizations, people have needs that can be supplied in organizational settings. Coordinated action can better help people meet their basic needs for sustenance through remuneration and safety through collective action. Within the organizational context, people interact with others and generate feelings of friendship and affection. They develop attachments through years of association that provide identity and belonging. Through both financial and social rewards, esteem needs may be enhanced and individual motivation can be leveraged for greater overall performance. Finally, by answering the "Why of Work,"[10] organizations help people meet the full range of human needs, including self-actualization that both creates and derives from high performance.

- *Create and leverage talent:* Even the most seemingly self-made entrepreneurs with substantial individual talent were initially groomed through early organizational training (e.g., Bill Gates with his unique access to early computers and programming opportunities at his junior high school and Steve Jobs with his early grooming at Hewlett-Packard while still a high school student). As Malcolm Gladwell argues, "We are so caught in the myths of the best and the brightest and the self-made that we think outliers spring naturally from the earth."[11] Rather, in addition to having the right opportunities as a result of being born at the right time, it is frequently their early organizational exposure and the "cultural legacies" to which they were exposed that enabled them to excel. Many high-performing "outliers" become high performers by leveraging their inherent abilities through organizations of their making. Furthermore, no one can achieve 10,000 practice sessions that are required for individual excellence without support from coaches, cooks, cleaners, encouraging families, and practice settings.

For these reasons, organizations exist. Competitive advantage is determined by leveraging specialization, by optimizing information costs, by integrating complementarities, by making the organizational whole greater than the sum of the parts, and by using organization to create and leverage talent. For all of these purposes to be fulfilled, HR departments must provide processes, structures, talent, incentives, training, and communications that create and sustain the organizational capabilities.

How Should We Think About Talent in the Context of Organization?

Over the last couple of decades, the talent paradigm has gained considerable momentum. Dozens of books have been written on the importance of the processes of hiring, developing, nurturing, and retaining talent. Talent management consulting practices have proliferated. Even more telling is that many HR departments have formalized talent functions, and in some cases, HR departments have changed their titles to formally recognize the centrality of talent to their HR paradigm.

We suggest that if the focus on talent becomes overly emphasized, it might well be counterproductive to HR's ability to optimize its impact on business performance. The vulnerability of the talent paradigm is that it focuses on optimizing individual contributions. The term *talent* inherently focuses on ensuring that companies have the individual talent necessary to achieve their purposes. Certainly this is a critically important agenda for any organization. However, by focusing primarily on individual contributions, the talent movement, by definition, succeeds in making the organizational whole equal to the sum of the parts—and no more.

The talent paradigm was strongly amplified by the publication of McKinsey's *War on Talent*.[12] The authors proposed that "best" companies were obsessed with talent. They hired the top graduates from the top business schools. They paid them lavish signing bonuses and compensated them beyond their next-best alternatives. They identified star performers and turned them loose. Star performers could apply for any internal job that struck their fancy, and no manager could hold them back. Organizations empowered the entrepreneurial flair of their stars and moved them quickly into senior positions. All of this reinforced the superstar mindset, sometimes to the point of potential narcissism in which the best interest of the organization was sublimated to the self-interest of the superstar.[13] As Gladwell argues, such was the case for a major superstar-based organization that followed the war for talent prescription to great detail[14]—Enron.

This is not to say that companies should not do their very best to hire and nurture very good individual talent. However, we caution that talent in and of itself will tend not to create competitive advantage. Every year in dozens of forums around the world, we ask groups of line and HR executives, "How much time and effort do you spend trying to hire really good people?" They uniformly respond, "Quite a lot." We continue, "And how good of a job do you do?" They again uniformly respond, "Reasonably good." We continue, "Now all of you leave the room and have your exact counterparts from your most aggressive competitor take your seat in the room. Now we ask your competitors the same two questions. How do they respond?" The executives confirm, "Our competitors will respond just as we did." Then we ask, "So who is right, you or your competitors?" They respond, "We are both right." With that response, they confirm what labor economists have known for many years; over time major competitors will have roughly the same raw specialized talent.[15] In your hiring processes, you will win some and you will lose some. The critical issue is not the individual talent that you have; the competitive advantage is what you do with the talent once you have it. *And that is an organization issue.*

This conjecture is supported by both empirical and anecdotal evidence. Groysberg, Lee, and Nanda (2008) found that star security analysts who moved between employers exhibited an immediate drop in performance that lasted for at least five years.[16] However, when they take their teams with them, their performance stays constant.[17] Ulrich and Ulrich have noted that in the National Basketball Association (NBA), the team with the top scorer wins the NBA championship only about 15 percent of the time.[18] Against the bookmakers' odds of 5,000 to 1, Leicester City recently won the Premier League, the association of football clubs at the top of the English football league system. The average wages paid for top talent by the top five teams in the league was 191.2 million pounds. Leicester's wages were a paltry 48.2 million pounds. *Teamwork tends to beat the best talent.*

This is not to say that you can let up for one minute in striving to have the best talent. But competitive advantage is found in making the organization whole greater than the sum of the parts. It is this integrating and leveraging function of organization that creates competitive advantage. So if companies focus primarily on talent and fail to understand and focus on building and leveraging organization, their ability to create competitive advantage is severely limited.

The implications of the talent versus the organizational approach are far-reaching. If a company says it has a "people" or "human resource" strategy, the question is, "What does the company mean by *people*?" Do they mean people in the singular sense of "people as individual talent," or do they mean people in the plural sense of "people as a team or organization"? This distinction goes so far as to determine what one might select as a college major. For example, a college advisor asks a newly enrolled freshman, "What do you want to major in?" The student answers, "I am interested in people." Then the college advisor might ask, "What do you mean by *people*?" The freshman states, "You know, people as individuals: how they think and act." The advisor responds, "If you mean people as individuals, you will want to major in psychology." If in response to the first question, the freshman responds, "You know, people as teams or organizations." Then the advisor would respond, "Oh if you mean people as organization, you will want to major in economics (theory of the firm) or sociology (which has its roots in economics)." Thus the theory and practices that you use to manage people as individuals tend to be different from those you use to manage people as organization.

From a variety of perspectives, it is important for HR professionals and leaders to understand that talent and organization have very different though compatible agendas. And it is through the creation of capable organizations and not just through talented individuals that competitive advantage is achieved.

Organizational Capability: The Construct

Many alternative conceptualizations of organization have been proposed. Organization structure is probably the most frequently cited approach to organization.[19] People who focus on organization in this manner emphasize how to divide up specialized activities along different dimensions such as geography, products, markets, technologies, and functions. They then propose alternative mechanisms by which the horizontally differentiated parts can be reintegrated (e.g., hierarchy, meetings, rotating assignments, integrated goals, common values or culture, mutually compatible goals and measurements, information sharing and control, and cross-functional task forces).[20] Within this same approach, these writers propose how to segment the organization across vertical lines by addressing questions such as "How many layers of management does a company need?" "What is the optimal span of control?" "What is the grant of decision-making authority for each level?" They then address how to bring the differentiated layers into alignment. Such vertical aligning mechanisms include management by walking around, town halls, delegation, delayering, cascading objectives, vertical messaging, and employee surveys.

Among other approaches to framing the organization are the following:

- *Process approach:* Organizations are thought of as a set of step-by-step processes that begin with customer requirements and conclude with marketing, sales, and service. This approach is consistent with the value chain approach by which each step in the value chain is identified and emphasized as potential sources of competitive advantage.[21]
- *Culture approach:* Organizations are thought of as shared values, beliefs, and assumptions that give focus, integration, meaning, and purpose to employees as well as to customers.[22]
- *Systems approach:* Organizations are thought of as a set of HR, leadership, and organizational practices that integrate to accomplish the organization's strategic direction. This approach was popularized in the classic *In Search of Excellence*[23] and eventually became the foundation for McKinsey's 7-S model and other related approaches.

- *Core competency approach:* Organizations are thought of as bundles of technical competencies[24] (e.g., designing and building internal combustion engines) that are most valued by customers. In this approach, technical know-how is built and leveraged to create competitive advantage.[25]
- *Strategic goal approach:* Organizations are thought of as mechanisms through which the strategic goals can be achieved. Goals reflect the market forces that determine whether or not the organization and its members will be rewarded by society for accomplishing the purposes for which society allows their organization to exist.[26]

We propose that the most powerful way to think about organization is through the logic of "organizational capability."[27] Capabilities represent what the organization is good at doing toward implementing its strategy and creating value for its stakeholders. Capabilities include how the organization patterns the collective human intelligence and activities through integrated infrastructure processes, structures, incentives, skills, training, and information flow. Our approach to organizational capability builds on and leverages all of the preceding approaches. By so doing we provide a logic that will optimize the likelihood of achieving competitive advantage and business success. We suggest a four-step process.

- *Step 1:* Firms should first identify the organizational capabilities that they must have to *meet the requirements of customers and shareholders.*
- *Step 2:* We then suggest that companies *identify the core technical capabilities* that will be required to meet these market-based requirements.
- *Step 3:* To fully leverage these technical capabilities and to guide the workforce toward the market-based outcome, the firm must *specify its desired culture,* that is, how people need to think and behave together in ways that are consistent with market requirements.
- *Step 4:* The *full system* of organizational practices must then be designed and delivered to build the core technical capabilities of the firm and to encourage people individually and collectively to think and behave in ways that will meet the requirements of their customers and owners.

From here, we elaborate on the four steps.

Organizational Capability: The Application

We start from the premise that organizations exist to fulfill fundamental social purposes that are represented primarily by customers and shareholders. If a company fails to deliver on its socially derived purposes as well as others, then customers and owners withdraw their support. Thus organizational capabilities must be defined from the outside in. The driving question is

> *Does your firm have the organizational capabilities that ensure that it meets the current and future requirements of the marketplace better than its competitors?*

Step 1: Defining the Required Organizational Capabilities

With this premise in place, we then obviously assert that not all customers are equally important. Having a clear understanding of the requirements of your most important present and future customers is paramount. In addition to customer requirements, other criteria may also be applied to identifying a firm's required organizational capabilities. Other potential requirements might include shareholder expectations, process or product technology, economic health of the industry, suppliers' market power, level of industry competitiveness, globalization, the availability of human capital, product life-cycle trends, and the speed of technological innovation.

From the HRCS done in 2016, we have identified 11 basic organizational capabilities that guide or influence organizational performance. We have factor-analyzed these 11 capabilities into three categories. We mapped these 11 capabilities on a matrix according to those that have the greatest impact on business performance and that are done best and most poorly; that matrix is shown in Figure 3.1. Within this mapping, we have also grouped the 11 capabilities into three capability categories.

The 11 specific capabilities can be grouped into three categories: Market-based Innovation, Customer-based Speed, and Human Capital.

Figure 3.1   *Organization capabilities by effectiveness and business impact*

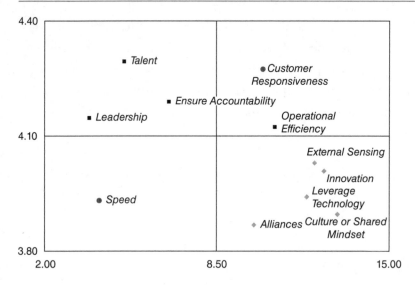

Market-based Innovation

Market-based Innovation capabilities include External Sensing, Innovation, Leverage Technology, Alliances, and Culture or Shared Mindset.

All of the capabilities that comprise Market-based Innovation are done at below-average levels and have above-average impact. This is the capability of potential competitive advantage. Firms such as GE, BlackRock, and Unilever aggressively leverage technology (e.g., big data analytics) to sense external market trends; they also continually search the marketplace for qualitative information that helps them interpret current market preferences and clarify future trends. They embed the value of such information into the culture of the firm by internal and external collaborative alliances. Such collaboration may occur within teams, across teams, across layers of management, with new acquisitions, and with external stakeholders such as suppliers, customers, consultants, and other technical experts. With this rich and comprehensive flow of reality-based information, these firms are able to innovate ahead of their competitors, thereby creating present and future competitive advantage.

Customer-based Speed

Customer-based Speed capabilities include Speed of Acting and Customer Responsiveness.

The differing levels of effectiveness and business impact of customer responsiveness and speed are noteworthy. Firms do a relatively good job in responding to customer demands, and doing so results in above-average performance. What firms tend to do considerably less effectively is to respond with speed and agility. It appears that responding to customers accurately is more important than responding quickly. Such have been the strategic approaches of Apple and Tata Consultancy Services (TCS). Whereas Samsung continually pushes cell phone updates into the market, Apple works to ensure that its products are carefully crafted to excite and engage customers. TCS has recognized that its brand hinges on the quality of its consulting services. As it moves into the Internet of Things, big data analytics, and carbon footprint reductions, it does so with precision and care. In so doing, TCS creates digital competitive advantage in retailing, healthcare, financial services, and other market segments.

Human Capital

Human Capital capabilities include Talent, Leadership, Ensure Accountability, and Operational Efficiency.

In the Human Capital capability category, we found an integration of individual talent and leaders both being accountable for getting things done with high levels of operating efficiency. Two features of the Human Capital factor are noteworthy. First, individual talent, leadership, and accountability are all done relatively well but have below-average impact on business performance; thus they tend to provide comparatively less opportunity for competitive advantage. Second, of the three, operating efficiency is the only one that has above-average impact on business performance. Accountability matters, and companies tend to do it well.

Once a company's organizational capabilities are clearly selected, it is then useful to develop measures of success for each. These measures can be used to track progress, to communicate capabilities to customers and shareholders, to reveal areas for improvement, to specify operational definitions for selected organizational capabilities, and to provide the basis for performance evaluation and rewards. For example, innovation might be measured by revenues from products that are less than three years old and customer responsiveness might be measured by a customer service index. Other organizational capabilities should be measured in a manner that is consistent with the individual firm's conceptualization of its required organizational capabilities.

Step 2: Building Technical Competencies

Virtually every industry has at its foundation a core technical competency. In the oil industry a company must know how to discover oil reserves (geology), drill wells to access those reserves (mechanical engineering), refine crude oil into gasoline (chemical engineering), and market gasoline and other products (distribution logistics). In the pharmaceutical industry, firms must excel in molecular biochemistry and pharmacogenomics (how a person's gene configuration responds to specific drug treatments). For these firms, every other activity builds on these technical competencies. Without this technical core, firms cannot exist. However, the shrinking shelf-life of technical knowledge indicates that technical knowledge as a competitive differentiator is on the decline. The key issue is not the technical talent that you have; the key issue is your ability to create and use technical knowledge once you have it. And that is an organizational capability issue.

Nevertheless, firms must honestly take inventory whether or not they have the quantity and quality of technical competencies at a competitive level.

Step 3: Specify Cultural Capabilities

Culture is perhaps one of the most widely cited, highly disputed, superficially referenced, and instinctively important constructs in business. In 2014 *culture* was identified by Merriam Webster as the Word of the Year. In Deloitte's *Global Human Capital Trends 2015*, executives stated that culture was rated as their most important overall and challenging issue. Numerous anecdotal examples permeate the popular press explaining the central importance of culture in the success in companies across virtually all industries, such as automotive (e.g., Toyota), transportation (e.g., Southwest), pharmaceuticals (e.g., Johnson & Johnson), investment services (e.g., BlackRock), and fast-moving consumer goods (e.g., Procter & Gamble). Perhaps more important than anecdotal evidence are numerous empirical studies that support the significant influence of culture on firm performance.[28] One recent article, for example, indicated that CEO personality influences firm performance primarily as it is moderated through the means of organizational culture.[29]

Given its importance, the lack of clarity and precision with which culture is defined is a bit surprising. Multiple definitions have been offered: beliefs, norms, values, behaviors, customers, knowledge, assumptions, shared cognitions, artifacts, symbols, and social structure, and the list goes on. In the first six months of 2016, every issue of the *Harvard Business Review* had at least one article that addressed aspects of culture, ranging from ignoring culture ("You Can't Fix Culture") to emphasizing cultures of collaboration, empathy, emotion, innovation, originality, agility, intensity, and so on.

Arguably, the most comprehensive overview of alternative cultural conceptualizations was done by Kroeber and Kluckhohn.[30] They reviewed and summarized 164 definitions of culture across sociology, anthropology, economics, and psychology. Their results are informative. Four percent of the 164 major writers about culture defined culture in terms of shared ways of thinking (i.e., collective ideas, values, and ideals). Thirty-seven percent framed culture in terms of behavior (i.e., patterns of behaviors, shared habits, collective problem solving, and activities to achieve outcomes). A noticeable 49 percent of the cultural constructs indicated that culture is best conceived in terms of how social groups share common ways of both thinking and behaving.

Building on the preceding theoretical and empirical work and on our own work with hundreds of companies on their cultural agendas, we have found the following to be the most useful way to think about culture within the organizational context. We found that it is useful to think about culture as *both* a perceived construct *and* a reality-based construct. In this context, all words that are used to describe culture are based on perceptions. They are linguistic categories that represent aggregations of behavior.

For example, let's assume that Disney Theme Parks want to create an organizational capability of customer responsiveness. It would therefore want to create a culture that would create and sustain that organizational capability. If you were to ask someone who has visited a Disney theme park, "What words would you use to describe Disney's culture?" most people would respond with "friendly." Actually Disney employees are not necessarily friendly. What Disney's customers had seen was Disney employees behaving in certain ways[31] and then they concluded in their minds that Disney employees are friendly. "Friendly" is a generalized perception that Disney wants to create in the minds (i.e., in the perceptions) of its customers. However, these perceptions are created from people experiencing the reality of how Disney employees behave together. The perception of culture is in the mind of the observer. The reality of culture is in employee behaviors. The same is true for all culture words such as *fast, responsive, sensitive, aggressive, stylish, obsessive, relentless, creative, efficient, bold, collaborative*, and so on. These are linguistic categories that we use to describe aggregations of behaviors.

Creating Cultural Perception: An Example

One company with which we are familiar decided that it wanted its identity in the minds of its customers to be "Disciplined Innovation." The company then asked itself, "How do our employees need to behave so that our customers will conclude that this is a company whose identity is best described by *disciplined innovation*?" For this company, such behaviors included the following:

- When mistakes are made, teams meet to discuss why a faulty decision occurred (e.g., lack of information, knowledge, or logic) and what needs to be done in the future to ensure that the mistake is not repeated.
- When faced with change initiatives, people make the change happen within prestated performance and time-frame parameters.

- When meetings, reports, approvals, and paperwork inhibit speed and responsiveness to customers, people meet to discuss how to eliminate the inhibitor and gain approval for its removal.
- New ideas are accessed by reaching to outside experts and sources of information to build global networks and partnerships. These networks are leveraged to make better decisions and create new market opportunities.
- Each department compares its practices and results against those of internal and external best practices, determines how to bridge the gap, and monitors progress. Forums are created to facilitate internal and external best practices sharing.

Through this logic, companies are able to capture both the powerful *perception* of culture as well as the *reality* of culture that is embodied in how people think and behave together. All of this is based on the requirements of customers and other stakeholders.

Step 4: Implement Organization Practices

In the first three steps, we have specified the organizational capabilities and their accompanying metrics based on customer and other contextual conditions. We then identified the technical and cultural capabilities that are required to create and sustain the organizational capabilities. In Step 4 we summarize the organizational practices that are necessary to build the technical skills and cultural behaviors needed to encourage performance toward the organizational capability metrics that are specified in Step 1.

Six categories of organizational practices can be differentiated. We have provided substantial detail for each of these in previous publications[32] and will also provide greater detail on these practices in subsequent chapters of this volume. By way of quick review, the six categories include the following:

- *Staffing* consists of the generic talent cycle of hiring, transferring, promoting, and exiting.

- *Measurement and rewards* includes goal setting, performance management, output and behavioral measurements, and financial and nonfinancial rewards.
- *Training and development* covers both internal and external classroom training as well as on-the-job development.
- *Information management* consists of the flow of internal communications as well as the coordination, dissemination, and utilization of externally based information.
- *Structure and process* covers all dimensions of organizational structure, including horizontal and vertical differentiation and integration as well as the design of individual processes in the context of the integrated organization-wide value chain.
- *Leadership*, last but not least, includes both the developing and leveraging of leadership talent in the short run while ensuring a pipeline of competent and results-oriented leaders over the long run.

The first consideration for Step 4 is to determine how many of the preceding organizational, leadership, and HR practices can be redesigned and implemented in a reasonable time frame. The answer is, of course, as many as you need to create your required organizational capabilities. Research by Mark Huselid[33] indicates that high-performance practices (generally as listed previously) reach the inflection point of business impact when around 77 percent of them are implemented.

The second consideration is to identify which of these practices are out of alignment with the required technical competencies, cultural behaviors, and organizational capability metrics. This can be done on a simple three-point scale with 1 equaling high and 3 equaling low.

The third consideration is to identify which of these practices would have greatest impact if they were brought into alignment. This might also be evaluated on a three-point scale. In this case, 1 equals low and 3 equals high. The assumption behind this step is that not all practices will have equal impact. For example, if a firm wants to improve its speed capability, it would probably not initially rely on staffing or promotions; rather, the first practice to be addressed would probably be work processes ("structure and process").

If the work processes are inherently designed to be slow due to redundant and unnecessary steps, these maladies must first be addressed before other practices such as measurements or rewards would be implemented.

You may then multiply the two results for each practice area together. The multiplicative relationship of these two considerations tell us which practices are out of alignment of your desired organizational capabilities and which would have greatest impact if we brought them into alignment.

Organizational Capability: The Audit

We'll finalize this chapter by providing an example of an organizational capability audit, which you can use to assess the current state of your organization with respect to the 11 key capabilities described earlier. The audit focuses on assessing the extent to which your firm has specific organizational capabilities relative to its competitors.[34] A content audit may be customized to your firm's specific organizational capability requirements. The following provides a starting point for constructing a customized content audit.

The scale that we suggest for this audit is as follows:

1. My company is significantly below others in my industry.
2. My company is somewhat below others in my industry.
3. My company is as good as others.
4. My company is somewhat above others in this area.
5. My company is best in class in this area.

Customer Responsiveness	1	2	3	4	5
We are good at building long-term relationships of trust with our target customers.					
All employees can create a line-of-sight between their personal activities and external customer value.					
Customers experience minimal hassle in getting their questions answered or problems resolved.					

External Sensing	1	2	3	4	5
We keep ourselves in touch with marketplace reality through continually accessing qualitative and quantitative information.					
We bring customer information into the direct experience of all employees.					
We communicate positive or negative market performance throughout our organization.					

Innovation	1	2	3	4	5
We are good at creating new products and services that drive growth.					
We anticipate future market trends and seek to respond to those trends before they occur.					
Employees understand how to shepherd new ideas through the organization to full implementation.					

Agility	1	2	3	4	5
We quickly reconfigure the organization based on changes in the market environment.					
We quickly eliminate obstacles to organizational speed and agility.					
We excel at making change happen quickly.					

Culture	1	2	3	4	5
We define our culture from the outside in based on the requirements of our targeted customers.					
We translate our cultural requirements into specific competitive behaviors that drive business performance.					
We ensure the alignment of our organizational practices with our required culture.					

Alliances	1	2	3	4	5
We co-create new products and services with our targeted customers.					
We encourage employees to cooperate within and across teams and departments.					
Information is shared across the organization so that our organizational intelligence is greater than the sum of individual intelligence.					

Leverage Technology	1	2	3	4	5
We use social media to optimize our brand coverage.					
Our information systems get the right information to the right people at the right time.					
We use big data analytics to identify insights into market opportunities.					

Operational Efficiency	1	2	3	4	5
We continually examine how to reduce operating costs.					
We have clearly defined and frequently used processes to improve our processes.					
Employees have the information, incentives, training, and measurements necessary to function with minimal supervision.					

Leadership	1	2	3	4	5
Our leadership selection process is free of political considerations.					
We have a pipeline of leaders with the potential for upward institutional mobility.					
Our leaders are regular and consistent role models of our cultural behaviors.					

Talent	1	2	3	4	5
We have an optimal level of skills in our highest value-added technical capabilities.					
We attract and retain the highest quality talent.					
We provide challenging and rewarding work assignments for our high-potential employees.					

CHAPTER 4

HIGH-PRIORITY HR PRACTICES—INFORMATION MANAGEMENT AND INTEGRATED HR PRACTICES

4

In this chapter we will review HR department practices that are generally *not* done well around the world but that when they *are* done well have the greatest potential to impact stakeholder value. Since many of these high-impact practices are done well by a relatively small set of high-performing companies, they may seem "foreign" to many HR and line executives. But it is through these practices that the greatest potential for differentiating HR performance resides. This chapter has potentially important implications for those who are responsible for the design and delivery of high-performing HR departments, those who are interested in ensuring that their personal efforts contribute to the overall HR performance, and those in line management who seek to create and sustain high-performing organizations.

In Chapter 3 we provided the case that competitive advantage is found when we consider organizations as a whole instead of as a summation of talented individuals. We emphasized that this is especially true for competent HR professionals when compared to well-integrated HR departments. By way of review, Table 4.1 (which is also shown as Tables 2.13 and 3.1 in the last two chapters, respectively) shows that HR *department* activities explain much more of the value created for all stakeholders and overall business performance than does the sum of competent individual HR professionals.

These findings naturally raise the questions, "Which HR department activities have greatest impact on stakeholder value along with short-term business performance, and which have the greatest room for improvement?" Examining these questions in detail is the focus of this and the next chapter.

Table 4.1 Relative impact of HR professional competencies and HR department activities on alternative stakeholder categories[a]

	Business Performance	External Customers	Investors/ Owners	Communities	Regulators	Line Managers	Employees
HR Professional Competencies	7.7	19.8	12.2	17.8	22.4	15.3	16.2
Activities of HR Departments	31	46.5	52.4	52.8	41.7	60.7	59.8
Other Variables (e.g., strategy, capability, culture)	61.3	33.7	35.4	29.4	35.9	24	24
Multiple Regression adj. R^2	45.2	52.5	49.5	39.5	36.9	51.6	57.2

[a]The rows sum to 100 percent, representing the percentage of explained variance in the model that can be explained by each factor category.

Understanding Key HR Department Activities

We identified four categories of HR departmental activities:

- HR's role in information management focuses on HR's involvement in helping ensure the optimal flow of information, including identifying, accessing, importing, analyzing, and disseminating important external information and to facilitate its use in decision making that impacts the business.
- Integrated HR practices focuses on the integration of business strategy, culture, technical capabilities, and HR policies and procedures.
- Employee performance HR includes the HR practices of performance management, rewards, training, and empowerment.
- HR analytics focuses on applying metrics to track HR's measurement scorecard.

In Chapter 2, we distinguished between two outcomes for HR professionals and HR departments: business performance and stakeholder value. Since the distinction between the two is central to this and the next chapter, we briefly repeat it here.

Our measures of business performance look at the past three years of competitive performance relative to several dimensions, including profitability, labor productivity, developing new products, customer satisfaction, attracting talent, and regulatory compliance. These are important indicators of performance looking backward. Research on market capitalization suggests that 50 percent of a firm's future performance might be predicated on the past. But the other 50 percent is predicated on creating sustainable value for external stakeholders of the business, including customers, investors, communities, and regulators, in addition to internal stakeholders such as line managers and employees.

Table 4.2 shows that for HR departments to have the greatest impact in *short-term business performance*, they should focus on employee performance HR, consisting of measurement, rewards, training, and empowerment. The relationship of these items to short-term performance makes sense in that they tend to be designed and implemented to incentivize short-term results.

Table 4.2 *Relative impact of HR department activities on different stakeholders*[a]

	Business Performance	External Customers	Investors/Owners	Communities	Regulators	Line Managers	Employees
Employee Performance HR	**44.1**	(6.5)	10	16.2	(6.1)	15.3	**19**
Integrated HR Practices	16.9	**21.6**	**30.8**	**28.5**	**33.6**	**57.2**	**56.1**
HR Analytics	17.3	**26.7**	23.3	18.1	**31**	15.2	(13.2)
HR Information Management	21.7	**45.2**	**35.9**	37.2	29.4	12.2	11.7
Total Percentage Explained by HR Department Activity	31	46.5	52.4	52.8	41.7	60.7	59.8

[a]The rows sum to 100 percent, representing the percentage of explained variance in the model that can be explained by each factor category. Bold numbers represent results that are statistically significant. Numbers in parentheses are negative.

To create value for *regulators, line managers, and employees*, HR departments should focus on Integrated HR Practices. These stakeholders expect HR departments to provide integrated HR practices that are predictable, consistent, and comprehensible.

To create value for *external customers, investors,* and *communities,* HR department emphasis should be on optimizing the flow of information throughout the institution. In today's information-rich environment, managing and leveraging the flow of external information is a primary mechanism for sustainable performance.

Finally, HR analytics have relatively small impact on both short-term business performance as well as stakeholder value. These somewhat dramatic and unanticipated results will receive detailed discussions in this chapter and the next.

The Biggest Opportunities in HR Activities

To identify the HR department activities that have the greatest room for improvement, we calculated the average effectiveness scores for each activity category.[1] They are presented in Table 4.3.

Table 4.3   Relative effectiveness of HR department activities

HR Department Activity	Mean
Integrated HR	3.93
HR Analytics	3.57
Employee Performance HR	3.52
HR's Role in Information Management	3.49

This table shows HR departments are most effective at integrated HR activities. The other HR department activities cluster around the mid-3s with HR's role in information management coming in last.

Four high-level conclusions stand out from the preceding information:

- Integrated HR activities create the greatest value for regulators, line managers, and employees and are done at the highest effectiveness level.
- Employee performance HR practices generally have modest effectiveness scores but have the greatest impact on short-term business performance.
- HR's role in information management creates the greatest value for customers, shareholders, and communities and is done least well in HR departments around the world. Given that this HR department activity is done most poorly but has greatest impact on sustainable stakeholder value, we will provide extensive descriptions and analyses for this potentially important HR agenda.
- HR analytics are done at a moderate level and have low influence on either short-term business performance or sustainable stakeholder value.

These results encourage HR departments to address three defining issues. The most basic issue is, "Who is the customer of HR? Is our target customer external buying customers or our internal clients?" Achieving success with one will not necessarily achieve success with the other. The second issue is, "Should HR departments focus on short-term performance or sustainable, long-term value creation?" The third issue is, "How seriously do we take the business partner aspiration?" For years, HR has been talking about being a business partner. Probably a more accurate way of framing the agenda is HR's aspiration to be a partner *in the business*. If such is the aspiration, then the customer of the business partnership is the external customer. The company does not exist to make management or employees happy; the company's mission or purpose is to make external stakeholders happy.

The previous data indicate which HR department activities create value for which stakeholders; notably they are largely mutually exclusive. HR professionals must obviously work closely with line executives and employees, but the data indicate that HR professionals can create value for them without contributing substantially to the organization's purpose. Finding the balance is the key. In subsequent chapters, we will address the HR mandate for HR professionals to work successfully as Paradox Navigators.

HR's Role in Information Management

The importance of HR's role in information management is rather remarkable and to a great degree unanticipated. The importance of this agenda is further amplified by the fact that it is done least well of the four HR department activity factors in HR departments from around the world.

It should be noted at the outset that information management is not HR applying information to itself. This is rather HR's role to help design and facilitate the flow of information throughout the organization.

To explain why HR's role in managing information is so important, we first need to clarify the nature of today's information environment. In this section, we will discuss the driving characteristics of today's information-rich environment and the implications of the information environment for changing business models, organization design, and talent. We will then provide an information management framework that is indicated by our data and will conclude by possible steps that an HR department might take to increase its involvement in applying the framework.

The Information Environment

On virtually everyone's list of major trends that are transforming the nature of business is information.[2] Information is a much broader construct than information technology. It includes the generation of facts or knowledge that are then conveyed from one source to another, analyzed to create useful insights, and finally utilized to create economic or social value. The information agenda includes designing and implementing the hard and soft processes by which firms may create and eventually leverage information for competitive advantage. In this regard, the information agenda is related to but goes far beyond technology per se.

Four factors characterize today's information flow within and between organizations: speed, pervasiveness, ubiquity, and structure.

1. *Speed:* The speed of information has catapulted from really fast to faster than the speed of thought. Moore's law is often referenced as an example. In 1965, Gordon Moore projected that the speed of information processing would double every two years. This projection was eventually popularized to 18 months. Fast forward to 2016, the speed of information would have increased over the ensuing years by 4.8 trillion percent. In one Internet minute in the year 2015, 2.4 million searches occur on Google, 701,389 Facebook logins occur, and 150 million e-mails are sent.[3] By December 2015 it would take you five years to view all the video content that crosses the Internet each second.

   The speed dimension of information is played out in virtually all aspects of business. During the 10 years from the first Facebook post, more people have created Facebook accounts than the population of China. In the two years between 2013 and 2015, the Wall Street Journal International site increased its traffic from 21 to 33 percent. To respond to its speed-accustomed customers, FedEx has provided instantaneous package location through tracking mechanisms in each package. Finally, people will visit a website less often if it is as little as one-half of a second slower than a close competitor.

2. *Pervasiveness:* Today there are well over a billion transistors for every person on Earth. By 2020, 44 zettabytes of data will be available, roughly equivalent to the amount of digital memory required to record all human speech ever spoken or written. That is enough for a stack of single-spaced pages of data to reach the moon and back 79,000 times. U.S.-based Acxiom provides clients from multiple sectors more than 500 million customers with 1,500 data categories representing more than 50 billion transactions. In 1997, 2 percent of the world's population was online; in 2016, it was 40 percent.[4] In the United States the number is 98 percent. SpaceX and OneWeb are racing to provide fast, high-quality connection to the remaining 60 percent through cheap, low-flying satellites. Cross-border Skype calls have increased 500 percent from 2009 to 2014, while traditional calls grew a paltry 4 percent. This has

been facilitated by a 4,500 percent increase in cross-border bandwidth used since 2005.[5]

3. *Ubiquity: The Internet of Things:* The technology that propels the information agenda is enabling machines to bypass much of the involvement of their human creators. Information processing allows machine-to-machine communications with minimal human intervention. Cisco predicts that by 2020, 50 billion "things" will be communicating with each other. Applying Internet of Things algorithms, General Electric (GE) tracks the functioning of its aircraft engines while the engines are still in the air. By so doing GE can identify needed repairs so that when a plane lands, the repair materials are ready. This decreases the plane's time on the ground, thereby, eliminating 60,000 late flights per year and significantly boosting revenues per plane for GE's customers. Perhaps the most well-known example of the Internet of Things is found in the fast-growing trend toward "smart cars." Led by Google, embedded in a single smart car is the computing power of 20 personal computers (PCs). This will enable smart cars to communicate with other machines to find parking places, determine the easiest routes home, warn of traffic dangers, signal if traffic police are around, and drive themselves in the safest lanes at the safest speed.

4. *Structure:* In the midst of this morass of information, a primary challenge is how to identify patterns of information that can be applied to decision making. The mechanisms through which information patterns may be identified depend on whether people are accessing and analyzing structured or unstructured information.

   - *Structured information* is information that can be embedded in the columns and rows of a spreadsheet. The application of big data analytics facilitates the analysis of structured data for business and government decision making. Structured big data tends to be stable, predictable, and fact-based. This data can be readily categorized and interpreted. Because of its numeric attributes, it is relatively easy to reach consensus about its meaning. For example, by finding patterns in your online buying habits and by comparing your habits to millions of others, Amazon makes product recommendations that you are likely to buy. Using face-recognition technology, GAP will be able to identify who you are, your clothes and related buying habits, and make product recommendations that are most likely to appeal to you. Structured information also assumes that large-scale data are available along with algorithms that make predictive analytics possible. For example, predictive analytics in healthcare enable faster diagnostics, reduce length of in-patient stays, ensure better equipment utilization, and optimize clinical procedures.

• *Unstructured information:* The overwhelming proportion of global information is available in unstructured formats that cannot be quantified or organized on a spreadsheet. As opposed to structured information, unstructured information is unstable and less predictable. Its patterns are difficult to identify and its interpretation is problematic; therefore, reaching consensus about the meaning and implications of unstructured data is more difficult and thereby creates opportunities for competitive advantage. Unstructured information exists in two forms: electronic and social interaction.

  • Electronic-based unstructured information exists in YouTube videos, online chat rooms, e-mails, speeches by senior executives, medical records, and so on. While still in its infancy, the analytical processes for identifying patterns in electronically based unstructured information is quickly progressing in the forms of Hadoop, nSpace 2, and word pattern algorithms (tag clouds). JP Morgan, for example, identifies the issues that employees at all levels are considering and discussing through the application of language-based algorithms to meeting minutes, speeches, and e-mails.

  • Socially based unstructured information exists in the forms of hallway conversions, social networks, phone calls, and debates in meetings and town halls. Through these means many insights are generated, and most are subsequently lost. How does a company capture insightful, focused, spontaneous, and transient human interactions that are spread through thousands of "chance" occurrences? To facilitate, capture, and use socially unstructured information through "orchestrated spontaneity," leading companies such as BlackRock, Pfizer, and State Street are developing well-defined, disciplined yet flexible, high-impact "social algorithms." These companies argue that substantial competitive advantage may be gleaned from this type of information. How they do so will be discussed later in this chapter.

The implications of these distinctions for HR departments are potentially profound. HR departments may build the organizational capability and ensure individual talent that can electronically access and analyze structured information and electronically formatted unstructured data. Doing so can make a fundamental difference in a firm's competitive advantage. Perhaps more important for HR departments is their potentially central role in creating a social mechanism by which socially based unstructured information is created, shared, and utilized.

Implications for Business Models, Organization Design, and Talent Management

Virtually every industry is transforming under opportunities and threats that result from the information revolution. Highly digitalized sectors such as media, finance, insurance, and information technology have grown four times since 1997, while growth in other sectors is barely keeping pace. Traditional sector barriers are blurring, and new sectors are emerging. Amazon started in books and now sells almost everything. Google has expanded from its search engine roots into biotech research, venture capital investments, and longevity research. Examples of five business model disruptions include the following:

- *Distribution channel control:* Web-enabled control over distribution channels has grown substantially, enabling remarkable topline growth of Facebook, iTunes, eBay, and Airbnb. Craigslist enables customers to bypass real estate agents to more quickly and efficiently rent out apartments. Between 2000 and 2014 online hotel bookings increased 10 percent, but the number of travel agents in the United States fell by 48 percent.[6]

- *Cost-based efficiency:* Companies that are leveraging web-enabled cost savings have experienced remarkable success. At the expense of traditional telephony carriers, Skype has shifted $37 billion of communication value to consumers. In Europe, as a result of making online price comparisons, customers have moved billions of euros to discount retailers at the expense of the traditionally dominant retailers. By providing substantially lower-priced car services, Uber grew in six years from one driver to 327,000.[7] Perhaps most remarkably, Wikipedia is now the world's largest repository of knowledge, virtually displacing traditional encyclopedias and almanacs. It is written and supported by unpaid volunteers and is easily accessed without cost.
- *Innovation:* Web-enabled innovation is a hallmark of the current generation. For example, Linux, the open-source software, has been created by thousands of unpaid programmers who have never been at the same place at the same time. It is now the dominant software for mobile devices and has extended its reach into far-flung sectors, including movies where it is used by more than 95 percent of the servers and desktops at large animation and visual effects companies.[8] In the six years since the advent of the first app, more than 1.5 million are now available. The intersection of creativity with web-enabled market opportunities led OKCashbag from Korea to create a mobile app that accesses and categorizes pools of product promotions for more than 50,000 merchants.[9]
- *Globalization:* In 2014, $2.8 trillion of the global GDP stemmed from information flow. This is larger than the impact of the trade of hard goods.[10] Digital platforms have especially allowed small and medium-sized enterprises (SMEs) to quickly diversify their customer base by accessing global markets. Of eBay's top 1,000 sellers, 35 percent are involved in significant cross-border trade.[11]
- *Service quality:* The quality of service has become substantially more transparent through web-enabled customers' comments. For example, the UN World Tourism Organization estimates that 70 to 92 percent of travelers from developed countries consider online guest reviews as an important consideration when booking a hotel. Trip Advisor currently reaches 340 million monthly visitors and logs 350 million reviews and opinions that

evaluate more than 6.5 million accommodations, restaurants, and attractions in 48 markets worldwide.[12]

Effects of the Information Revolution on Organization

The information revolution is having significant influence on the logic of enterprise organizing. These influences range from flattened and empowered structures to focused outsourcing and networked value chains.

- *Flattened and empowered structures:* Organizations may flatten their structures, reduce hierarchical layers, and increase spans of control to the extent that they apply information technology to accelerate individual and team learning, track output performance, provide feedback, and facilitate improvements. A well-known alternative investment firm conducts regular senior management meetings to which all employees are invited. For those who cannot attend, the proceedings are recorded and made available through the firm's intranet. By these means senior leaders communicate with bottom-line employees and reduce the need for intermediate layers of management. Perhaps the most visible example is Zappos, the online shoe company that eliminates hierarchy and empowers its employees by applying the principles of holacracy. In a holacracy, the organization is self-managing at the individual, team, and institutional levels. At Zappos, holacracy is enabled through Glass Frog, the firm's information system, which clarifies roles, activities, accountability, and performance metrics. It monitors employee performance and provides feedback against standards.
- *Focused outsourcing:* In the 1990s, Nike was among the first to recognize that market capitalization could be increased by the company focusing on core activities and outsourcing the rest. Nike now concentrates on those activities, which create the greatest value such as product design, branding, and marketing. Its other activities are outsourced through a network of suppliers and distributers. The inherent paradox of *Nikefication* is that shareholders want the benefits of concentrated wealth-creating activities,

but they also demand, via social networking, social justice throughout its globally distributed value chain. Balancing social responsibility with profitability is made possible by a robust information system.

• *Networked value chain:* In the same vein as Nikefication, many global start-ups can move quickly to scale by creating and leveraging networked value chains that are held together by a rigorous flow of integrated information. coModule is a European firm that designs, builds, and sells electric bikes and scooters. Its designs originated in Estonia. Its funding came from Germany. Its components are produced in China. And its prototype went public in Barcelona. Its network of continuously flowing information holds the firm together and is key to its success.[13]

New Talent Requirements for the Information Age

As a result of changes in business models and organization design, firms and individuals are grappling with the new talent requirements of the Information Age. Between 2000 and 2014, a net 2.5 million traditional production and transactions jobs have been lost.[14] Sixty percent of occupations could have up to 30 percent of their activities automated, including radiologists, design engineers, market researchers, and HR professionals. They are being replaced by big data analysts, social media experts, cloud builders, app developers, and other types of information specialists. Software engineering jobs will grow at a rate of 18.8 percent by 2024, tripling the rate of overall job growth rate.[15] As a rough indication of the growth in the demand for information specialists, information sectors wages will grow at twice the U.S. national average. These trends are accentuated by the skill gap. Half of the large industrial, energy, and healthcare companies surveyed by Accenture and GE indicated a noticeable skill gap in data gathering, analysis, and integration.[16]

New Cognitive Models and Thought Patterns

In addition to emerging technical skill requirements, new cognitive models will also emerge. We are likely to see changes in work-related thought patterns, from discovering nuggets of truth in quantitative data to finding and interpreting patterns in qualitative data, from narrowly focused sequential thought to the lateral integration, from data systems architecting to visualizing story lines out of complex information, and from spreadsheet algorithm application to unstructured data mining.[17]

These new thought patterns are leading to talent deficits. Several mechanisms are emerging to mitigate these deficits.

- Labor markets are becoming more efficient at identifying and allocating talent where it can create the greatest social and economic value. Labor market efficiency is facilitated by information technology, which can efficiently identify people who have talent and match them with institutions in need of talent. Online talent portals such as LinkedIn, Monster.com, and Indeed .com provide information about available talent. These allow companies to proactively recruit individuals whether or not they are active in the job market. Firms are able to temporarily access core talent through crowdsourcing websites such as Innocentive.com, which matches tough technical questions (e.g., cure for Lou Gehrig's disease) with anyone with Internet access (e.g., Dr. Seward Rutkove) and provides financial incentives (e.g., $1 million to Dr. Rutkove for his research on Lou Gehrig's disease). P&G and IBM have established similar web portals for online idea-sourcing. Finally, 44 million people find freelance work through Freelancer.com, Upwork.com, and other digital platforms. All such information-based initiatives efficiently bring together labor supply with labor demand.[18]

- Learning processes that are either internal or external to firms are emerging to quickly move individuals up the skill development ladder. Companies are increasingly making professional development the responsibility of individual employees. As the shelf life of technical knowledge shrinks, employees must continually update their skills. Firms may provide self-paced and self-learning portals for employees to enhance their skills in their heretofore free time. Portals such as Lynda.com, Khan Academy, and GCFlearnfree.org are either free or make learning at all levels available at low prices.

- The good news is that a considerable number of NetGenners, digital-savvy millennials, come to the game with many of the required technical skills and cognitive orientations that enable them to fill the talent gap. They are fast at information processing. They are inherently collaborative in sharing information on a global scale.[19] They are intellectually curious, cognitively flexible, and excel at multitasking. However, they may also be accustomed to being coddled (i.e., living at home), ignoring intellectual property rights, and centering on themselves (even while promoting social and ecological justice). In sum, they are the product of and the accelerators of the Information Age.

Information Management Framework

So far we have focused on explaining the probable reasons for the emerging importance for HR departments to focus on the information agenda. We have provided the data that highlight the statistical relationship between customer, investor, and community value and HR's role in information management. Before proceeding with an actionable HR agenda, it would be useful to place HR's role in information management in the larger institutional context.

HR's Role in Information Management

HR can play differing roles relative to the information agenda: central coordination, key support, or basic enabling. Other departments and functions will undoubtedly play important roles. Each of these has strengths and limitations relative to the information agenda. For example, IT departments are responsible for the pipeline through which information passes. They tend to focus on the technical aspects of information and less on the total flow and utilization of information through the entire institution. Marketing departments have direct responsibility for accessing and analyzing market information. Ensuring the full prioritizing, disseminating, sharing, debating, and utilizing of information tends to be less emphasized in many marketing departments.

Public affairs and investor relations are responsible for tracking and analyzing information about capital markets, community concerns, and regulatory perceptions of the firm. Finance departments are centrally interested in the gathering and processing of financial information but tend to be less interested in information about competitive markets. Thus the challenge of specifying accountability for conceptualizing, coordinating, integrating, and embedding the information logic remains elusive while still being critical to an organization's success. Our data and our consulting experience underscore the substantial role that HR can play in helping companies succeed in the increasingly information-rich environment.

Specific Activities

Within the turbulent information environment and the resultant rapidly changing business models, organization design, and talent requirements, we may now examine the specific activities HR departments might engage in to act on the information imperative. In our research we identified and measured nine actions* through which HR might add value to the firm's information capability. We have summarized these into an actionable five-step framework (Figure 4.1).

---

*The specific items that we statically examined in the 2017 HR competency study are as follows:

- HR is heavily involved in identifying centrally important external information (i.e., social, political, technological, economic, industry, customer, and competitive trends).
- HR imports external information into the organization for decision making.
- HR is heavily involved in identifying patterns in important data to generate insight.
- HR ensures the application of big-data analytics in the organization's decision making.
- HR is heavily involved in bundling centrally important external and internal information to create competitive advantages.
- HR is heavily involved in bringing in centrally important external information to share across the organization.
- HR determines a policy for monitoring employee use of and access to key information.
- HR ensures the consistent utilization of a common corporate language.
- HR ensures the full utilization of information in the organization's decision making.

Figure 4.1   Information management framework

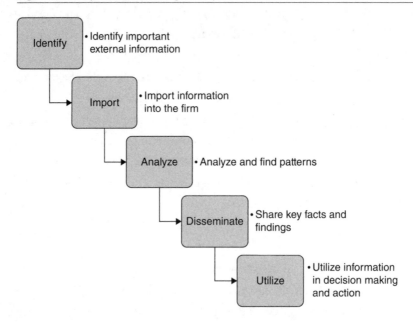

Effective HR departments may consciously contribute in each of these five steps:

- *Identify:* HR departments may help the firm identify and focus on the most important sources of external information. While in most cases HR professionals are not experts in market analysis, they can be in the position to ask simple but critically important questions such as, "How do we segment our markets?" "How do we access the most important information?" "On what information should we focus most?" Some time ago the HR department in Baroid (an oil field service company that is now part of Halliburton) partnered with its marketing department to segment customer markets and facilitate the gathering of customer information that led to a rapid increase in market share.
- *Import:* With HR's involvement, companies are finding creative ways to ensure that the most important information is imported into the firm and that the less-important information is filtered out. For example, Hindustan Unilever Limited (HUL, Unilever's Indian operation) hires some of the best

young talent out of the best Indian universities. To ensure their intellectual and emotional connection with the masses of India, HUL has its trainees travel to remote villages and live with the poor of India for several weeks to several months. They then bring this understanding with them as they serve customers and as they rise in HUL's leadership ranks.

- *Analyze:* Once important information is identified and imported, the challenge is then to analyze the information in innovative ways that results in key insights. HR can play an obvious role in championing the importance of hiring and utilizing data specialists who analyze the ongoing stream of both structured and unstructured information. Apple and Google provide well-documented examples of accessing and using such talent for competitive advantages. In addition, firms such as Qualtrics and Pimco conduct forums in which senior executives analyze, discuss, and debate emerging trends.

- *Disseminate:* HR departments may be involved in three categories of activities related to disseminating information. In companies like GE, HR has played a role in structuring town halls and customer-focused WorkOut sessions in which market and other information is widely communicated. HR professionals may also facilitate specific interactions that result in collaborative insights. In a leading financial institution, the learning function works with the senior leadership team to identify emerging trends in global finance and facilitate cross-boundary forums for key middle managers and high-potential investors to discuss and debate the emerging trends. Finally, for reasons of self-interest and ego, those who have information occasionally do not want to share and those who do not have it do not want to receive it. This dynamic has been popularized as the "Kerr paradox," in reference to Steve Kerr, former chief learning officer for GE and Goldman Sachs who was the first person to enunciate the problem and its solutions. CalSTRS helps overcome this tendency by hiring, promoting, and retaining people on the basis of their ability to share information. The Walt Disney Company provides training and incentives that encourage individuals to share information and leverage synergies across its different businesses.

- *Utilize:* All of the preceding practices have little impact unless information is finally used in improved decision making. HR departments can encourage the utilization of information by including it in behavior-based performance evaluations. A more subtle mechanism is to create a deeply purposeful organization so that employees at all levels are personally driven to fully utilize information in furthering the institution's purpose. Such is the case with Medtronic, a leading medical service and device company. Medtronic sponsors annual social gatherings for its employees and customers, including medical specialists and their patients. The specialists explain how they have used Medtronic projects in their practices. The patients tell the gathered Medtronic employees what they have done with their lives since Medtronic products have kept them alive. The patients frequently end with deeply emotional expressions of gratitude. These expressions impact the minds and the hearts of Medtronic employees that enhance the urgency of their day-to-day decisions and activities.

Action Steps

To act on the information agenda as discussed earlier, we have seen HR departments apply the following action steps:

- It almost goes without saying HR professionals who work on this agenda must know the core business value proposition, that is, how the company leverages information to make better decisions than its competitors.
- By its very nature, the information agenda requires a cross-department perspective. Therefore, HR may convene a team of insightful individuals who represent key segments of the firm's business model. The team may document how information has been historically used to make effective decisions and how information should be used in the future to create competitive advantage.
- From this information, the team may then create a customized model of how information flows through the organization.
- An employee survey may then be developed to examine which stages of the customized information framework are most important for the firm's success and which stages need the most improvement.

- With the framework and the accompanying survey data in place, the team is ready to engage the firm's senior leadership in a detailed discussion of how to improve the flow and utilization of information to create an information advantage.

Integrated HR Practices

One of the authors was asked to observe a two-day meeting in which the HR department of a leading energy company was preparing its HR strategy for the firm's executive committee. At this point in time, the company had experienced two years of extraordinary profitability. This resulted in each section of HR being allowed to hire its own consulting firm to develop the section's state-of-the-art approach. Over the two days, the head of each section (e.g., performance management, diversity, leadership development, benefits, technical training, recruitment, succession planning, rewards, organization development, and communications) presented its plans for the coming year.

At the end of the two days, the author was asked to provide his observations. He emphasized how impressed he was as each section presented its state-of-the-art recommendations; however, each section had used different criteria from their different consultants in the design of section strategies. He then noted, "I understand your state-of-the-art approach for each practice area, but I am unclear about what you as a total HR department are trying to do. My guess is that some of your senior line clients are asking the same question." Because inconsistent criteria had been applied to each section, the department whole was less than the sum of the parts.

The HR department of one of the world's leading financial institutions worked with its line executives to answer three questions: "What are our assumptions about the future of global investments? What must our firm do to outperform its competitors? What culture do we need to have to outperform our competitors in the emerging world of global investments?" With this alignment clearly defined, the HR department redesigned a substantial number of its HR practices to be consistent with this alignment. Over the ensuing years the firm experienced considerable super-normal investment success, and the HR department's contributions were recognized by the board and the senior leadership team.

In the 2016 Human Resources Competency Study (HRCS), we found broad statistical support for the preceding anecdotes. It is clear from Table 4.2 that to create value for line managers and employees, HR departments should focus their efforts on providing integrated HR practices. What line managers and employees overwhelmingly want from HR departments is an integration of its practices around its culture and core competencies that, in turn, reflect the strategic requirements of the business.[†] This integration provides a clear focus and direction to what HR contributes to the business in a way that makes sense to HR's internal clients.

The integrated approach to HR has been discussed under a variety of different terminologies including high-performing work systems, strategic human resource management, and HR systems. We believe that the most accurate terminology is integrated HR practices. The empirical research on the impact of integrated HR practices is quite extensive.[20] One of the largest research projects on this topic was conducted in the United Kingdom among 2,906 organizations of multiple sizes across multiple industries.[21-30] It concluded that no single subsystem of HR has significant influence on business performance in isolation. However, the integrated combination of staffing, training and development, talent engagement, job design, and information management does have powerful statistical influence on a wide array of organizational performance measures.

[†]The specific items that make up the statistical factor of integrated HR practices are as follows:
- Develops an HR strategy that clearly links HR practices to |ORGUNIT|'s strategy
- Ensures that HR is a cultural role model for the rest of the organization
- Contributes to building and/or maintaining |ORGUNIT|'s core competencies
- Ensures that the different subgroups within HR work effectively with each other to provide integrated HR solutions
- Creates policies, practices, and procedures that help frontline managers in their jobs
- Effectively manages external vendors of outsourced HR activities
- Resolves employees' complaints and issues
- Ensures that managers follow correct procedures in order to avoid legal repercussions

Steps to Create Integrated HR Practices

The following four steps can be followed to create and deliver a clean set of integrated HR practices:

Step 1: Differentiate Between Corporate and Business Strategy

- *Corporate strategy* asks the question, "Where do we compete?" When Microsoft recently purchased LinkedIn, it made a corporate strategy decision to enter the social networking business. While this issue may seem relatively straightforward, many corporations struggle with the question: "Are we one company in which all of the business units are treated the same, or are we multiple companies that have different business models?" From an HR strategy perspective, the importance of these distinctions cannot be overemphasized. If a corporation has a differentiated business portfolio but HR attempts to treat these differentiated units as the same, customer focus is lost and chaos ensues. On the other hand, if a corporation's portfolio consists of related businesses and HR treats the relatively similar units as though they were different, then synergy and efficiencies are lost.

- *Business strategy* asks the question: "How do we compete in the context of our business environment?" The first phase of business strategy is to ensure an accurate understanding of the following: supply/demand economics and the entry and exit barriers of the industry, the market segments and the customers' buying criteria within the segments, the nature of relationships with suppliers, the trends among the industry's competitors, the dynamics of process, product and information technology, the directives of the regulatory environment, and owners' expectations. With this contextual analysis, you may then formulate an accurate business strategy of the combination of unique and inimitable products and services and financial infrastructures that enable you to outperform your competitors.

Step 2: Identify the Culture That Is Required for Your Firm to Win Its Customers' Hearts and Wallets

As discussed in Chapter 3, culture is the organizational capability that enables all other capabilities. It is both a perceived construct and a reality-based construct. As a perceived construct, culture may be defined as the identity of the firm in the minds of its key customers. A firm must then ensure that the desired customer perceptions are reflected in employee behaviors. Customers may then directly experience these behaviors or indirectly experience the outcomes of these behaviors, both of which contribute to the identity of the firm in the minds of its key customers.

Step 3: Clarify the Required Technical Competencies

Every industry is based on technical competencies. Without these technical core competencies, the firm cannot exist. In addition to technical competencies that are discussed in Chapter 3, other technical competencies include automotive design for car companies, skin composition and chemistry in the cosmetic business, and biomedical engineering in medical equipment firms. Such technical competencies are required to enter the competitive environment; however, in today's world of shrinking shelf-life of technical knowledge, competitive advantage is created not by having them but by how they are created and leveraged in the context of an organization's culture.

Step 4: Design and Implement HR Practices and Policies

Six categories of HR practices and policies include the following: staffing cycle, measurement and reward, training and development, information management, organization structure and process, and leadership. With these six categories in place, we may then ask specific questions about the alignment of HR practices with cultural requirements. Assume for a moment that the cultural requirement is focused responsiveness along with its accompanying behaviors. Then the following questions are to be asked:

- *Recruitment:* To what extent do we hire people on the basis of their prior track record of creating focused responsiveness?
- *Promotions:* To what extent do we promote people on the basis of their contributions to a culture of focused responsiveness?
- *Rotations:* To what extent do we rotate people around so that they can be exposed to excellent role models and practices of focused responsiveness?

- *Outplacement:* To what extent do we move people out of their jobs or out of the company on the basis of their not exhibiting focused responsiveness?
- *Measurement:* To what extent do we measure focused responsiveness and give people feedback on the extent to which they exhibit the behaviors of focused responsiveness?
- *Rewards:* To what extent are people rewarded for exhibiting the behaviors of focused responsiveness?
- *Training:* To what extent do we use classroom training to train people in focused responsiveness?
- *Development:* To what extent do we use on-the-job development to develop the skills of focused responsiveness?
- *Information Management:* To what extent do we use the voice of external customers and shareholders to communicate the importance of employees focusing on being responsive to customer requirements?
- *Systemic Communications:* To what extent do the formal communication processes (e.g., newsletters, speeches by senior executives, in-house video systems) communicate the importance of focused responsiveness?
- *Information System Design:* To what extent is the information system designed to provide people the information they need to demonstrate focused responsiveness?
- *Organization Structure:* To what extent does the structure of the organization encourage focused responsiveness?
- *Process/Work Design:* To what extent are work processes designed to encourage employees to be focused on being responsive to each other and customers?
- *Physical Setting:* To what extent does the design of the physical setting encourage focused responsiveness?
- *Leadership:* To what extent are leaders regular and consistent role models of focused responsiveness?

With a clear understanding of both the desired culture and required technical competencies, the full breadth of HR practices and related policies may then be designed and delivered to create the HR department capable of delivering integrated HR practices.

CHAPTER 5

HIGH-PRIORITY HR PRACTICES—EMPLOYEE PERFORMANCE AND HR ANALYTICS

5

In the preceding chapter, we examined HR's influence on the entire organization through information management and through what we refer to as integrated HR practices. This chapter covers two additional HR department activities. We will first focus on the HR department practices that have direct influence on the performance of individual employees—which not surprisingly include performance measurement, rewards and compensation, and employee development. We will then discuss key issues relative to HR department analytics. Since much has been written on these topics, we provide overviews of the major issues or emerging themes. This chapter will conclude with a checklist that summarizes the key messages of Chapters 3 through 5. The checklist reviews the actions that an HR department should consider as it seeks to add greater value to the business.

Employee Performance HR Practices

The HR department practices that influence the performance of individual employees include measurements, rewards, development, and involvement.*

---

*The specific items that make up the statistical factor of employee performance HR practices are as follows:
- Performance appraisals provide employees with feedback for personal development.
- Employee salaries and rewards are determined by the employee's contribution to the success of |ORGUNIT|.
- On average, the pay level (including incentives) of our employees is higher than that of our competitors.
- Employees are provided comprehensive training throughout their careers (i.e., training beyond the skills required by the trainee's current job).
- Employees are empowered to recommend necessary changes in the way they perform work.
- If a decision affects employees, usually their opinions are asked for in advance.

Performance Measurement

Once an employee is hired, the challenge emerges of how to encourage and optimally motivate individual employees. The starting point of the talent cycle is having robust and credible performance measurements. Measurements are the basis of rewards, training, development, and employee involvement initiatives.

The measurement cycle consists of goal setting, measurement, and feedback. One of the world's largest fabric companies desired to improve its measurement system. It started by clarifying the purpose of its measurements, including specifying its strategic direction at multiple levels, then tracking progress so that additional improvement could be made and achievements could be communicated to customers and shareholders. In addition, they sought to have operational definitions of their desired sources of competitive advantage, including quality and efficiency. Until they placed a measurement on quality, it remained an abstract concept. But when they developed the three measures of rejects per production unit, product returns, and customer survey results, they had an operational definition of quality.

The HR department then took the lead in developing the company's measurement framework. The HR measurement team realized that it was possible to set goals and measure results for individuals, for departments or teams, as well as for the company as a whole. They also realized that for each of these three levels, they should be able to measure output results (lag indicators), cultural behaviors (lead indicators), initiatives (throughput indicators), and technical competencies (skill indicators). Combining these two dimensions led to a comprehensive measurement matrix (Figure 5.1).

HR professionals then worked with line executives to determine which of the 12 cells needed the most immediate work. Since organization and department output metrics were already in place and a process was being tested to more rigorously monitor the progress of major institutional initiatives, the line leadership decided to focus on improving the measurements of individual output results and cultural behaviors. The individual output measures were based on semiannual goals. The cultural behaviors were measured by

Figure 5.1   *Comprehensive measurement matrix*

	Output Results	Cultural Behaviors	Initiatives	Technical Capabilities
Individual				
Team/ Department				
Organization				

360-degree survey instruments with HR assisting supervisors in providing feedback for developmental purposes. Since the utility of their measurement system hinges heavily on specificity and clarity of the goals and the credibility of the information sources, the company has worked to make its output and behavioral measurement processes more transparent and accessible.

The Performance Ranking System—Ready for an Update?

The company has grappled with the same measurement issue that is debated within the global HR community. This debate centers on whether measurement should be based on power distribution assumptions or on assumptions of normal distributions. For years, performance rankings have been based on normal distributions in which the employee population is force ranked into the top 10 percent, the next 20 percent, the middle 40 percent, the next lower 20 percent, and the lowest 10 percent.

Recent authors have argued that normal distributions do not reflect the performance reality. The so-called power distribution logic has been most strongly argued by O'Boyle and Aguinis, who conducted five studies that included 633,263 individuals in 198 samples of researchers, entertainers, politicians, and athletes.[1] They found that in almost all cases, a small number of hyper performers created the greatest proportion of results, followed by a broad range of average performers and a small number of lower performers. They further argued that focusing the measurement and reward system on the assumptions of normal distribution results in a loss of star performers. On the other hand, focusing on the power distribution results in retaining the stars and losing the low performers.[2] Another study qualifies the pure star logic by arguing that stars are partially a product of an institution that consists heavily of the mid-level "B" performers and that stars are stars because of their ability to leverage the total organization for competitive advantage.[3]

Pitfalls of the Employee Feedback Process

The measurement cycle is completed by feedback sessions. In most companies, these sessions are codified in the performance appraisal process whose capstone is the quarterly, semiannual, or annual performance review meeting. Even as we write, the HR department of the fabric company case is grappling with the perennial problems that beleaguer HR departments around the world: how to improve the company's performance management process. The myriad of problems surrounding the traditional performance-appraisal process are well documented and include the following:

- The characteristics of the rater produced 62 percent of final evaluations as compared to only 21 percent of the person's actual performance.[4]
- Gender and race projections play a significant role.[5]
- Performance reviews are heavily influenced by the ratee's negotiation skills, especially when short-term outputs are difficult to measure (i.e., R&D).
- Performance appraisals tend to focus on individual rather than team or firm performance, thereby contributing to making the human whole less than the sum of the parts.
- Almost everyone thinks they are above average, which results in disappointment by a large number of employees.
- Bosses are not well trained and generally don't like doing performance appraisals. As Steve Kerr, former chief learning officer for General Electric

and Goldman Sachs, has stated, "Annual performance reviews are unnatural acts in unnatural places."

• Work is becoming more team and knowledge based and more globally integrated. These job attributes make measurement more problematic.[†]

Rethinking the Feedback Process

As a result of these problems, many companies are rethinking their feedback processes. Consider the following examples:

• IBM has recently modified its performance review system.[6] Employees may now request feedback sessions as frequently as they want, at least once per quarter. Employees evaluate the quality of the feedback. They may elicit electronic feedback from peers. These changes are based on the assumption that the annual single numerical feedback is overly simplistic and vague, and is therefore not very credible or useful.

• Deloitte is taking a somewhat similar reformulating of its performance management system.[7] At Deloitte team leaders evaluate employees quarterly or at the end of a major project by applying a five-point scale that focuses on four questions of what the leader would do relative to a team member's performance rather than what the leader thinks about the team member (e.g., "Given what I know about this person's performance, and if it were my money, I would award this person the highest possible compensation increase and bonus," and "Given what I know of this person's performance, I would always want him or her on my team." Factored into these considerations are the person's overall contribution to the company and the difficulty of the person's assignments.

• Perhaps most important at Deloitte is institutionalizing performance feedback from an "event" to a "way of life" by weekly "check-in" meetings with

---

[†]We are indebted to our colleague Dick Beatty for several of the preceding insights.

each team member. The foundational assumption is that feedback is not a leader's side responsibility; it is the leader's primary work.

- Similar to IBM, Accenture is refocusing its performance process toward more frequent conversations with the supervisor as coach. The coach-subordinate conversation emphasizes the employee's strengths—what they are and how to further develop and leverage them. In this way, the conversation is encouraged to create priorities rather than a litany of objectives.

- Another firm that we are familiar with has worked to create a culture of extensive and yet informal peer feedback. Work team members are expected to give and receive regular feedback not only to and from their respective supervisors but also to and from their peers. If a team member goes a couple of months without giving or receiving feedback to and from peers, the team senses that an underlying problem is at hand. The issue then escalates to the team as a whole to ensure that a culture of lateral feedback continues and its accompanying performance improvement is maintained.

Rewards and Compensation

As Nobel prize winner, Herbert Simon, and his coauthor James March have asserted compensation systems have two primary purposes: to attract people to join and then to motivate them to perform. If the primary purpose of a reward system as linked to performance management is to motivate performance, then let us briefly review the criteria for effective rewards as argued by Steve Kerr.[8]

- *They are available.* Rule: Do not publicize rewards if they are not available. Companies that want to motivate the entire workforce and then provide bonus incentives only to executives will motivate the executives but not the rest of the workforce that are the source of quality improvements, cost-reduction efforts, innovative ideas, and time-to-market enhancements.

- *They are linked to performance.* However, some years ago Ed Lawler estimated that up to 90 percent of U.S. compensation dollars might be given on the basis criteria that are not linked to performance such as tenure, age, gender, showing up, unionization, hierarchical level, seniority, company size, department size, last name, past performance, anticipated future performance, and relationship with the boss.

- *They are visible.* A major company offered a large bonus to the company's greatest innovation of the year, but the innovator could win it only once and could not tell anyone that she or he had won it. Compare that to Nobel Prize winners who are publicly acknowledged throughout the world. Or the University of Michigan whose faculty compensation numbers have traditionally been published in the local newspaper. Why are rewards not visible in most companies? Much of the reason is probably because of the lack of credibility of the measurement system on which they are based.
- *They are timely.* We know from ample research that the sooner a reward is given for an achievement or behavior, the more motivating the reward will be. Compare that to what happens in most companies. A person achieves a major success in March; sometime in the following January she receives her bonus. On the other hand, many airlines provide their high-level frequent fliers the opportunity to recognize exceptional employee service at the time the service is rendered by personally handing the employee a card or token that is worth cash, prizes, or frequent-flier points.
- *They are reversible.* One company HR executive estimated that the time from giving a bonus for one year's performance to people feeling entitled to receiving the bonus the next year is about 15 minutes. As soon as a reward has any vestige of an entitlement, it undermines its motivating potential.
- *They are valued by the receiver.* The good news is that people like money. The bad news is that money is not unique to the institutional context; it provides relatively little idiosyncratic traction to the giving institution. Its motivational impact may be immediately transferable to other institutions.

With these criteria in mind, we may then assess the extent to which alternative financial and nonfinancial rewards meet these criteria. Base compensation weakly meets the preceding criteria. Bonus-based compensation (including stock options and other deferred compensation schemes) does a little better but is still weak on half of the criteria.

Let us then examine alternative forms of nonfinancial rewards. Time off, gifts, training, travel, visibility, office space, and notes of recognition from the boss have been tried and generally have weak or inconsistent motivating potential. Voice in decision making is more interesting. Recently a major high-tech company was in danger of losing several of its senior employees. These employees were fully vested and were each worth many millions of dollars. When asked, "What would it take for you to stay?" they responded, "To have a voice in the future of the company in creating the future of the industry." The HR department, in turn, responded with more bonus money and many of the folks left. Finally, consider adding challenging and valuable work. When people are given challenging responsibilities, autonomy to control their outputs, participation in decision making, and visible and valuable recognition, it meets virtually all of the criteria for effective rewards. The challenge is to organize the work in a way to meet all of these criteria. Providing work with these attributes is clearly a silver bullet in a motivating reward system.

Referring back to Table 4.2, we see that while employee performance HR practices have strong influence on short-term performance, it has relatively low influence on most stakeholders, especially investors and owners. This relationship may be strongly reflected in the current shareholder revolt against executive compensation. In the 1980s, the ratio of CEO pay to bottom-line employees was 40-1; now that ratio ranges from 140-1 to 335-1.[9] The perceived inequity of these numbers, especially in light of the net loss of worker purchasing power over the last decade, has led shareholders to reject senior executive bonuses and pay raises in many companies, including BP, Smith & Nephew, and Anglo American. As additional evidence of shareholder dissatisfaction, Norway's Government Pension Fund Global that owns on average 1.3 percent of every publicly traded company in the world is launching a crackdown on executive pay. If shareholders were getting value for their executive pay allocations, it is unlikely that these revolts would be happening.

In sum, there is a lot of opportunity for HR—and lot of work to do—to improve employee measurement and reward systems. But if completed successfully, they will have high impact on individual employees and ultimately on the organization as a whole.

Employee Development

Employee development occurs through feedback and coaching, from classroom and media-based training and from on-the-job development. To be optimally effective, feedback should come from a multilevel, informal loop. The first level of feedback and coaching is from individuals themselves. Do they learn from their mistakes and do they build on their successes? They may then learn and receive coaching from their team members through direct conversations, through elicited feedback, through 360-degree evaluations, and from chance meetings (of which Steve Jobs was so fond). They may learn from their boss and receive coaching as described in the preceding section. They may learn from their internal clients who can provide blunt feedback about the extent to which the quality, quantity, and timeliness of support is adequate. Finally, and perhaps most important, they can learn from the company's customers.

Customer Feedback

Companies are experimenting with different avenues through which to connect customers to employees. Such avenues include locating employees in the customers' facilities (GE), having customers visit the company's site to speak to employees (Timken), arranging for employees to spend time with customers as they use your products (P&G), engaging employees in market research efforts (Disney), having customers participate in employee training courses (GE), having employees listen to customer service phone calls (Unilever), and having employees summarize company references on social media (McDonald's). Our experience is that very few HR development specialists apply this logic in framing their development efforts. Companies that concurrently utilize these multiple loops will find their learning cycles will quickly move employees toward greater performance.

Classroom and Online Training

Classroom training continues to be a mainstay but is quickly morphing toward online learning experiences. Online learning, including Lynda.com, GCFlearnfree.org, and a multitude of YouTube sites, provide basic learning for standardized disciplines such as accounting, basic manufacturing, supervisory skills, computer programming, math, cake baking, swimming, and other disciplines where imparting facts is the goal. Networked online learning provides the opportunity for groups of people to learn, provide feedback, and solve interdependent problems on a global scale. It enables education on demand. It provides a broad range of learning topics at virtually costless levels. Perhaps most important is that the online offerings are becoming the learning platforms of choice by tech-savvy millennials.

To optimize the value of online learning, its limitations should also be addressed. Considerable research has been done to confirm that the majority of information transmission is not through what is formally stated but rather through nonverbal means such as body positioning, facial expressions, hand gestures, and voice intonation. Internet learning groups severely truncate these modes of communication. Conversations in which nuanced subtleties are being explored may frequently be done best by fast-paced face-to-face or voice-to-voice interaction. Furthermore, some people learn best from speaking; that is, their brains are wired such that they don't know what they mean until after they hear themselves say it. For these people, communication with faculty and colleagues through online learning networks may not be ideal. Online learning is optimal for linear sequential learning protocol but may not be ideal for individuals whose learning style is more holistic and iterative. Finally, online learning is generally best applied to content that is more rote and standardized, such as accounting and benefits administration and may be less effective for more paradigm-building concepts such as might be found in business strategy or business ethics.

Classroom learning likewise has its pros and cons. Its advantages include the following:

- Accelerates learning through fast iterative discussions.
- Facilitates both verbal as well as nonverbal communications.
- Better at building relationships among class members. This has implications for learning to value diversity. Also, if customers are involved in the classroom training, more solid relationships with customers may be created.
- Trust is more likely to be developed by face-to-face learning interaction as opposed to anonymous Internet-based team learning.
- The relatively more intense learning environment may be more likely to create paradigm-breaking insights.
- Materials may be more readily customized to specific strategic, tactical, and cultural environments.
- It is more personal, and there are fewer distractions, as time is fully committed to the exercise.

With these positives also emerge several drawbacks, including expense, lack of time flexibility, tendency toward greater interpersonal groupthink, and underleveraging of existent technology that may have greater appeal for the Internet generation.

Regardless of targeted content of learning, four general trends may be delineated. In traditional training programs, the materials are presented and the burden of application is solely on the shoulders of the students. The trend is toward teachers working with students in the classroom context to facilitate application. The traditional business classroom tends to be heavily case-based. The emerging pedagogy is to create live cases from student projects or from previous organizational experience of students or participants. In a traditional classroom, the teacher teaches generic materials. The emerging trend, especially for in-house training programs, is to customize materials to the corporate context. Generic training is likely to create generic skills, enhance the market value of participants, and thereby enhance employee turnover. Customized programs on the other hand will provide idiosyncratic learnings that are less transferable across companies, thereby reducing employee turnover. In the traditional corporate classroom, employees are taught about customers and shareholders. The current trend is to involve customers and shareholders as either participating students or as presenters or teachers.

It has long been assumed and empirical research supports the conjecture that the most effective development occurs on-the-job.[10] Laundry lists of development alternatives are available from multiple sources. They include suggestions such as integrate a cross-department process, serve on a new project or product review board, teach a new process to a team, do a competitive analysis of an emerging market trend, mentor a new hire on an important department initiative, or act as a consultant to a community volunteer organization. These are undoubtedly useful and have developmental value. However, truly high-potential individuals are likely to be only moderately interested in such laundry lists.

Companies such as Intel, GE, and Northrop Grumman have learned that high-potential individuals are interested in on-the-job assignments that are both challenging and valuable. Challenging work means the work is difficult and not a lot of people can do it. If the work is difficult and a lot of people can do it, the market value of the work is low and high-potential individuals will be less interested. The work must also be valuable to the company, to customers, to shareholders, or to any combination of these. If the work is challenging but not valuable, high-potential individuals are less likely to be interested, because they want to create a track record of documented results. They tend not to be interested in challenging work for its own sake (the history of HR notwithstanding). Building on this logic, Microsoft is offering employees the opportunity to select their next assignment.[11] To understand better how global companies develop local talent through on-the-job logic, McKinsey studied 21 multinationals. Two-thirds of these companies located local talent who were studying for their MBAs abroad and then brought them back to their countries of origin where they were quickly thrust into leadership positions. The most successful development initiative from these companies was the rotation of these high-potential individuals for 6- to 18-month assignments for specific developmental needs. These assignments were offered along with the promise for greater responsibility upon their return to their country of origin.[12]

Employee Involvement

Employee involvement or empowerment programs have been an ongoing topic of discussion among behavioral scientists for 30 years. Driven by ebbs and wanes of cost and innovation cycles, employee involvement programs have wavered in and out of popularity over these decades. Such programs enable employees to make decisions and take action based on minimal supervisory oversight or approval.

A Tier 1 automotive supplier faced enormous pressures to reduce its costs. An element of its cost-reduction program was the reduction in the number of expensive middle managers and corporate staff. These moves required the restructuring of the workforce into self-managing teams. The effectiveness of these teams rested heavily on the involvement of each team member and the organizational infrastructures that enable the desired involvement. Seven practices had to be put into place to enable the success of the involvement teams:

- Teams received considerable amounts of training in reading and understanding financial and operational reports; in team problem solving and conflict resolution; in the company's strategy, market position, and competitive requirements; and in the continually emerging technical skills, such as computer-facilitated manufacturing.
- Performance expectations for each team had to be made explicit. Each team received information about the requirements of its downstream internal clients and its upstream supplier capabilities.
- Based on this information, each team set its production targets that were then horizontally communicated to its partner units.
- Each team then received a steady flow of performance information that enabled the team to adjust its performance.
- Each team evaluated itself and its members through 360-degree evaluation tools that were sharply focused on defining how each member and the team as whole needed to function to achieve high performance.
- Compensation was then linked to the lag indicators of production accomplishments and to the lead behavioral indicators. The compensation

system was designed to heavily favor team performance over individual performance.

- New definitions of leadership were formulated, communicated, and applied through a rotating team leadership protocol.

In a less comprehensive but equally effective manner, companies such as Ritz-Carlton, Best Buy, and Disney encourage employees to identify and rectify customer complaints without obtaining permission from management to do so. By so doing they provide faster and more targeted customer service. Recently one of the authors left his room card in his room at a Disney resort. When he and his family arrived at Epcot, he discovered his error. He talked to a Disney guest relations manager who quickly issued a temporary pass. The empowered employee salvaged a potentially negative experience and elevated herself and Disney to hero status. In the era of social media, such "Wows!" can be multiplied thousands of times over; the reverse can also be the case when employees are not empowered to respond quickly and effectively to customer complaints or needs.

Employee involvement in decision making is frequently facilitated by several institutional factors. The information system must be designed to provide employees the information that they need to make fast and accurate decisions. For comprehensive empowerment initiatives to be implemented, it is usually necessary to reduce the influence of middle management and corporate staff. When GE implemented its bureaucracy reduction program called Work-Out, Jack Welch determined that the only way to reduce the influence of middle management and corporate staff was to reduce the number of people in middle management and in corporate staff. Finally, teams may have to be more proactive in staffing issues, including determining who joins the team as well as occasionally identifying who may need to leave the team.

Analytics in Measuring HR Practices

How does an HR department determine if it is doing a good job? To make and communicate that determination requires the application of data analytics to HR departmental activities and to the functioning of functional areas within HR. Furthermore, a considerable amount of writing has been done on the application of analytics to the functioning and outcomes of HR practices.[13] The challenge resides in the fact that measuring HR tends not to be done very well and is, in fact, among the most poorly done of HR activities.[14] In addition, it has the least impact of the four categories of HR department practices on HR's overall impact on stakeholder value creation (see Table 4.2). In light of the findings and discussion in Chapter 4, the main value of HR's role relative to analytics is not the application of analytics to the HR department but HR's role in helping the organization apply analytics to the rest of the organization as part of an overall information strategy.

Nevertheless, there are several purposes to be achieved by measuring HR departmental impact:

- To improve HR department performance and thereby improve the company's performance
- To help HR professionals make better informed decisions
- To identify how HR adds the greatest value so as to focus its resources where the greatest good can be achieved
- To help drive unnecessary costs out of HR activities

To achieve optimal value from HR analytics, several guidelines should be considered:

- Measuring HR is relatively easy and straightforward; knowing what to measure is more difficult. This guideline requires that HR departments have a clear vision of how it adds greatest value. Does HR create the greatest value by optimizing talent? By optimizing organization capabilities? By providing the most efficient administrative services? By developing high-performance leaders? Depending on the answer to the preceding questions, different approaches to measurement will result.
- Effective measurements help you know what you know but also help you know what you don't know. Three types of errors can be distinguished. Good HR measurements can help you avoid accepting as truth something

that is not. It can also help you avoid rejecting something that is true. Good measurements can also help you ask the right questions in the first place.

- Effective measurements help you gather data when you know what you will do with it and to avoid asking questions when you don't know what you will do with it.

- Effective measurements answer the important "Who?" questions. Who owns the data (e.g., the boss, the individual, HR, CEO)? Who has access to the raw data (e.g., HR, line managers, consulting firm)? Who uses the data for what purposes (e.g., the individual for developmental purposes, the supervisor for evaluation purposes, HR for talent management purposes)? Such issues should be fully discussed and decided before any HR measurement initiative is undertaken.

- The interpreters of HR analytics should understand and account for the difference between causality and correlation. Equating the two might result in erroneous decisions and actions. For example, are people productive because they are satisfied, happy, and engaged at work? Or are people satisfied, happy, and engaged at work because they are productive?

- The users of HR analytics should also understand the distinction between the terminologies of *statistical significance* versus *statistical meaningfulness.* *Statistical significance* is a technical term that states that the relationship between two variables does not occur by chance. It implies that a "linkage" exists between the two variables, but it does not state that the relationship between two variables is meaningful. For example, one widely used employee engagement survey claims an empirical linkage of its employee engagement questions and customer satisfaction, productivity, and profitability, but the statistical magnitude of the relationship (i.e., the correlation) between the questions and the outcome variables is an unimpressive 3.6 percent.

Three Categories of Analytics

We have found it useful to distinguish among three categories of HR analytics: foundational HR metrics, organization capability, and talent.

Foundational HR Metrics

Foundational HR metrics may be expressed as absolute numbers, quantity or quality of completed initiatives, percentages or as cost/benefits ratios. Absolute numbers include number of employees, number of people hired, number of teaching hours, cost of employee benefits, number of HR employees, and so on. These are the basic fodder of HR measurement. These are to HR as counting money is to finance. Initiative metrics refer to the quantity and quality of completed initiatives. Examples include the following: Was the HR information system implemented on time and on budget? Was the HR restructuring completed per schedule with minimal disruption to the line organization? Foundational HR metrics may also be expressed as percentages that measure departmental efficiency such as the percent of performance appraisals that are completed on time, the percent of targeted jobs filled per month, and the percent of employees with development plans.[15] HR's efficiency may also be expressed in terms of cost/benefit ratios such as cost per hire, HR expenses per employee, profitability per employee, and benefits of any HR initiative minus program costs divided by program costs, resulting in the program's return on investment.[16]

Organization Capability

In preceding chapters, we have argued that HR creates competitive advantage through the HR value chain. As summarized in Figure 5.2, the HR value chain includes the outcomes of marketplace performance, HR's primary contribution to the firm in creating and sustaining organizational capability and its enabling culture, and finally, the HR activities that create and sustain the culture, which, in turn, creates the required organizational capabilities, which then drive performance in the marketplace. Once the HR value chain is understood, its measurement is quite straightforward (see Figure 5.2).

With this logic flow in place, we can identify how HR adds greatest value and build a protocol to measure the integrated value chain. As an example, let us assume that the company's business strategy focuses on growing revenues through new product development. The required organizational

Figure 5.2   *Measuring the HR value chain*

capability of innovation may be measured through the percent of revenues from products that are less than two years old, number of new patents, or number of new products. To achieve these targeted metrics, employees must exhibit behaviors consistent with a culture of customer-focused innovation. Such cultural behaviors might include (1) employees meeting with customers to co-create new products or sales, service, product design; and (2) manufacturing engineers and customers jointly design new products and their efficient production. These behaviors may be measured through a 360-degree survey, through a pulse survey, or through a regularly scheduled employee survey.

Once the desired behaviors are identified based on their ability to achieve the desired organization capability metrics, we are then in a position to design and deliver the HR, organization, and leadership practices that need the most improvement to create and sustain the desired behaviors. We may then measure the extent to which employees are experiencing these practices via an employee survey. One question on the survey might be "To what extent are you measured and rewarded for contributing to improvements in the efficient design or production of new products?"

Thus we can measure each phase of the HR value chain. If the practices and behaviors are measured on the same survey, the correlations may be generated that assess the extent to which the measurement and reward practices are encouraging the desired cultural behaviors. Such correlations can be useful in improving the relevant practice areas. For example, with a recent client we found through the employee survey a negative correlation between training program attendance and team-oriented behaviors: The more employees attended training programs, the less likely they were to exhibit the desired teamwork. Of course, the head of training and development was not pleased with the results. We asked him to show us the materials from his most visible leadership development program. The title was: "Individual Excellence: Unleashing the You Who Is in You." It was clear that the more people attended this individually focused program, the less likely they were to think and behave in terms of teamwork. The training programs were subsequently redesigned around teamwork and teamwork scores improved.

Because many factors might influence revenues from new products, it is more difficult to measure the impact of culture and its behaviors on organization capabilities. At this point executive logic and insight must play a role. If the culture and its accompanying behaviors are designed and delivered with the organizational capability metrics as the design criteria and if then as a result of the HR, organization, and leadership practice alignment the desired behaviors improve along with improvements in the organizational capability metrics, then HR has done its part in building the organization capabilities that are desired by the marketplace.

By following this protocol, an HR department may create a measurement line of sight from the marketplace, to the most important organizational capabilities, through culture and on to HR, organization, and leadership practices.

Talent

Much of the HR analytics agenda over the past few years has focused not on organization-level analysis but rather on individual talent. This focus is due partially to the inflow of HR professionals from psychology backgrounds but also due to the relative ease of measuring individual talent and its related processes as opposed to measuring organization effectiveness. A major question for talent measurement is "What do we meant by talent?"

In our experience two categories of talent may be differentiated with each category having different measurement implication. First, talent may be differentiated by the importance of the work that is done and by the quality of the individuals who do that work. This has been popularized by the question, *"Do you have A players in A positions?"*[17] "A positions" may be indicated by the direct value that the position creates for customers and shareholders, by the ability of the position to provide products or services at the desired cost, and by the ability of the position to enable the company to charge its desired price.[18] We like to address this issue by asking, "What percent of your people create 90 percent of the value? Who are they and what do they do?" We find this to be a reasonably thought-provoking question that hits at the heart of how the company creates sustainable value.

Once this first question is resolved, then the second question must be addressed: "*What percent of the employees in your A positions are high performers?*" The measurement goal is to have the maximum proportion of your A players in A positions. Then you may measure the extent to which such individuals are being continually productive and are voluntarily exiting or staying.[19] A players may or may not include the company's leadership. Regardless, the HR department should have the numbers that answer the question, "Do we currently have leaders with the technical capabilities and leadership competencies that ensure short-term performance, and do we have a measurable pipeline of leaders who will take the companies into the future?"[20]

Second, every industry is built on a foundation of technical knowledge (e.g., automotive design engineering for automotive companies, molecular biology for pharmaceutical companies). To ensure that your company has the technological capabilities that are required for sustained success in its industry, these capabilities should be clearly identified and measured. They may be measured by a calibration meeting of the most knowledgeable technical experts in the firm. The meeting should focus on reaching agreement on which capabilities are most important for sustainable success and which need the greatest attention or improvement (i.e., a gap analysis).

A Talent Measurement Tool Kit

The following questionnaire, or tool kit, can help with organizational talent assessment. The talent tool kit consists of the basic HR functions, each of which has associated measurement options. While the possibilities are almost endless, the following represent a sample of the options.

- Recruitment
  - What percent of hires remain after two years of being hired?
  - Which selection criteria are the best predictors of performance and retention?
  - What is the percent acceptance rate of the top talent?
- Development
  - What percent of promotions come from inside versus outside the firm?
  - How does the individual performance after training compare with performance before training?
  - Which employee groups benefit most from training (e.g., level, age, experience, nationality)?
- Succession
  - What percent of key risk positions have ready-now candidates?
  - What percent of the ready-now candidates are actually moved into positions?
  - What is the balance of cultural versus technical promotion criteria as they are actually applied?
- Rewards
  - What is the correlation of pay increases with improvements in performance?
  - What is the performance improvement following nonfinancial reward?
  - Which form of compensation results in the greatest short-term and long-term performance?
- Communications
  - What percent of employees know the company's mission, long-term objectives, and business strategy?
  - What percent of employees know the company's external brand identity?
  - What percent of employees listen to or read executive speeches on the intranet?
- Retention
  - What percent of exits are voluntary versus involuntary?
  - What percent of people leave for different reasons?
  - From what jobs and leaders do the voluntary leavers tend to leave?

Summing Up: A Final Checklist for Effective HR Departments

The following checklist summarizes the findings and analyses of the last three chapters, which focus on the characteristics and practices of effective HR departments. In these chapters we have emphasized the importance of organizational capability as the most essential HR agenda along with the HR department practices that have greatest impact on business performance and that create the greatest value for HR's internal and external customers. To complete the checklist, the following scale may be applied:

1 = Very weak

2 = Weak

3 = Okay

4 = Strong

5 = Very strong

STEP	1	2	3	4	5
We recognize the importance and logic of organizational capability as competitive advantage.					
We align our HR organizational structure to be consistent with the structure of the business.					
We conduct a thorough examination of the external environment with focus on present and future customer segments and other competitive considerations.					
We identify those organizational capabilities that are required for us to win in the context of our competitive environment.					
We format the key metrics that measure our success in creating and sustaining our targeted organizational capabilities.					
We identify the technical capabilities that are required for us to fully achieve our organizational capabilities.					

STEP	1	2	3	4	5
We define the culture that we must have in order to fully implement our organizational capabilities.					
We formulate the cultural behaviors that are required to achieve better performance relative to our organizational capability metrics.					
We identify and implement the HR, leadership, and organizational practices that will have the greatest impact on creating and sustaining our requisite technical and organizational capabilities and will most strongly reinforce our organizational capability metrics.					
We understand which information is most central for our company's success.					
We assist in developing institution-wide processes to identify, access, import, analyze, disseminate, and utilize information as a competitive advantage.					
We ensure that all HR policies, processes, and practices are fully integrated around key business results.					
We leverage all talent management tools to optimize individual performance.					
We measure each stage of the HR value chain to ensure HR's ongoing contribution to business success.					

PART III

INDIVIDUAL

CHAPTER 6

CREDIBLE ACTIVIST— GETTING INVITED TO THE TABLE

6

Introduction

Before HR professionals can consistently have an impact on the organization, they must be invited to be a part of the business conversation. Getting invited to the conversation is a clear prerequisite for HR to create real business value within any organization.

In earlier rounds of this research, we found that HR professionals had to be trusted advisors to gain access to business decisions—a message we've emphasized for more than two decades. We evolved this metaphor to the term *Credible Activist* because our research found that trust comes not just from doing what is expected in a predictable way, but also from having a unique and proactive point of view. To get a seat at the table, HR professionals need to demonstrate the competence of trust—which comes in part from taking proactive positions with a point of view about the business and HR's role in business success. They need to be Credible Activists.

For the last 30 years, the findings of the HR Competency Study (HRCS) suggest that demonstrating trust or becoming a Credible Activist is the best way to get invited to the business conversations. These findings continue; being a Credible Activist continues to be the crux of HR's being actively involved in management discussions.

This chapter shows how to get invited to the table.

Competency in Action

In preparing this book we interviewed seasoned HR professionals whom we truly felt exhibited the nine HR competencies we found (see Chapter 2). We share a couple of their cases as examples.

General Electric/Varian Medical Systems—David Staffanson

If you speak with David Staffanson, currently VP of HR for Varian Medical Systems, he will tell you that the credibility piece of the competency is really HR 101. It is foundational, but too often missed by both young and seasoned HR professionals. Before one can become an effective activist, one must establish credibility at all levels of the organization.

Reflecting on his first HR site leader role at a GE manufacturing plant, he said that his initial order of business was to "pound the pavement," in other words, walk the plant floor and get to know all of the employees personally and understand what they did. Most HR professionals would offer similar advice, but Staffanson took it a step further. In addition to getting to know the employees' names, roles, and personal stories, he carried a notebook and would write down the things that were important to the employees and ask them what he could do to help. He was notorious for this personal checklist.

The most important part of this exchange was that he would reliably follow up. He always completed what he committed to do, and this established credibility with the employees, from the production workers to the business leaders. At times, the checklist appeared to be mundane, and as a new HR manager, he wanted to work on more strategic deliverables, but Staffanson felt that he first had to establish credibility—one person, one conversation at a time. The trust earned on the floor came to be immensely important when he and the leadership team had to reorganize the workforce. He had several change champions at his disposal, and they trusted him to advocate for their interests. Without that trust, those same employees would have likely resisted any change from the business.

Fast-forward a decade, he was partnering with a new CEO of a division of GE Healthcare. His approach did not change; he used the same fundamental practices to establish credibility with the entire workforce and earn the trust of the CEO. He personally connected with the team, worked closely with the CEO to determine business priorities, and figured out how he could deliver results. He still carried a notebook with an action checklist. The trust he gained came in handy when he needed to influence significant change in the business to better align the organization with customers. When he asked for buy-in to attempt some out-of-the-box ideas—like taking the leadership team to a cadaver lab to gain hands-on experience and customer perspective—he was able to get it. Over Staffanson's career, genuine interactions and dependable execution have been instrumental in establishing credibility and enabling him to be an activist, giving him the trust he needed to get people on board with his ideas.

General Mills—Brad Taylor

In the mid-2000s, the General Mills R&D and technology function was facing two issues: brain drain and the need for increased innovation. The function included a substantial baby boomer population who were beginning to retire, taking with them significant technical and institutional knowledge. Regarding innovation, the reward system discouraged collaboration and rewarded the earning of individual patents. The lack of collaboration slowed the pace of innovation and inhibited open innovation (looking for great new ideas external to General Mills).

Brad Taylor, a seasoned HR leader, had partnered with the R&D and technology function for several years and had built up credibility. As Taylor was contemplating the issues the function was facing, he came across a novel solution. In a conversation with a colleague at Procter & Gamble, he learned that a few companies, including Procter & Gamble, from different industries were thinking about setting up a platform to share retired technical talent for short projects and consultancy work on a temporary basis. When pitching the idea,

Taylor received pushback over three related issues: (1) General Mills' R&D culture was not based on collaboration (internal or external), (2) the retirees would be coming from different industries and there was a strong "not invented here" mentality at General Mills, and (3) people were too busy to get involved. These barriers did not stop Taylor; he believed in his idea. It was a low-cost, low-risk solution to a complex problem. He continued to proselytize his idea until it took hold.

General Mills joined Procter & Gamble, Eli Lilly, and Boeing to create a retiree knowledge-sharing program, which was called YourEncore. The idea grew like wildfire. It started with 50 knowledge workers and four companies. Today, 1,000 companies are members of YourEncore, and they have access to 11,000 experts. More important, YourEncore has created a vehicle for infusing GM with tremendous external innovation and a method for extending the shelf life of retiree knowledge contribution. Taylor attributes the success of YourEncore within General Mills (in part at least) to the trust he had gained over years of delivering results as well as his willingness to take a stand for an idea that he believed in.

What Is a Credible Activist?

Credible Activists understand that they cannot have a real impact without first having built trust. Staffanson understands this principle, which is why he dedicates so much time entering a new role to build relationships that develop trust. He earns trust over time, moving the needle with each interaction, consistently following through on commitments and obligations. For Staffanson, trust is important across the entire organization—the ideal situation. However, at a minimum, HR professionals need to have strong trusting relationships with the leaders they partner with to be effective and have an impact on the business. Credible Activists use the earned trust to get invited to business conversations where they can drive the right kinds of business conversations and initiatives. They build upon the trust by focusing on matters important to business outcomes and by delivering impactful results for the business.

Once the trust is obtained, Credible Activists take risks that may be outside their comfort zone to challenge organizational norms, practices, and ways of thinking. They do not shy away from the hard work required by the business; they are willing to contribute to new organizational strategy and priorities. When they see opportunities for improvement, they voice their opinions and marshal the resources needed to move their ideas forward.

Their opinion or point of view need not be solely HR related, but also about the expectations of customers, investors, and other stakeholders. In the earlier example, Taylor felt strongly that General Mills needed to shake up cultural norms to tackle issues related to talent management and innovation. He was fighting against long-standing norms and thinking at General Mills. Although initially against the idea, business leaders listened because they trusted him. He had delivered in the past; he had credibility. He also had perseverance, another attribute of Credible Activists. As business leaders pushed back on his idea, he continued to push his idea, garnering enough support to make it stick.

Credible Activists are exceptional communicators with the ability to frame complex ideas in simple and useful ways. Using their effective communication skills, they relate facts, facilitate discussion, and enable agreement on a course of action. In their interactions with coworkers, they exhibit both confidence and humility. They communicate downward with employees, horizontally with peers, and upward with supervisors.

Finally, Credible Activists carry a sense of pride in the HR profession and the contribution they make in their roles. They are likely to be members of a local or industry-specific HR association. They keep up to speed on innovative HR practices and new ideas in research—and what other organizations are doing to improve people management in their own organization. They are more likely to be certified by their professional association.

It is interesting to note that the relative importance of Credible Activist (or its antecedent, trusted advisor) has remained critical for HR professionals to gain access to business dialogues. We would suggest that the Four Forces in Chapter 1—STEPED, VUCA, stakeholder expectations, and the personal context of today's worker, which describe higher rates of environmental change and greater employee malaise—reinforce the need for HR professionals to be Credible Activists. In VUCA times, it helps to manage at the speed of trust.

Credibility and Activism

It is the combination of credibility and activism that allows HR professionals to establish trusting relationships with those they support as well as their HR colleagues. They use the trust they have gained to influence others. Credible Activists are respected and proactive. Credible individuals who are not activists may be respected for their insights or expertise, but have little impact. Activists who are not credible may have good ideas, but no one pays much attention to them. The matrix in Table 6.1 illustrates this concept and continues to be valid today:

Table 6.1   *Credible Activist matrix*[a]

	Less Credible	More Credible
More Activist	Risk of being seen as impetuous, arrogant, or uninformed	Opportunity to have impact
Less Activist	Risk of being seen as a marginal or poor performer	Risk of being seen as irrelevant, not having anything to say, resting on past laurels, or not knowing the business

[a]*Source*: Ulrich, Brockbank, & Ulrich, 2010

History of the Credible Activist Competency Domain

We have seen the Credible Activist domain emerge and evolve over the last 30 years of HR competency research through three phases:

• *Phase 1: Personal credibility is central*
  • Credibility was the central competency in the HRCS model during the late 1980s and 1990s. It is personal, based on relationships with individual managers. HR professionals considered to demonstrate personal

credibility did so by developing chemistry with the managers they supported and by understanding and acting on their needs.

- *Phase 2: Backseat to strategy*
  - The data from the fourth round of the HRCS study (2002) showed that while personal credibility was still incredibly important, strategic contribution became the center of HR competence. Ultimately, maintaining a relationship with line management was no longer sufficient; HR professionals established credibility based on business contribution.
- *Phase 3: Credible Activist 1.0 and 2.0*
  - *Credible Activist 1.0:* Personal credibility became Credible Activist and was once again the center of the HRCS model. Our 2007 findings illustrated how the performance expectations of HR professionals had evolved to match the increasingly competitive, complex, and global business environment. HR professionals need to comprehend internal needs and external realities, taking greater initiative in setting the HR agenda and contributing business priorities. Another factor introduced with the Credible Activist competency is "HR with an attitude," which suggested that HR professionals should have an informed and proactive opinion about both HR and overall business issues.
  - *Credible Activist 2.0:* In 2012 Credible Activist was still at the center of the HR competency model, but a new, key aspect of the competency was knowing and focusing on the external market environment. Continuous improvement, self-development, and self-awareness became increasingly important with added emphasis on participating in professional organizations. The "HR with an attitude" leads HR professionals to associate oneself with the HR profession and progressing the field. Credible Activists do the right things in the right ways with the right people. We might evolve HR with an attitude to HR with business insight where HR professionals understand how to position their organization to win in changing market conditions. This evolution is similar to sales where the evolution is from relationship sales to insight selling, where sales increase through new ideas that deliver customer results. As Credible Activists, HR professionals inform with new ideas and perspective that achieve business results.

While the Credible Activist is no longer at the center of the model, it continues to be a differentiating competency for HR personal effectiveness. The current round of research builds upon Credible Activist 2.0, but simplifies the competency to focus on the core elements that drive an invitation to the business conversation. Credible Activist becomes the foundation for getting invited to the proverbial table (or to engage in business dialogue). Effective HR professionals become Credible Activists as they achieve trust and respect within the organization by exhibiting integrity, strong interpersonal skills, and business acumen. Undeniably reliable, they do what they say they will do. The HR professionals translate the chemistry that they have built up with key stakeholders into positive influence, using clear, consistent, and impactful communication to get the right people moving in the required direction. They remain persistent through adversity, learning from both successes and failures. Finally, the Credible Activist must be self-aware, demonstrating the appropriate balance between confidence and humility.

Who and Where Are Today's Credible Activists? Key Findings from HRCS Round 7

The following are key findings from HRCS Round 7:

- Credible Activist is the highest-scoring competency domain in the study, suggesting that in general HR professionals are successful as Credible Activists (see Table 2.7). This finding is consistent in self-ratings and ratings from supervisors, HR, and non-HR associates.
- North American HR professionals tend to score higher on the Credible Activist competency than HR professionals outside of North America (see Table 2.9).
- Women tend to score slightly higher than men on the Credible Activist domain (see Table 2.8).
- Credible Activist is the most important HR competency for explaining the overall effectiveness of individual HR professionals and the value that HR professionals create for employees (19.3 percent, with the next highest being Strategic Positioner at 14.5 percent).

Credible Activist Subdomains

In HRCS Round 7, the Credible Activist domain remained a critical competency for high-performing HR professionals, and we saw two subdomains particularly driving the overall competency domain: influencing and relating to others and earning trust through results. We see in Table 6.2 that the "influences and relates to others" subdomain scores slightly higher than "earns trust through results" for all raters other than HR associates. This suggests that from the perspective of most raters, HR professionals are generally better able at influencing than they are at delivering results. It is also interesting to note that self-ratings on "influences and relates to others" is higher than HR associate ratings (4.39 to 4.29), which is an anomaly in the findings (generally self-ratings are lower than associate ratings). Line managers are extremely high on their view of HR trust (4.45). Maybe HR professionals could spend more time building relationships with other HR colleagues.

Table 6.2   *Credible Activist subdomain scores by rater group*

	Credible Activist				
	All Raters[a]	Self-Ratings	Supervisor Ratings	HR Associate Ratings	Non-HR Associate Ratings
Influences and relates to others	4.35	4.39	4.30	4.29	4.45
Earns trust through results	4.30	4.28	4.21	4.29	4.36

Influencing and Relating to Others

Credible Activists are conscientious about their relationships with colleagues and business partners, and invest in these relationships. They build relationships up, down, and across the organization. They also look beyond the organization to develop relationships that will provide an outside-in perspective to help tackle challenges. From our work helping HR professionals build influence, we have found the following actions help develop relationships and support the "influences and relates to others" subdomain of Credible Activists:

- They show a genuine interest in others.
- They act with an appropriate balance of humility and confidence.
- They seek to learn from both successes and failures.
- They demonstrate personal integrity and ethics.

We explore them here one at a time.

Shows a Genuine Interest in Others

In his perennial work *How to Win Friends and Influence People*, Dale Carnegie (2010) wrote, "You can make more friends in two months by becoming interested in other people than you can in two years by trying to get other people interested in you." It is going to be a lot easier to get people to listen to and follow you if they like you. In the book, Carnegie gives six timeless ways to make people like you:

1. Become genuinely interested in other people.
2. Smile.
3. Remember that a person's name is to that person the sweetest and most important sound in any language.
4. Be a good listener. Encourage others to talk about themselves.
5. Talk in terms of the other person's interests.
6. Make the other person feel important.

Two of the six principles on Carnegie's list directly relate to showing genuine interest in others, while the other four are means to show the other person that you are interested in them. According to Carnegie, American president Teddy Roosevelt was an exemplar of these traits. Whenever Roosevelt expected a visit from someone with whom he was not well acquainted, he would stay up the night before and learn about that person's interests or profession, so he could more easily discuss the things that were important this new acquaintance. Roosevelt himself is considered one of the most interesting characters in U.S. history, and he could have very easily spent the time with guests talking about his life and experiences. Yet he knew that the interaction would be more meaningful if he took the time to get to know what's important in the lives of others.

Here are some effective practice principles related to this concept:

- Find out something new about a colleague; ask follow-up questions. You can use a technique similar to the one used by Dave Staffanson. When you are new to an organization, you generally have many people to meet and it can be a bit daunting. Carry a notebook and use it to remember names and information about the people you meet. When you go to lunch or dinner with new colleagues, work to learn something new and interesting about each one of them.
- Avoid using "I" for the entire day. At a minimum, you will see how often you speak about yourself as you resist the tendency to do so.
- Ask questions to find out more about a person; for example, why did you take this job? Why do you like your job? What are the challenges you face on the job and why? What do you think?
- Follow the Teddy Roosevelt example. When you are about to spend a significant amount of time with a new acquaintance or meet someone of influence to your role, take some time beforehand to learn about what that person does and what interests him or her professionally and personally. Social media can provide powerful insights you can use as you honestly invest in learning about others. Do your homework.

Acts with Appropriate Balance of Humility and Confidence

We are saying that HR professionals need to be both humble and confident. On the surface this can seem somewhat paradoxical, but these concepts are tied at the hip. Jim Collins (2005) offers a similar characteristic for leaders who want to transform companies from "good" to "great". The term Collins uses is *Level 5 leadership*, which is the combination of personal humility and professional will. "Level 5 leaders are a study in duality: modest and willful, shy and fearless." For Collins, American president Abraham Lincoln is the exemplar of a Level 5 leader, and we cannot argue. He was shy and quiet, yet showed no weakness leading the Union army against the Confederates in a battle that cost the lives of more than 600,000 soldiers. Lincoln was truly special in the way he managed the duality of traits.

Collins describes a person who exhibits personal humility in the following way:

- Demonstrates a compelling modesty, shunning public adulation; never boastful
- Acts with quiet, calm determination; relies on inspired standards, not inspiring charisma, to motivate
- Channels ambition into the company, not the self; sets up successors for even more greatness in the next generation
- Looks in the mirror, not out the window, to apportion responsibility for poor results, never blaming other people, external factors, or bad luck

We often coach leaders to be Teflon in success by sharing credit and Velcro in failure by absorbing blame. Effective leaders or HR professionals inspire confidence in others. We find that one subjective but reliable indicator of someone's personal credibility is the extent to which someone leaves an interaction with the leader or HR professional feeling better or worse about him- or herself.

Seeks to Learn from Both Successes and Failures

Learning requires a commitment to improve. Self-improvement begins with self-awareness and a belief in the need for change. Self-awareness is a valuable skill for a successful career. Self-awareness is an informed understanding of one's strengths and weakness. While it sounds easy, it is not. People often judge themselves by their intent (which they know), while others judge them by their behaviors (which others observe). To be self-aware requires a person to see him- or herself as others see him or her without the person's inevitable filters.

It also requires personal after-action reviews after engagements to candidly learn what worked and what did not. It also involves thoughtful consideration for strengths that will be important in the accomplishment of one's goals.

Organizations have many tools to help HR professionals evaluate their own competency and performance. There are also many low-cost tools for self-assessment that individuals can use without the resources of their respective organization, including this book. Nevertheless, here is a sample of tools that your organization may employ to help you become a more polished HR professional:

- *Competency frameworks:* Most organizations have them, and in our opinion, all organizations *should* have them. The basis for self-awareness is an understanding of the performance standard. Too often competency frameworks are created, but not used. Once in place, the organization must make sure it is well communicated and used.
- *Individual development plan (IDP):* The best organizations promote discussions among managers and employees that focus on the development needs of each individual. IDPs should outline strengths, prioritize areas for improvement, and summarize development opportunities and agreed-upon outcomes. As an HR professional, you have the responsibility to ensure that your organization is doing something to promote this type of discussion among your managers and employees.
- *Training:* Top organizations provide immense opportunities for training. Training is an opportune time for HR professionals to build self-awareness, to recognize strengths and weaknesses, and to develop plans for improvement.
- *Supervisor, customer, and peer feedback:* 360-degree feedback tools can be very effective for identifying strengths and weaknesses, depending on the level of candor in your organization. More companies are focused on real-time 360-degree feedback. PwC and GE, for example, each offer a phone app that promotes real-time feedback, giving the employees the opportunity to share feedback with anyone in the organization at any time.
- *Seek out coaching or mentorship:* Many organizations now use internal or external coaching to help leaders and other professionals understand

how they can be more effective. Formal mentorship programs still pop up in some organizations, but we have found that the best mentor relationships form organically. HR professionals should take ownership of the self-improvement and career navigation. Decide on a cadence that works well with your mentor(s), and be consistent with your discussions.

- *After-action review (AAR):* A structured process invented by the armed forces to review or debrief the impact of action, understand why it happened, and what could and should be done differently in the future. Since Shell Oil began using them in the late 1990s, they have become an effective business tool. Effective AARs use descriptive rather than evaluative language to focus on the behavior of individuals and groups and provide a more positive environment for improvement, self-awareness, and self-reflection.

Self-improvement is not easy to achieve. There are countless examples of personal and professional change efforts that have failed. A successful self-improvement plan has five elements:

1. Recognition of the need for change
2. A specific goal, time frame, and plan of action for changing
3. Support before, during, and after taking action
4. Rigorous monitoring of progress
5. Help from a spotter or admired individual who reinforces and supports change motivation and commitment

Demonstrates Personal Integrity and Ethics

At times, members of your organization may view HR as the policy police and others view HR as the creator of or cheerleader for company culture, values, and ethics. Regardless of how your organization views HR, the expectation for HR professionals is that they will do the right thing in the right way. Integrity and ethics are foundational personal traits for HR to influence; personal integrity is a key element of the credibility. HR professionals have a special obligation to act in a way that is in accordance with the culture that the company hopes to create. Employees should be able to look to HR for an example of how to act toward others in the organization, or externally with customers or suppliers.

Here are some tips on how to exhibit integrity and reinforce ethics within the organization:

- Develop a personal code of conduct or a statement of ethical values.
- Identify and discuss *gray-zone issues* in your organization. These are ethical issues where there are legitimate differences in points of view or the direction from the company is unclear. It is important to stay ahead of these issues, and where possible, try to find some agreement or clarity, so they do not become a problem in the future.
- Help others understand consequences for violations to colleagues or the organization as a whole. This approach has the added benefit of helping the HR professional, and leadership in general, develop more thoughtful and insightful perspectives on how to deal with the issue now and similar issues in the future.
- Review ethical principles or values of the organization and help others apply them to real situations. Use a case study to evaluate the actions or behaviors of other organizations through the lenses of your company's values or code of conduct. Not only does this help reinforce the ethical principles and values of your organization, it offers an opportunity to see gaps in those principal statements or values.
- Additionally, case studies could be used merely to open dialogue and help employees understand the practical implications of unethical behavior. Bring in case studies from other organizations to help illustrate problems or change behavior with your own organizations. We have found that every semester we teach or quarterly executive program we facilitate there are live case studies of ethical choices. Using current events from the headlines shows the timeliness of ethical behavior.

Learning the skills to influence and relate to others matters a great deal to being a Credible Activist, which in turn shapes personal HR effectiveness. The ability to influence is a learnable trait through the behaviors we identitied earlier.

Earning Trust Through Results

Influence and relationships build trust, but ultimately professional effectiveness starts and ends with results. HR professionals earn trust by following through on commitments and delivering results, thus maintaining and building effective relationships. The following are attributes of earning trust through the results subdomain:

- Has earned trust with key internal and external stakeholders
- Frames complex ideas in simple and useful ways
- Persists through adverse circumstances
- Has a history of delivering results

We explore them here one at a time.

Has Earned Trust with Key Internal and External Stakeholders

Trusted advisor principles continue to be reinforced in our research. These principles related to trust are foundational. Consider the example of David Staffanson at the beginning of the chapter. His notebook, the days spent walking the shop floor, the personal conversations with the CEO, and so forth were efforts to build the requisite trust with his coworkers. He understands that that trust is foundational and seeks to build it right away. In gaining trust through results, we have found a few hints that may help:

- Listen to the nagging concerns of employees, which may be as basic as lighting for an office or comfortable chairs. Observe the inevitable logistical annoyances in any work setting.
- Start small. We have found change begets change, and it is useful to find small and simple things to start with. There is often low-hanging fruit around physical setting, but also reports, approvals, meetings, and policies. These things are often small but can lead to larger and more substantial changes.
- With success in the simple things, work to deliver more complicated results. In doing so, share the credit for success and take the blame for failure. When things don't work as intended, quickly learn how to improve for the future.

Frames Complex Ideas in Simple and Useful Ways

Credible Activists are good communicators. They take communication skills seriously. They seek to ensure that their conversations are clear and accurate. HR professionals gain and keep credibility when they are able to articulately and persuasively communicate ideas, particularly complex ideas. Such sharing of information occurs in both spoken and written forms. If you feel like your communication skills are lacking, here are a few ideas for improvement:

- Seek out opportunities to present at a conference or offer in-house training.
- Publish an article about a business issue in a journal, magazine, or blog.
- Join your local Toastmasters or other social setting.
- Have written material critiqued by a writing professional.
- Observe great speakers or writers, and take notes less on what they say and more on how they say it.
- Practice drawing visual images of complex problems that clarify key issues.

Persists Through Adverse Circumstances

Life as an HR professional is no walk in the park. We find that often HR professionals are under enormous demands, being frontline in sharing bad news and central to creating a new culture. When nearly all of your daily activities and the decisions you make on the job every day involve people, you are in for a ride. People are an organization's only emotional asset. As an HR leader, you are at the forefront of difficult decisions that affect employees and their livelihood. Those decisions can be popular or very unpopular; you must approach both with stamina and conviction.

Take the VP of HR for Air France, for example. During October 2015, 100 workers who were upset about an upcoming restructuring plan forced their way into a meeting of the airline's work council. The executive team was in the process of finalizing a restructuring plan involving the layoff of 2,900 employees by 2017. The angry employees attempted to rip off the shirts of the senior leaders' backs. The VP of HR lost his shirt and was forced to scale a fence to evade the protesters. Though understandably shaken by the incident, he returned to work and continued to insist on the need to cut costs to stay competitive.

Though most HR professionals will not experience what the Air France executives experienced, they will go through trials and uncomfortable situations. Credible Activists look at these adverse circumstances as growth opportunities and struggle through them.

Has a History of Delivering Results

As mentioned earlier, perceived professional performance begins and ends with results. A track record of meeting commitments and delivering results is essential for establishing and maintaining trust in any organization.

After New York Yankees closer Mariano Rivera tore his ACL just one month into the 2012 season, some thought his career was over. Rivera, who had already discussed retiring after the 2012 season, was 42 years old and had suffered a season-ending injury, plus his replacement was younger and performed exceptionally in his stead. When Rivera indicated that he wanted to return and promised that he would be in shape for the 2013 spring training, there was no doubt in the minds of Yankee leadership he would be ready and that he would perform at a high level. He had given 16 years of consistently strong results and had always been among the most physically fit players on the team, so they signed him to a one-year deal. The 2013 season turned out to be another exceptional one for the Yankee closer.

If Rivera had had only a couple years of strong performance under his belt before the injury, the probability would have been very low that the Yankees would have paid an injured player at his age $10 million to play one season. He had built trust over time. HR professionals must do the same. Credible Activists build trust by consistently following through on their commitments. Here are a few suggestions to help you deliver results over time:

- Set clear performance goals.
- Meet commitments (obvious, but sometimes we need a reminder).
- Under-commit and overdeliver.
- Focus on meeting prenegotiated or prestated commitments.
- Strive to be error free.

- Create HR measures that track both the output of HR and the means of generating the output.
- Apply Six Sigma quality standards and processes to improve the accuracy of all HR activities and practices.

Conclusion

HR professionals who want to add value to the business need to be involved in business discussions. To get invited to those discussions, HR professionals must first exhibit Credible Activist competency traits. They need to be credible, and they need to have an opinion and be willing to voice that opinion. Credible Activists build credibility over time by delivering results, improving personal and professional performance, developing relationships of trust internally and externally, and using the trust to influence others.

CHAPTER 7

STRATEGIC POSITIONER— GOING BEYOND KNOWING THE BUSINESS

7

In Chapter 6 we discussed the importance of becoming Credible Activists so that HR professionals can be invited to the table to be a part of business discussions. However, we know that just sitting at the table or having access does not ensure impact, nor is it enough to rely on one's personal relationships to have influence.

HR professionals need to be an equal partner in setting the direction for the organization and getting it moving in the right direction. Getting to the table or discussion is different from knowing what to say when the discussion starts. Without addressing the right issues in the right ways, HR professionals will be ignored or discounted in business discussions. When HR professionals bring unique information, insights, and recommendations about talent, leadership, and organization, they become Strategic Positioners who help deliver competitive advantage. Nevertheless, the pattern of HR professionals who are Strategic Positioners adding value to external stakeholders is clear for individual HR professionals who participate in business meetings and who design and deliver HR practices.

The Strategic Positioner Competency in Action

In the fall of 2007, Blackstone Group, a multinational private equity firm, purchased Hilton, Inc. By the time Hilton's new CHRO Matt Schuyler arrived in 2009, tourism was in a severe slump with the global recession in full swing. Blackstone purchased Hilton with an aggressive growth strategy to capitalize on its investment and was intent on carrying it out as quickly as possible.

Hilton's growth opportunities were promising. The company had an iconic history, well-known brands (including Hilton and its derivatives, DoubleTree, Embassy Suites, Hampton Inn, Homewood Suites, and Waldorf Astoria), and very talented employees, which they refer to as "Team Members." However, Hilton lacked integration, saw only average top-line and bottom-line performance, and had stagnant organic room growth. Hilton was in need of a global transformation to realize its full potential.

After understanding the implications of the external environment on the business, Hilton business leaders decided to focus its strategy on four key priorities: aligning its culture and organization, maximizing performance across the entire enterprise, strengthening its brands and commercial services platform, and expanding its global reach. Working closely with Hilton's president and CEO Chris Nassetta and other members of the executive committee, Schuyler and his team sought opportunities to drive the alignment that would support these priorities and contribute to the company's success. While on a tour of their hotel properties, it quickly became apparent how his team could help Hilton deliver on its strategy.

Schuyler found that each Hilton-branded hotel he visited was operating under different vision and mission statements and sets of values. This created a lack of focus and identity. The team also identified more than 320 HR policies that were causing confusion. Many of these policies were out of date and negatively impacting Team Member engagement. For a hospitality company, employee engagement and alignment are critical and have a direct impact on the guest experience and, ultimately, the bottom line. Hilton's inconsistent policies made it difficult for the company to establish a common approach that its Team Members could follow to ensure guests enjoyed a great stay regardless of which hotel they visited.

The first step the team took was to create new, simplified vision and mission statements as well as company values. They wanted something that was simple enough for any Team Member to understand and remember, but also aligned with the company's four key strategic priorities. They created a vision from the words of company founder Conrad Hilton: "to fill the earth with the light and warmth of hospitality," and a straightforward mission to guide Hilton's path forward. The company's resulting HILTON values remain consistent today and stand for Hospitality, Integrity, Loyalty, Teamwork, Ownership, and Now. The HR team took an active role in communicating the changes to Team Members, who received them well.

The next step was an overhaul of the HR ecosystem. With the right people in critical HR roles, the team was ready to improve and standardize the infrastructure, process, and systems across the organization. The HR team focused on delivering great environments, great careers, and great rewards to Hilton Team Members. As part of this effort, HR rebuilt and simplified its approach to talent life-cycle management. The team created dedicated recruitment systems and resources to help Team Members join. Once Team Members were in the door, they sought to simplify the talent, performance, and compensation processes, as well as offer benefits that truly mattered to their workforce. They also improved how they managed departures by enhancing the company's workforce planning processes.

Now that Hilton had designed a unified culture based on common vision, mission, values, and key strategic priorities, they were in high-performance mode. Using these new inputs as a guide, Hilton's leadership team realigned the business, drove industry-leading growth, and generated outstanding financial results, despite the global economic downturn. When the company went public in 2013, it was the largest U.S. real estate IPO, the largest global lodging equity offering, and the 12th largest market capitalization in history. Since 2007 Hilton's physical global room count has increased by more than 56 percent, rooms in the development pipeline have more than doubled, and rooms under construction have more than tripled.

The impact for Team Members has been remarkable. There was 99 percent recognition of the values in Hilton's last employee engagement survey, indicating that HR has excelled at communicating and integrating the new values. Team Member engagement and trust scores reported through the survey have also steadily increased year after year. Additionally, Hilton made Fortune's list of the 100 Best Companies to Work For, surpassing several of its main competitors. Matt Schuyler and his HR team were truly Strategic Positioners in helping architect Hilton's transformation.

What Is a Strategic Positioner?

When we ask groups of HR professionals what they have to do to be effective, the most common answer is the proverbial "know the business" response. This response is consistent with findings from early rounds of the Human Resources Competency Study (HRCS), but "knowing the business" is not sufficient any more. This business-related competency domain has evolved over the years to what we now refer to as Strategic Positioner. In this round of research we continue to use the term *Strategic Positioner competency* and find that it is even more relevant in delivering value to external stakeholders.

The use of the word *positioner* is deliberate on our part. HR professionals contribute to business strategy by first understanding the business context in which the business operates. Positioning refers to the HR professional's ability to understand the business context and create a future for the organization—recognizing emerging trends and responding to them. For example, Schuyler at Hilton recognized that Airbnb with over 1,500,000 listings would be the largest lodging business in the world. For Hilton to win customer loyalty, they had to have more than a room and bed, but also exceptional service. And the key to customer experience would come from Hilton Team Members who ensured great service. By knowing this logic, HR helped position Hilton to win. Positioning is more than being able to identity and flex to respond to new opportunities, *it is being able to transform the organization to fit those opportunities*. Schuyler and his team understand customers, investors, and communities and bring innovative solutions to their problems.

The essence of this competency domain is that HR professionals must be able to evaluate both the external and internal business contexts, including social, technological, economic, political, environmental, and demographic trends (see Chapter 1) to effectively translate business strategy into the right talent, leadership, and organization actions. Strategic Positioners must understand the underlying competitive dynamics of the industry and the market that their organization competes in, including the customers, competitors, and supplier channels. They also familiarize themselves with the expectations of shareholders and potential shareholders (either debt or equity). They use their knowledge and experience to co-create a vision for the organization's future. Finally, they help apply this vision to the development of the organization's strategy, always aligning the actions of the organization to meet the expectations of external stakeholders and to anticipate trends in the competitive environment.

We have seen the Strategic Positioner domain emerge and evolve over the last 30 years of HR competency research. We can break the evolution into four distinct phases, which follow. In *HR from the Outside In* (2012), we showed that these phases are not separate, but rather interconnected, building upon each other to make a Strategic Positioner. As the Four Forces for business identified in Chapter 1 intensify, these four phases of being a Strategic Positioner are even more relevant today. Strategic Positioners have to master the skills for each of these phases to deliver both their personal and departmental values, particularly to external stakeholders (phases 3 and 4).

The four phases of being a Strategic Positioner are the following:

1. Master the language and flow of business.
2. Recognize and deliver strategy and sources of competitive advantage.
3. Understand and co-create with external stakeholders.
4. Anticipate and react to external business trends and context.

We discuss them here one at a time.

Phase 1: Master the Language and Flow of Business

The language of business primarily emphasizes finance but includes any category of the business that is central to a company's business success (marketing, strategy, IT, etc.). Today, more than ever, HR work crosses functional boundaries with marketing (building firm, leadership, and employee brands), finance (using HR to manage financial returns as well as intangibles for investors), and IT (ensuring that information capabilities are part of a firm's success as discussed in Chapter 4). HR professionals have traditionally avoided learning finance due to fear or discomfort with math and complex financial equations. Nevertheless, we found that HR professionals needed to know enough of the language to get by in, understand, and contribute to the business conversation. Early in our research, we created a business literacy test (see Table 7.1) for HR professionals, which they should still strive to pass today.

Table 7.1 *Business literacy test*

Who is our largest global competitor, and why do people buy from them?
What is our stock price? Market value?
What is our P/E ratio? What factors shape the P/E ratio? How does our P/E ratio compare to competitors?
What was the profit and revenue of our division and/or company last year?
What is our firm brand and reputation in the marketplace? How does this shape our internal culture?
What is our market share?
Is our market segment growing or shrinking?
What are the emerging technology trends facing our industry?
What are the top two or three priorities for our business leaders this year?
Who is our largest customer and why do they buy from us? Who are key customers we have recently lost and why did they leave us?
Who are our primary competitors? What do they do better than we do? What do we do better than they do? Which do customers value most?
What social and political trends might be disruptive to our industry?

Phase 2: Recognize and Deliver Strategy and Sources of Competitive Advantage

In 2002, the "business" competency domain evolved into what we called strategic contribution. We found that knowing the business meant also understanding the organizational strategy and competitive advantage.

HR professionals needed to know how the business made money and what the key differentiators of the business were. Strategic decision making, fast change, infrastructure design, and culture management were key elements of this competency domain.

Phase 3: Understand and Co-Create with External Stakeholders

HR professionals need to know the niche, the customers, competitors, suppliers, investors, and so on. There is a new focus on external stakeholders. HR needs to know who they are, how to build relationships with them, and how to use them to set criteria for effective people management. For example, customer expectations should inform and become criteria for hiring and promotion, performance management, training and development expectations, and leadership behaviors. We have conducted extensive research on the collaboration with targeted customers and find that such collaboration results in sustainable value and validates the practices of integrating customer expectations. At Hilton, Schuyler learned that guest experience was highly correlated with Team Member sentiment. Additionally, HR professionals should be aware of not only customers, but also investors. We have also found through our research that investor confidence (expectation of future earnings potential) is in part the product of their perception of intangibles (or organization capabilities as discussed in Chapter 3), which are in turn shaped by what we refer to as leadership capital.

Phase 4: Anticipate and React to External Business Trends and Context

In our 2012 research, we evolved this logic to define the Strategic Positioner. HR professionals need to know the context within which their organization operates. They understand social, technological, economic, political, environmental, and demographic (STEPED in Chapter 1) trends and how they affect their respective industries and/or geographical regions. They translate their knowledge of the external environment and trends into internal action. Hilton first understood the economic climate before developing company strategy and aligning organizational practices to that strategy. Since articulating this outside-in logic from the 2012 research, we have seen an increased pressure for HR professionals to ground their choices in customer, investor, and community stakeholder expectations. *It is no longer enough for HR to merely implement strategy created by others; HR must help co-create it by understanding emerging market opportunities.*

Most HR professionals recognize and do Phase 1 or 2, but we argue that to position your organization to anticipate and match external implications, you have to do all four. Business literacy has become the table stakes of the Strategic Positioner. HR professionals must do more and be more proactive in positioning their organizations for future success. They must master business fundamentals (beyond financials), contribute to and be the architects of strategy, align with external stakeholders, and anticipate and react to external trends to more fully contribute to business discussions.

What We Learned from the 2016 HRCS

Business success comes when HR professionals can effectively envision external opportunities, help translate these opportunities into business strategy, and then create the right talent, leadership, and culture to respond. This round of research suggests that HR professionals are acting as effective Strategic Positioners in general, but it is not easy, which is one reason we consider the competency to be a value differentiator.

- Strategic Positioner was the third highest-scoring competence domain overall behind only Compliance Manager and Credible Activist. The highest rating came from non-HR associates, suggesting that line managers view HR's contribution to the business discussion favorably.
- There is wide variance across regions in the Strategic Positioner score with North America highest (4.25 average) and Japan the lowest (3.85 average),

suggesting that different regions may have different expectations for how HR professionals engage strategy.

- Strategic Positioner is the second most important competency for explaining the overall effectiveness of individual HR professionals and the value created for line managers and employees.

- Strategic Positioner is the most important competency for the value HR professionals create for external stakeholders. This critical insight helps demonstrate the importance of identifying whom HR serves once invited to the table. If the HR professionals want to primarily serve the employees and line managers inside the organization, they should continue to rely on their Credible Activist competencies (i.e., listen to me because you trust me). But if the HR professional wants to influence external stakeholders (customers, investors, communities, and regulators), they need to become Strategic Positioners (refer back to Table 2.10). If HR focuses on credible activism without also playing the role of Strategic Positioner, then HR professionals will be invited to the table but offer no opinion regarding the strategic direction of the business. By becoming Strategic Positioners, HR professionals can use their seat at the table to help the company focus on value creation for the key external stakeholders that keep the organization in business.

- This same pattern of external stakeholder influence generally applies for HR professionals acting on their own (Table 2.10) and for HR professionals designing and delivering HR practices that add value (Table 2.11). The only shift in this Strategic Positioner stakeholder external influence pattern comes when the HR professionals represent the design and delivery of HR practices; being a Strategic Positioner is negative related to value created for line managers. Evidently, to increase line manager–perceived value, HR professionals should not just focus on design and deliver of HR practices, but also demonstrate Human Capital Curator skills (Table 2.11). Line managers expect HR professionals to deliver human capital (talent) more than shape strategic choices. This may be that line managers see strategic decision making as their domain, and/or they may not have experienced HR professionals who add value in this space.

- Being a Strategic Positioner was also the second most critical HR competency to drive business financial results behind Paradox Navigator (see Table 2.11).

Clearly, being a Strategic Positioner remains a core driver of personal HR effectiveness and using HR to serve key stakeholders and to drive business results.

Strategic Positioner Subdomains

In HRCS Round 7 the Strategic Positioner domain subfactored into three subdomains: interpreting business context, decoding customer expectations, and understanding internal business operations. A summary of the subdomain scores is shown in Table 7.2.

Table 7.2   Subdomain scores by rater type for Strategic Positioner

	Strategic Positioner				
	All Raters[a]	Self-Ratings	Supervisor Ratings	HR Associate Ratings	Non-HR Associate Ratings
Interprets business context	4.22	4.18	4.06	4.22	4.30
Decodes stakeholder expectations	4.07	3.95	3.86	4.07	4.16
Understands internal business operations	3.97	3.81	3.73	3.98	4.05

It is interesting to note the score variations among these three subdomains. HR professionals are much better at interpreting business context than they are at decoding customer expectations or understanding internal business operations. This means that the high overall score observed for the Strategic

Positioner domain is largely driven by the HR professional's ability to interpret business context. While this is critically important given our prior work emphasizing an outside-in perspective on HR, it is also insufficient to interpret the business context without being able to merge that interpretation with stakeholder expectations and internal business operations. The key to the Hilton success outlined at the beginning of this chapter was an integration of all three of these critical pieces.

We visit each subdomain, one at a time.

Subdomain 1: Interprets Business Context

This important subdomain, in turn, has four key components:

- Understand changes in the organization's external environment
- Understand who makes key decisions in the organization
- Understand expectations of external customers
- Understand how the organizational unit makes money

Again, we explore these components one at a time.

Understand Changes in the Organization's External Environment

Increasingly important for HR professionals is the ability to understand changes in an organizational unit's external environment (e.g., the Four Forces from Chapter 1). To help leaders in general, and HR professionals specifically, understand the world in which they operate, we developed a simple framework that captures the business context they should pay attention to in each country or region where they may operate. We introduced the STEPED framework in Chapter 1. But it is useful to discuss this in more detail here so that HR professionals can more fully leverage this logic in their efforts to understand the external context:

- *Social trends:* healthcare, lifestyle, family patterns
- *Technological trends:* access to and use of the Internet

- *Economic trends:* inflation, recession, key industries
- *Political trends:* elections, regulatory requirements, political stability
- *Environmental trends:* issues around sustainability
- *Demographic trends:* age, education, race, gender, income issues

These STEPED issues redefine the nature of what work will be and how work will be done. When HR professionals have a working knowledge of STEPED issues, they are better aware of how these external business factors impact their organizations and the work of HR. They are able to oversee and guide decisions that affect that market.

Table 7.3 gives a list of questions that generate discussion and frame what HR professionals think of their external environment. These questions may be applied to a geography (e.g., a new country where an organization might compete) or to an industry segment (e.g., a new product line). In Chapter 1, we used the beverage industry as an example of using the STEPED model. Here we offer more specific questions that might help an HR professional understand the external context.

Table 7.3   STEPED framework questions

STEPED Category	Questions to Ask
Social	• What are health patterns (physical, emotional)? • What are family patterns (married, not married, divorced, number of children)? • What are religious trends (heritage, activity)? • What is the urban/rural mix and movement? • What is lifestyle (workday, weekends, dominant hobbies)? • What is homeownership (apartment, home)? • What are the social problems (e.g., drugs, crime)? • Who are the heroes or famous people from this area (past and present)? • What are the diet and eating patterns?
Technical	• What are their communication mechanisms (media, television) and how independent are they? • What is the level of technological maturity within the geography (Internet use, computer access)? • What is their use of social media?

Table 7.3 *STEPED framework questions (continued)*

STEPED Category	Questions to Ask
Economic	• What is the gross domestic product? Relative to others, how is it doing? • What economic cycle are they in (recession, growth)? • What is unemployment? • What are leading industries? Companies? • What is the economic gap between haves versus have-nots (size of middle class)?
Political	• What is their political history? • How much political stability is there? • How much regulation versus private enterprise exists? (What is the role of government in industry?) • How open (versus repressive) is their government? • What is their political heritage (democracy, socialism, parliament, king or family rule)? • What are the political "hot topics" that exist? • What is the relationship between the military and government? • How much corruption is there?
Environmental	• What are the environmental issues that people are worried about? • How does the organization deal with social responsibility issues? • How does the geography participate in global conferences and trends?
Demographic	• What is the average age? • What is the birthrate? • What is the education level? (public versus private) • What is the income level? (income disparity)

Social trends may impact the merits of an employee value proposition by shifting employee expectations of the company. Technological trends may affect the extent to which work can be done in remote sites. Economic trends may affect competitive opportunities for investment and growth of products and talent. Political trends may affect the regulatory and compliance obligations for a company. Environmental trends may shape the social responsibility initiatives that help attract talent. Demographic trends may affect where to source talent. In the future, HR professionals should be conversant with these general business conditions in a global context so they can anticipate what might happen next in their industry and organization and prepare to respond accordingly.

STEPED is one framework we can use to better understand the external environment, but there are other tools and activities that you can use to understand the business context and position your business to win in the market. Table 7.4 introduces another list of to-dos to gain this competency.

Table 7.4 *Activities for understanding business context*

How do HR Professionals gain external knowledge and insights?	
1. Read positive and negative analyst reports	11. Track financial analysis of market segments
2. Read magazines, newspapers, and articles about your company	12. Attend marketing meetings
3. Read magazines, newspapers, and articles about the industry	13. Attend product development meetings
4. Attend industry trade shows	14. Attend sales meetings
5. Master internal market reports	15. Invite customers, analysts, and shareholders to address training programs
6. Learn how internal market reports are generated	16. Invite customers, analysts, and shareholders to attend training programs
7. Visit customers in their buying context	17. Invite customers, analysts, and shareholders to address management meetings
8. Visit customers in their product or service utilization context	18. Invite customers, analysts, and shareholders to address HR meetings
9. Study competitors in detail	19. Invite customers, analysts, and shareholders to address meetings of line operators
10. Be personally involved in market research	20. Know what you don't know

Understand Who Makes Key Decisions in Your Organization

Key decision makers are often the people who control important resources, but it does not necessarily have to be that way. You will want to identify leaders in your organization and gain their commitment for the future through collaboration and openness. Remember that some of the most important leaders in your organization may not be considered leaders by their positions, but instead, because of the influence and trust that they have generated with time and experience. Finally, do not restrict yourself to understanding your department, site, or region and the decision makers there. Connect regularly with different departments and regions within your company to understand their outlook on business trends. You might do an influence map of key players in your organization. This network of influence map shows who connects with whom and how information is shared. It will help you recognize networks of influence patterns. Knowing network influencers will help you involve and collaborate with the right people to get your ideas implemented.

Understand Expectations of External Customers

Of all the potential stakeholders in your organization, we have found that customers require the most attention. Without a steady customer base who is willing to buy your products or services, organizations will no longer exist. Given the incredible pace of change (outlined in Chapter 1), staying connected to and anticipating customers becomes even more important for HR professionals as Strategic Positioners. This means that HR professionals should do the following:

- Understand customer buying criteria
- Help articulate a customer value proposition that guides internal organization actions
- Contribute to building the brand of the company with customers, shareholders, and employees
- Ensure that the culture (and brand) of your business is recognized in the minds of external stakeholders
- Design a culture that focuses on meeting the needs of external customers

HR professionals co-create customer focus by guiding their organization through three steps:

1. *Who are our targeted customers?* HR professionals can partner with marketing and sales to segment customers based on revenue, buying patterns, channels, size, and opportunity. We have worked with HR professionals who build marketing segmentation into training programs so that participants throughout the organization recognize target customers.

2. *What do the targeted customers value or what are their buying criteria?* HR professionals can help define target customers' value proposition (price, speed, service, quality, innovation, or value). HR professionals have trained marketing and sales professionals to do market research and collect customer value data. When internal employees learn to do market research (rather than contract this to market research consultants), the employees become more sensitive to customer buying criteria.

3. *How does the organization build sustainable relationships with targeted customers?* HR professionals may audit and tailor their HR practices to be customer centric. Customer-centric HR comes when customers participate (directly and/or indirectly through a detailed understanding of customer needs) in setting hiring standards, interviewing potential job candidates (particularly at senior levels), defining performance measures, attending training as participants or presenters, allocating financial rewards, participating in communication forums, and governing organization decision making.

We have also identified some additional activities designed to help HR professionals better understand customer expectations:

- *Conduct a study that includes a value chain analysis of your major customers.* Include a definition of who the customers are. What are their buying criteria? Who do they currently buy from? Where are you strongest and weakest versus key competitors?

- *Speak with customers about their current and future needs.* If this is not possible, spend time with members of the sales and marketing team and/or others on the front line, like support agents, to try to gather information that you would have otherwise gathered from the customers. We recommend that HR professionals set aside about 5 percent of their time to working with customers or a suitable proxy such as sales and marketing.
- *Review customer performance data to get a sense of their satisfaction and expectations.*
- *Serve on a cross-functional team.* This team's task is to identify customers' buying habits and recommend steps to improve market share.
- *Work with the marketing department to involve employees more extensively in market research efforts.* Ensure that information gathered through such an effort is used to solve customer problems and to improve customer satisfaction indicators.
- *Act as a customer.* That is, use your company's products or services.
- *Audit your HR practices.* See the extent to which they reflect customer expectations.

Once HR professionals understand customer expectations, they must put that knowledge into action. Integrating customer expectations into design HR practices and processes can help position their organization for long-term success.

Understand How the Organizational Unit Makes Money

Part of understanding how your organization makes money will come as you make an effort to understand who the customers are and why they are buying your product or services. Connecting with marketing, finance, and operations will also be necessary, as you understand who is buying what and why, what product lines carry the highest margins, and where there may be room for greater efficiency in operations. As you understand how your organization makes money, you will better understand and be able to contribute to conversations around business strategy and resource allocation.

Subdomain 2: Decodes Stakeholder Expectations

This subdomain has two elements:

• Understand investor expectations and how they value your organization.
• Help investors recognize the quality of leadership within the organizational unit.

We explain them one at a time.

Understand Investor Expectations and How They Value Your Organization

In today's hyper competitive environment, investors have become ever more active. Since intangibles explain up to 70 percent of overall market value (e.g., firms like Amazon have market value far beyond their earnings), HR work can begin to shape these intangible values in the minds of investors. Intangibles often represent the capabilities that a firm possesses, as seen by investors. Many of the principles with customers would apply to investors, for example, (1) who are our targeted investors, (2) why do they invest in us (intangibles as well as tangible results), and (3) how can we build sustainable relationships with these targeted investors? HR can use HR practices to build investor confidence in future earnings.

The methods used by investors to assess a company's market value have evolved. No two investors do it alike, but we have observed the following shift through three "phases" of evolution of the assessment methodology. As the methodology has evolved, it has become more guided by intangible factors such as brand, innovation, and leadership.

In Phase 1, investors define market valuation in terms of financial returns defined by accounting standards of earnings, cash flow, and profitability. In Phase 2, due to changes and uncertainty in markets, information, and globalization, the financial data publicly reported by firms has not reflected their value accurately. As a result, efforts at firm valuation by Baruch Lev and his colleagues have shown increased interest in intangibles like strategy, brand,

R&D, innovation, risk, and information flow. These intangibles predict firm profitability and market value (see Ulrich & Smallwood, 2003).[1] In emerging Phase 3, long-term investors recognize that leadership matters. In our research, we found that investors allocate about 25 to 30 percent of their decision making on the quality of leadership. Quality of leadership becomes a predictor of intangible value, which in turn produces financial results. We have created a leadership capital index that investors can use to determine the quality of leadership within a company. HR professionals can use this information to ensure that the HR practices that deliver leadership have meaning for investors. For example, one large company designed their leadership development programs to ensure that investors who co-created, attended, or presented in these forums would have more confidence in the leadership team. Given the increased investor attention to intangibles and leadership, HR professionals can play a more active role in building investor confidence.

Help Investors Recognize the Quality of Leadership Within the Organizational Unit

As with the evolution of investment analysis, the definition of effective leadership has also gone through three phases. In Phase 1, leadership theorists tried to identify a core set of demographic or personal traits that characterized an effective leader: height, gender, heritage, speaking style. Many leadership theorists and advisors emphasized one competence area (e.g., authenticity, emotional intelligence, strategy, execution, talent management, or human capital development [see *Leadership Code*]). In this phase, leader actions matter most. In Phase 2, leadership theorists recognized that effective leaders create value for those inside their organization (e.g., employee, organization, or strategic outcomes) depending on the task at hand. Situations may vary by maturity of team members, complexity of the tasks, time horizon for doing the work, or uncertainty in predicting outcomes of the work. In this phase, the outcomes of leader actions matter more than the actions. Leadership authenticity without creating value for others is narcissism, not real leadership. In the emerging Phase 3, the quality of leadership is determined by the value created for those outside the organization. Effective leadership is not merely what leaders know and do or how they drive internal organization outcomes, but how their actions shape the experiences of those outside the organization. External stakeholders may include communities, customers (see *Leadership Brand*), or investors (see *Leadership Capital Index*).

We see HR professionals as Strategic Positioners working to increase the perceived quality of leadership as seen by investors. Doing so increased market valuation as much as increasing financial earnings.

HR professionals can help investors have more confidence in the quality of leadership within their company. Traditionally, assessments of leadership, particularly from investors, have been subjective, reliant on a "gut feel" approach. We wanted to create something more rigorous. We felt there was a need for a Leadership Capital Index, similar to a Moody's or Standard & Poor's financial confidence index, so we created one (see Dave Ulrich's recent book on the Leadership Capital Index).[2] This index is based on interviewing and surveying investors as well as a thorough review of studies on the impact of leadership. From that analysis, we have an index that can be used by investors to value a company and by a company to help investors recognize the quality of leadership.

The Leadership Capital Index has two dimensions: individual and organizational. Individual refers to the personal qualities (competencies, traits, characteristics) of both the top leader in the organization and his or her leadership team. Organizational refers to the systems leaders create to manage leadership throughout the organization and the application of organization systems to specific business conditions. Each dimension in turn contains five elements: *Individual Dimension*

1. *Personal proficiency:* To what extent do leaders demonstrate the personal qualities to be an effective leader (e.g., intellectual, emotional, social, physical, and ethical behaviors)?
2. *Strategist:* To what extent do leaders articulate a point of view about the future and accordingly adjust the firm's Strategic Positioning?
3. *Executor:* To what extent do leaders make things happen and deliver as promised?

4. *People manager:* To what extent do leaders build competence, commitment, and contribution of their people today and tomorrow?

5. *Leadership differentiator:* To what extent do leaders behave consistently with customer expectations?

Organizational Dimension

1. *Culture capability:* To what extent do leaders create a customer-focused culture throughout the organization?

2. *Talent management:* To what extent do leaders manage the flow of talent into, through, and out of the organization?

3. *Performance accountability:* To what extent do leaders create performance management practices that reinforce the right behaviors?

4. *Information:* To what extent do leaders manage information flow throughout the organization (e.g., from top to bottom, bottom to top, and side to side)?

5. *Work practices:* To what extent do leaders establish organization and governance that deal with the increasing pace of change in today's business setting?

As the need for investors to analyze leadership capability grows, HR professionals can be proactive at assessing their executive leaders and their organizational leadership capabilities, but also helping their assessments become more visible to investors as they become more sophisticated at interpreting and understanding them. The factors outlined earlier create an effective starting point.

When HR professionals bring the discipline of a Leadership Capital Index to investors and boards of directors, they are dramatically influencing their value to the firm's market value.

Subdomain 3: Understands Internal Business Operations

Again, there are two to-dos within this subdomain:

• Contribute to creating the organizational unit's strategy.
• Accurately anticipate the organizational unit's risks.

We explore these to-dos here.

Contributes to Creating the Organizational Unit's Strategy

For many years HR professionals wanted to be part of the strategy conversation, but when invited, they primarily focused on *implementation* of the strategy. The expectation now is that HR contribute to both the *content* (vision of the future of the organization) and *process* (how it is crafted) of strategy.

The content of the business unit strategy asks two basic questions: Where do we compete and how do we win? HR professionals should be able to inform on both questions. Where a firm competes may be a function of the skills and abilities that a firm possesses. American Express finds business opportunities in data processing, a core competence from their credit card business; General Electric is moving into the Internet of Things, an extension of their technological skill base; IBM acquires PWC to develop its service and advisory business. How a firm wins is often tied to the disciplines of execution centered around talent (right people, right skills, right place, right time, and right motivation), leadership at all levels of the organization, and organization capabilities of information, innovation, service, collaboration, and efficiency. HR professionals bring value to these strategy questions. As such, they help shape the content of strategy.

HR professionals also influence the process of strategy by informing who should be participating in the strategy-making process. Given the complexity of the business environment in which we operate, part of the strategic process is to articulate a simplistic, easily digestible strategy that is widely shared and acted on. We see HR professionals adding value to the strategy discourse by framing complex ideas in ways that are useful and easily understood by leaders. They help identify and manage risk, while providing alternative insights to ensure diversity of thinking. HR professionals then need to translate business strategy into talent and culture initiatives. As HR professionals seek to do these things, they ultimately help facilitate the process of making strategy happen by playing three roles:

- *Storyteller:* HR professionals' responsibility is to first understand the organization's vision and strategy, then turn it into a specific experience.

People tend to remember stories better than facts. Well-told stories can make memorable points that lead to action.

- *Strategy interpreter:* One of HR's primary objectives is to turn strategy into actionable items for talent, culture, and leadership. HR professionals need to discover the implications of any strategy discussion on talent, culture, and leadership.

- *Strategy facilitator:* HR professionals must ensure good governance around the strategic discussion. We advise HR professionals who are invited into strategic discussions to be very aware of the processes connected to these forums:
  - Are the right people in the room?
  - Are the strategic decisions grounded in the reality of customers and competitors?
  - Are the conversations in the room the same as those outside the room?
  - Are the choices being made balancing aspiration and stretch with accomplishment and realism?
  - Is the group focused on strategic choices or decisions rather than vague ideals?
  - Is there a rationale process for taking ideas conceived in the discussion into the organization?
  - Who else needs to participate at what level of strategic thinking (e.g., creating, implementing, tracking, investing in the strategy)?
  - What follow-up and accountability will occur to make sure people deliver what they promise?

If strategy discussions do not occur in an organization, HR needs to ensure that they happen. They can gather key decision makers to hash out and formulate a clearly articulated vision for the future. For HR professionals who want more exposure and experience with strategy formulation, they can volunteer on a future scenario-building team. Or if the organization does not have such a team, they can establish a team whose task it is to develop a vision for the future of your company and the industry within which you compete.

The message here is that HR has spent years wanting to contribute to the strategy agenda—start contributing!

Accurately Anticipate the Organizational Unit's Risk

There has been increased focus in recent years on the importance of enterprise risk management in organizations. The 2008 financial crisis revealed multiple ways in which organizations were vulnerable and unprepared for the radical shifts that occurred almost overnight in the global economy.

At its basic level, risk deals with two processes: (1) uncertainty and the ability to predict the future from the present, or the probability something will happen, and (2) variability, or the range of difference in an activity. By reducing uncertainty and variability through control processes, risk is reduced and organizations more predictably accomplish their goals. Enterprise risk assessment occurs when a governing committee identifies the major potential risks, and then filters these risks against the criteria of uncertainty and variability to prioritize risks that management must pay attention to.

To guide this risk assessment, frameworks have been provided that help predict categories of risk.[3] The Committee of Sponsoring Organizations of the Treadway Commission (COSO) is a joint initiative of five private sector organizations dedicated to providing thought leadership about risk management. This commission has developed a framework to guide enterprise risk assessment with four major risk domains: strategic, operational, financial, and compliance risks. As HR professionals more fully grasp the risk portfolio, they can ensure that employees and line managers also understand the organization's risks, and they can help mobilize resources toward risk training and risk mitigation.

Not all organizations will have a formal enterprise risk management function, and organizations may vary in the sophistication of their risk management strategies, but HR professionals can engage in activities to better anticipate and understand the organization's risks regardless. Some suggestions to consider to better assess risk include the following:

- Include a short amount of time each meeting to allow others to share problems and ideas for improvement. Identify the areas that give experts within your organization the greatest discomfort.
- Talk to ground floor employees to find out their perspective on the company direction, problems they face, and solutions they suggest for the company.
- Identify leaders (not by position but by influence and trust), and explore with them the chinks in the organization's armor.
- Take time to evaluate how your company's strategy aligns with other elements of the organization through an organizational analysis tool, such as Galbraith's Star Model or McKinsey's 7S. Determine which areas may be out of alignment and, therefore, that create the greatest operational risk.
- Engage in failure-imagining experiences. Rather than directly asking people to reveal weaknesses and risks (which may be politically charged issues), we have found that asking people to do a post-mortem on their current project, as if it had failed, can help reveal potential concerns. Shifting to a hypothetical world may help individuals open themselves up to talking about the risks in project implementation and success.

Conclusion: The State of the Strategic Positioner Competency

We are heartened by the progress we see in the HR profession around the Strategic Positioner competency. As we travel and speak, we are pleased to see more and more HR professionals adopting the language and logic of the business. We also see more HR professionals embracing the realities of outside so they can be more effective inside. We see, and the data confirms, Strategic Positioner as one of the most critical competency domains, and we believe it will continue to be an essential opportunity for growth in the HR profession in the coming years.

CHAPTER 8

BECOMING A PARADOX NAVIGATOR

8

Paradoxes exist when seemingly contradictory activities operate together. We experience paradoxes in daily life as captured by such popular phrases as "tough love," "do more with less," "oil and vinegar," "sweet and sour," "work/ life balance," "catch-22," "go slow to go fast," "good and evil," and so forth. When these inherent contradictions work together, success follows. Instead of focusing on either/or, paradoxes emphasize and/also thinking.

Why Paradox? Historical Roots

The concept of paradox, which shows up in today's management thinking, is rooted in ancient philosophy. In Eastern philosophy the yin-and-yang concept views the world as holistic where all phenomena are "shaped by the integration of two opposite cosmic energies, namely Yin and Yang."[1] Yin represents "female" energy, and yang represents "male" energy; both forces operate both independently and together, shaping all universal phenomena and generating constant change. In Western thought, philosophers have also discussed the essence and value of paradox. Ancient Greeks were well aware that a paradox can take people outside their usual way of thinking. They combined the prefix *para-* ("beyond" or "outside of") with the verb *dokein* ("to think"), forming *paradoxos*, an adjective meaning "contrary to expectation." Latin speakers picked up the word and used it to create their noun *paradoxum*, which English speakers borrowed during the 1500s to create *paradox*. Søren Kierkegaard, a prominent Western philosopher in the 1800s, said, "But one must not think ill of the paradox, for the paradox is the passion of thought, and the thinker without the paradox is like the lover without passion: a mediocre fellow."[2] F. Scott Fitzgerald added, "The test of a first-rate intelligence is the ability to hold two opposed ideas in mind at the same time and still retain the ability to function."

In management thinking, concepts of paradox have shown up in many terms: *behavioral complexity, polarity, flexible leadership, duality, dialectic, competing values, dichotomies, competing demands, ambidexterity,* and so forth.[3] These concepts have applied to accounting, marketing, technology, and strategy literatures. In the HR field, we have talked about paradoxes for many years, proposing that the traditional shift from operational, administrative, and transactional to foundational, strategic, and transformational evolve to and/also thinking. For example, in *HR Champions,* we suggested that HR has to be both operational and inspirational, administrative and strategic, and transactional and transformational.

Why Paradoxes Matter Today: Emerging Organizational Requirements

Due to the Four Forces from Chapter 1 (STEPED, VUCA, stakeholder expectations, and the personal context of today's workers), *navigating* paradox is more important than ever for organization, leadership, and HR success. We chose the term *navigating* rather than managing since navigation implies constantly steering, adjusting, adapting, and evolving more than the disciplines of managing, which implies controlling, resolving, administering, and solving. The logic for the increased importance of paradox comes from the evolution of the concept of organization.

Traditional views of organization, grounded in the work of German sociologist Max Weber, drew insights from bureaucracies like the Catholic church and the German military. In these legacy views, organizations succeeded and survived by responding to external complexity by scalar principles, line of authority, chain of command, decision rights, spans of control, specialization and division of labor where each employee knows his role and responsibilities. The assumptions of bureaucracy have pervaded management practice. Scientific management encouraged standardization which led to mass production. Business historian Alfred Chandler talks about the "visible hand" of management in creating coordination and control processes in organizations. Balance scorecards ensure controls and governance through strategic maps that help employees know their role and the rules they follow by assignment and position as captured in a job description. As argued by Nobel Prize–economist Oliver Williamson, hierarchical organizations reduce transaction costs and increase efficiency. Organization thought leader Jay Galbraith proposed that organization coordination and control managed information, which clarified power and authority. In all of these (and other) ideologies, the hierarchical organization assumptions coordinate work through strategic and role clarity, process efficiency, and disciplined routines. For decades, these organizational assumptions enabled organizations to respond to complex work settings.

But today the greater challenge for organizations is agility and change. The world is changing so quickly that what was right yesterday is not right today and will not be right tomorrow. In a world of rapid change, the assumptions of hierarchy (control by roles, rules, and routines) often impair organizations because of inflexibility. Organizations, to survive the Four Forces of change we introduced in Chapter 1, have to adjust to change, which is often referred to as agility, flexibility, learning, transformation, revitalization, and so forth. Such organizational adaptability comes from navigating paradox.

Without the tensions, debates, dialogues, and conflicts that paradoxical thinking encourages, change is less likely to happen. When people in an organization agree all the time or act out of their existing roles, adaptation is less likely. Navigating paradox accepts and heightens disagreements that enable organizations to change and evolve.

Exploring Current Paradoxes for HR

To create more agile organizations, HR professionals are asked to move beyond the administrative/strategic paradoxes we have written about. In preparation for the seventh round of the Human Resources Competency Study (HRCS), the core research team and our regional partners conducted hundreds of interviews, focus groups, and workshops across the globe to identify what HR professionals require to be effective and to positively impact the business in the future. The feedback was largely consistent with the previous rounds of research, with ideas such as understanding the business strategy, having personal credibility, and designing HR systems. What was different was the rise of the new organizational assumptions as discussed earlier. Underlying these assumptions were several paradoxes.

Though the word *paradox* was not explicitly used, the tensions people described, such as centralization versus decentralization, globalization versus localization, flexibility versus standardization, top-down versus bottom-up control, freedom versus control, work life versus life work, and business versus social results, were clearly paradoxes at work in organizational life. These paradoxes are new business realities, for both line managers and HR professionals. HR professionals, to be effective, should not ignore them, but learn to face and navigate through them.

Given the emerging importance of these embedded tensions and their impact on the organization of the future, we chose to study them explicitly in this most recent round of research, resulting in a new competency for HR professionals that we have called Paradox Navigator.

A Leading Example

The following is an example of HR professionals as Paradox Navigators.

Staples, Inc.

In recent years, Staples, now the fifth-biggest Internet retailer behind Amazon, Apple, Dell, and Walmart, has had to diversify its business model to help capture the various shopping preferences of its customers. For approximately 15 years following the launch of Staples.com in 1998, the company had three distinct ways to interact with its customers, namely, its physical stores, B2B delivery, and online website. Discussions about how to make the customer experience more seamless and allow the customer to better dictate the experience really began to take hold around 2011. The retail world was no longer black and white. Staples leadership felt that the multichannel sales approach needed to be more integrated. The answer was an omnichannel strategy.

The goal of the omnichannel strategy was for customers to view Staples retail stores, mobile app, or websites as one and the same, not as separate places to shop. From an operations perspective, the integration introduced "buy online and pick up in store" and used in-store kiosks where customers could purchase items not in the store or look up product reviews.

From an organizational perspective, the strategy created both organizational and employee paradoxes. The company included seven divisions: U.S. Retail, Canada Retail, U.S. B2B, Canada B2B, Quill B2B, U.S. e-commerce, and Canada e-commerce. Under the omnichannel strategy, these divisions had to work together and better understand what each other was doing, particularly the retail and e-commerce divisions.

A contradiction existed between how things have always been run versus how they now needed to operate (in tandem), as well as the idea of centralization versus decentralization. Retail associates who previously were solely dedicated to their store's performance would now have to consider how to help lead potential online customers in their region to the company's online store. The challenge was not to see online as a threat, but as an opportunity to drive sales via an extension of the ability to offer 1.5 million products online instead of 7,000 in retail stores.

At the center of these paradoxes is the store general manager (GM)—part of a network of approximately 1,300 stores located in the United States and Canada. They are the ones who must deal with this transformation and have been challenged with navigating through these paradoxes (see Table 8.1).

Table 8.1   *Staples general manager omnichannel paradoxes*

General Manager Paradoxes	
Consumers (B2C)	Business (B2B)
Stores	Online
Products	Services
7,000 products in store	1.5M products online

(continued on next page)

Table 8.1   Staples general manager omnichannel paradoxes (continued)

General Manager Paradoxes		
Retail channels	**AND**	Omnichannel
Customer service "human touch"		Self-service "on your own"
Store operations excellence (internal focus)		Store business development (external focus)
Command and control		Innovation, autonomy, and flexibility
Long-tenure retail executives		New e-commerce team

To help employees navigate the paradox of being both a traditionally decentralized organization and a more centralized, cross-cutting organization, the HR team focused on unifying the associates across channels, incentivizing associates to contribute to the greater organization, and increasing the communication and knowledge-sharing across businesses.

The first thing the team did was to gather input from more than 25,000 global associates from all divisions on a set of new common values or language consistent with the business model. The new values decided upon follow:

- Work together.
- Own it.
- Say it like it is.
- Be caring.
- Keep it simple.

Once the values were in place, they were reinforced by a revised leadership behavior model called the Commitments that included the following:

- Put the customer first.
- Take risks.
- Raise the bar.
- Challenge yourself.
- Be fast and flexible.

After establishing the organization values and leadership commitments, the HR leadership team focused on incentivizing collaboration and communication. They recognized that rewards and recognition needed to align with the new strategy, sending the message to associates that they needed to work differently. Take the brick-and-mortar store managers, for example; part of their bonus now depended in part on the performance of the website in the zip codes covered by the store, which encouraged the store manager to get creative in marketing the website and also to collaborate with the e-commerce team.

To further collaboration between different channels, the organization has transformed the structure, bringing seven different groups (listed earlier) together into one business unit, centralizing corporate functions to provide common tools, processes, and solutions led by one senior executive.

As Paradox Navigators, the HR professionals enabled Staples to recognize and implement an omnichannel business model.

What Is a Paradox Navigator? State of the Art, and Science

In the Staples case, an effective HR professional navigated paradoxes inherent in the business. As introduced earlier, a paradox is a situation or concept comprised of two opposites, whose coexistence seems impossible (e.g., yin and yang, past and future, top-down and bottom-up). There is an increasing body of evidence that navigating paradox has positive implications within organizations. We highlight a few of these studies within organizations that enable us to define what it means for an HR professional to be a Paradox Navigator:

- Barry Johnson[4] offers tools to deal with what he calls polarity management. In his work he wants to help managers shift from solving problems with simple answers through either/or thinking to manage polarities for unsolvable problems. In managing polarities, managers recognize that there are multiple "right" answers, and by mapping the polarities, managers can find innovative options.

- Professors Kim Cameron and Bob Quinn[5] are professors who study competing values. They discuss the challenges associated with managing the tensions between competing values within an organization to drive organizational effectiveness. In their extensive research, they find that organizations have four competing values (collaborate, create, compete, control). As organizations manage these values as culture and leaders turn them into behaviors, the tensions inherent in these four competing values build effectiveness. Organizations avoid slow death by the deep change that comes from working across multiple value sets. Leaders with cognitive complexity and the ability to manage across the four values are more effective.

- Marianne Lewis offers a comprehensive review of paradox in management research and provides a guide for how managers and researchers may more effectively deal with inherent tensions. These scholars and practitioners she reviews have recognized the importance of paradox and have developed a number of practical and useful guides to dealing with paradox in general.[6]

- Wendy Smith, a management professor, provides frameworks for leaders to manage paradox and demonstrates how managing paradox helps senior leaders be more effective.[7] She found that successful firms deploy a dynamic decision model where paradoxes are surfaced, then managed by differentiating actions (focus on each paradox pole) and integrating actions (finding synergy across the paradoxes). Through dynamic decision making, paradoxical differences are less accepted or accommodated and more highlighted to find innovative solutions.

- Yan Zhang, David Waldman, Yu-Lan Han, and Xiao-Bei Li (faculty from the United States and China) explore the personal characteristics of leaders who cope with paradox.[8] They find that leaders who have personal skills of holistic thinking and integrated complexity are more able to manage paradoxical people practices that lead to productivity. Their insight reaffirms that navigating paradox applies at a personal level and that individuals may have more (or less) ability to do so. This work is extended to show that paradox savvy leaders who manage their personal paradoxes (sense of self and humility; maintaining control while letting go of control) are more able to manage organizational paradoxes. This work implies that HR professionals as Paradox Navigators have to personally model paradox so they can bring the ideas to their organization.

- The Center for Creative Leadership has summarized the paradox work and concluded, "Knowing how to manage paradox is a game changer. The research is clear: Organizations, leaders, teams, and individuals who manage paradox are better performers than those who do not."[9] They then offer tools for mapping paradoxes (and dualities) so that differences and synergies can be recognized.

Clearly, paradox has become relevant for organization and business leader success. If HR professionals are to help deliver on these paradoxical requirements, they must carefully maneuver their way forward through potentially hazardous waters. At any given moment emphasis may need to lean in one direction, but then a moment later emphasis may need to lean in the other direction. Rather than charting a straight line course, Paradox Navigators have to maintain high-level vision for where their organization is headed, and then make the necessary real-time adjustments to short-term directions to avoid downfalls and optimize how to get to this final destination. In our research, we are clearly not inventing the concepts around paradox nor offering new theoretical perspectives. We are evolving and adapting these ideas to the HR profession and by so doing, helping HR professionals create more value.

What Is a Paradox Navigator? Our Research on HR Professionals

The ability to effectively navigate the paradoxes that exist in the modern work environment has become essential for effective HR managers. To do so, they need to be flexible enough to move from *convergence* (focusing on priorities, making a decision, and reaching consensus) to *divergence* (exploring alternative perspectives, encouraging diversity) and back again. They must be able to disagree without being disagreeable and allow tension without contention.

We measured the Paradox Navigator competency by developing a set of competency items on the survey that reflected common and important tensions that HR professionals tend to face in their work.

- Effectively manages the tensions between global and local business demands
- Effectively manages the tensions between the need for change (flexibility, adaptability) and stability (standardization)
- Effectively manages the tension between taking time to gather information and making timely decisions
- Effectively manages the tensions between internal and external hiring
- Effectively manages the tensions between individual employee needs and collective organizational goals
- Effectively manages the tensions between internal focus on employees and external focus on customers and investors
- Effectively manages the tensions between top-down organizational control and bottom-up employee empowerment

What Our Research Tells Us About Paradox Navigators

HR participants (those doing self-assessment), HR associates, and non-HR associates scored the nine HR competencies (from Chapter 2, Figure 2.3) in terms of the extent to which the HR participant either does or is capable of doing the HR activities related to that competency. Paradox Navigator was the third lowest scoring domain for all raters (3.99 in Table 2.7). In other words, the overall results suggest that HR professionals have room to grow in their paradox navigation competencies compared to the other competencies we measured. Paradox Navigator skills are higher in North America (4.11 on Table 2.9) than the rest of the world. Paradox Navigator is generally the fifth most important competency in explaining individual effectiveness (11.7 percent, see Table 2.10) and the value that individual HR professionals and collective HR departments create for stakeholders (Table 2.11). However, here is a key finding from the entire study: *Paradox Navigator is far and away the most important competency in explaining business performance* (18.9 percent in column 13 of Table 2.12).

One of the most fascinating findings thus is that no competency is more important for business performance than Paradox Navigator, but this competency lags far behind in explaining the performance of HR professionals and HR departments. We offer two potential explanations for this surprising (to us) result.

First, employees tend to prefer clarity over ambiguity. As discussed, classic organizational theory suggests that most people come to work each day fully intending to fulfill their roles to do what will make the company, and their managers, happy. Some scholars refer to this as "normative intrinsic motivation."[10] *Normative* means that people feel they should do something and that there are some social norms or perceived social obligations associated with what they are doing. *Intrinsic* means that the motivation comes from the inside—that they naturally want to do something. They are not doing something against their own will. They get some personal satisfaction from doing something, and that is primarily internal. All this is a fancy way of talking about a robust phenomenon in organizations: People want to please their bosses and help their organizations succeed. Contributing to organizational success provides a great deal of personal satisfaction to many employees.

The problem, however, is that employees need to clearly know and understand how to make their bosses and the organization happy, and paradox introduces ambiguity. In the absence of very clear information, employees interpret what is expected of them and do the best with what they have. Employees can be very good at creating their own clarity out of ambiguous situations so that they can work hard in a way that is useful and comfortable to them while believing that they are doing great work for the organization. As long as employees are able to persist in their beliefs about what will create value and continue their comfortable work, then they can be happy in their work. When others force them to face the ambiguities that they have reconciled or address issues that they have implicitly ignored, then they may feel unusual unease and tension in their work. Thus when others push employees to face and navigate the embedded paradoxes in their work, then the world becomes less clear, less certain, and less comfortable.

While employees may benefit greatly from being challenged in this way, they may not fully appreciate the challenge and the associated work required. Thus those who encourage employees to face and navigate embedded paradoxes may do the organization a great service while creating ambiguity, discomfort, and tension for the individual employees.

Second, Paradox Navigators may seem very disruptive in meetings. Navigating paradox means managing divergence and convergence by identifying when we are moving too far in any given direction and helping pull us back into a more balanced, but tense, dialogue. Some meetings may be divergent, focused on generative brainstorming for creative ways to solve a problem. It is not uncommon for these meetings to rage onward for hours with great ideas proposed and wonderful potential solutions put on the table. But at times, the solution needs to come quickly and taking the time for engaging generative conversation may detract from a good enough solution that will help the organization address the current critical issue and move forward. A strong Paradox Navigator may step into this kind of situation, stop the divergent conversation and reground the group in the practical timelines required. Such adjustments and redirections can be painful for the group, and despite doing what is best for the business, the Paradox Navigator may pay a personal price among his or her peers for deciding to step in and cut back the idea generation.

The opposite also happens. It is not uncommon for people to very quickly converge on a solution and agree to move forward, without fully considering the embedded tensions and challenges in the decision. A strong Paradox Navigator might step in to encourage disparate thought and challenge the status quo. This person may bring up uncomfortable issues that the team has conveniently ignored and force the team to diverge in thought and process. Sometimes we call this person a "curmudgeon." Ironically, while we may not like that person, we frequently benefit from the opportunity to look differently at important issues when we might have converged too quickly.

So overall, we speculate that Paradox Navigators may increase tension and challenge which will make others uncomfortable and their work less clear, more ambiguous, and more challenging. While this is good for us, and likely very good for our businesses, we may not like these Paradox Navigators much for doing this important job.

Paradox Navigator as Center of the HR Competency Model

Given the preceding findings, it may be useful to clarify why we chose to position Paradox Navigator at the center of the HR Competency Model (Figure 2.3). It is clearly not the most important competency across all performance measures, so why does this competency deserve to be so central? We have at least four explanations for positioning Paradox Navigator in the center of the model.

First, no competency domain had a stronger impact on business performance than Paradox Navigator (Table 2.13). This, again, is fascinating to us. It does not show up as being critically important in the personal effectiveness or stakeholder outcome performance measures, but when it comes to prior business performance, no other competency is more important. Thus, being an excellent Paradox Navigator may not change how people view the HR professional's or HR department's overall effectiveness, and it may not directly affect the perceived value HR professionals create for stakeholders, but it does seem to relate to business performance.

Second, the Paradox Navigator concept seems to deeply resonate with the HR professionals we meet. In creating the survey and in sharing results, we have presented these results to thousands of HR professionals and we are consistently struck by how much these professionals express that we are describing their lives. We consistently hear them tell stories about their own paradoxes and how the concept of Paradox Navigator so effectively fits their lived experiences in the profession. So based on our field testing of the concept, it seems that paradox plays a central role in the experience of modern HR professionals.

Third, our portfolio of results reveals some interesting tensions within the HR Competency model itself. For example, should HR professionals worry more about satisfying external customers or line managers? The answer, of course, is "yes." Unfortunately, HR professionals do not have the luxury of ignoring one stakeholder while pandering to another. They must work to satisfy all stakeholders in their work. The irony, however, is that the competency that has the greatest impact on external customers and investors (i.e., Strategic Positioner) is NOT the competency that has the greatest impact on line managers and employees (i.e., Credible Activist). Also notice how fundamentally different the Strategic Positioner competency is from the Credible Activist competency. To become a better Strategic Positioner, we must focus our attention outside of ourselves. To become a better Credible Activist, we must focus our attention inside ourselves.

Fourth, given the emerging evidence we present about organizations, teams, and leaders being more effective through managing paradoxes, we believe that these more general findings also apply to HR. Others have found managing paradox to be a key predictor of leadership and organization success; we find it a key predictor of HR's ability to impact business results. To date, this is a mostly unexplored area in the HR profession.

So we placed Paradox Navigator in the center of our HR competency model. It does not stand alone, however. Each of the nine competency domains has a differing impact on personal effectiveness, stakeholder outcomes, and business performance, but navigating paradox is clearly an emerging HR competence that delivers business results.

Once the profession begins to more fully understand the value of paradox navigation, however, and line managers begin to see the impact of paradox navigation on business performance, we anticipate that this pattern will shift and change. Over time we may see employees and line managers who learn to recognize more fully the value that Paradox Navigators bring to the organization, and they may become more appreciative of the Paradox Navigator's efforts to push the organization to embrace and navigate the inherent tensions of business. We will explore in our future research whether a stronger relationship between paradox and all performance measures exists.

What Kinds of Paradoxes Should HR Pay Attention To?

It is not hard to find a list of paradoxes for organizations or individuals. Merely ask any employee to identify the challenges he or she faces in the job. By listening, you will discover paradoxes or tensions often come out. But it is helpful to be explicit about which paradoxes are most prevalent and require attention in an organization. In Table 8.2, we have prepared a list of 14 common paradoxes. We have done an exercise with executives to ask them to select the top two or three priorities given business goals. Once a leadership team recognizes the paradoxes, the HR professional can help navigate them with the ideas that follow.

Table 8.2   Common organization paradoxes

	Paradox	Pole A	and	Pole B	✓
1	**Work orientation (how work is done)**	Control • Disciplined, rigor		Freedom • Empowering, autonomy	
2	**Breadth of work**	Exploit, focus, prioritize, narrow, concentrate, unify		Exploit, explore, innovate, expand, broaden, diversify	
3	**Locus of control**	Centralized (top down)		Decentralized (bottom up)	
4	**Success criteria**	Bottom-line cost, efficiency, operational excellence		Top-line revenue growth, effectiveness, creativity, experiment	
5	**Stakeholder attention**	Inside (employees and organization)		Outside (customers and investors)	
6	**Unit of analysis**	Individual (personal success or performance)		Collective (team or unit performance)	

(continued on next page)

Table 8.2   Common organization paradoxes (continued)

	Paradox	Pole A	and	Pole B	✓
7	Line of sight	Stable (past)		Change (future)	
8	Employee philosophy	Equity (all the same)		Equity (differentiate, meritocracy)	
9	Measures	Hard financial, numbers		Soft Nonfinancial (well-being)	
10	Flow of work	Process: reengineer		Passion: renew	
11	Scope of work	Global reach		Local connectedness	
12	Accountability	Blame		Learn	
13	Skills	Hard: technical		Soft: cultural	
14	Time	Short term		Long term	
15	other				

How to Become a Better Paradox Navigator

As Paradox Navigators, HR professionals help their organizations and leaders navigate paradox by creating the right approach to paradox and developing the skills of a Paradox Navigator.

Approaches to Paradox

Based on our experiences and others' research cited earlier, we have identified six stages of paradox management that organizations and leaders often use. As Paradox Navigators, HR professionals should be able to assess where their organization is relative to these stages, and then play the appropriate role in moving to the next level.

Table 8.3   Stages of Paradox Management

Stage	Action	Implication	HR Role
1 Ignorance	Ignore the paradoxes and hope they go away.	• "You can't hide the truth." • "Ignorance is not bliss."	Gently point out alternatives.
2 Denial	Recognize paradox, but pick a pole and stick with it.	Fixed mindset . . . you better have picked right.	Suggest options; do site visits.
3 Spatial splitting	Create satellite organizations or internal competition. Leaders lead differently in different settings.	• Suboptimize by making parts more than the whole. • Leadership ambiguity leads to cynicism.	Look for common ground and create learning processes across units.
4 Temporal splitting	Sequence the poles; try one, then try the other.	• Hard to let go from one time to the other • Easy to get locked in and stereotype	Ensure learning from each sequence (after action review).
5 Small adjustments	Focus on learning from one setting or episode; run experiments.	Still separate, but encourages learning	Move quickly to identify small wins and weave into next steps.
6 Transcending paradox	Use information to clarify poles, explore new ideas, and exploit actions at same time.	• Manage convergence, divergence. • Seek common and higher purpose.	Become a true Paradox Navigator.

How Does One Transcend Paradox?

From a practical perspective, there are some simple steps any HR leader can take to become more comfortable confronting this reality. We base these steps on our experience and on the academic and consulting research and practices cited earlier.

1. *Clarify the poles of the paradox:* When paradoxes exist, organizations can sometimes get trapped into arguments about which side (pole) of the paradox to choose and emphasize. Many times this occurs because decision makers have not been able to explicitly identify the paradoxes at play and articulate why both outcomes are important and how they are in tension with each other. Taking the time to clarify the seemingly opposing poles of a paradox and how they relate and interrelate to each other can provide an important first step toward navigating that paradox.

2. *Define best outcomes:* Once we clarify the paradox, we can attend to the over-arching criteria for success in our organization, and we can begin to explore how the opposing sides of the paradox relate to our success criteria. Doing so can help clarify when to emphasize one or the other side of the paradox.

3. *See others' points of view:* Listen to others and try to understand how they experience the paradox in question. How does the paradox influence them and their work? What will happen to their work and outcomes if we emphasize one side more than the other? This may be done by a duality or polarity map where the alternatives are laid out with pros and cons for each. It may also be done by reverse role playing where advocates of one pole argue for the other and vice versa so that each side more fully appreciates the other's point of view.

4. *Find common ground:* Where do we agree and where do we disagree? Where do we agree to disagree? Can we agree on the conditions under which we lean toward one side of the paradox and the conditions under which we lean to the other side? In restructuring an HR group, there was a lot of quite animated debate about what work should go where (centralized versus decentralized). We asked each of the senior HR Team Members to draw on a flip chart their idealized organization. When they presented to each other, they realized that they had 80 percent agreement. We acknowledged this. We then looked at the 20 percent disagreement (which was taking 80 percent of the discussion) and laid out options and experimented with

an option for three months to see what would work. We then adapted and learned. Within nine months, an acceptable governance structure was in place and being acted on.

5. *Take first steps:* Once there is some common ground, begin to take small steps forward and learn as you go. This might include questions such as, "What is the plan for adjustments to the plan?" "How will we know when we have moved too far in any given direction?" "Have we established enough common ground that we can embrace this paradox together as we move forward?"

What Skills Make a Good Paradox Navigator?

HR professionals who are Paradox Navigators possess the knowledge, skills, and abilities proposed in Table 8.4. As an HR professional, you can do a self-assessment on these skills and you can use it with your business leaders or other HR colleagues. Paradox navigation is not an innate trait, but a learned set of behaviors that translate into skills.

Table 8.4   Personal skills of a Paradox Navigator

Skills To what extent am I able to . . .	Definition/Behavior What are specific behaviors associated with skill . . .	Rate (1 to 10)
1 Deal with cognitive complexity	• See different sides of an issue • Respect someone else's point of view • Learn new ideas (20 to 25% every 2 years) • See patterns in events	
2 Be socially endearing	• Disagree without being disagreeable • Allow for tension without having contention • Listen to understand • Help others feel better about themselves after meeting with me	
3 Be socially connected	• Spend time with people who are not like me (e.g., visit shop floor or other departments) • Observe and learn from those not in your zone of influence (competitors, customers, leading players)	

(continued on next page)

Table 8.4 *Personal skills of Paradox Navigator (continued)*

Skills To what extent am I able to . . .	Definition/Behavior What are specific behaviors associated with skill . . .	Rate (1 to 10)
4 Be personally aware	• Know my predispositions (e.g., introvert versus extrovert; judging versus perceiving) or style • Not be bound by my predispositions and see beyond my biases • Judge myself less by intent and more by my behavior	
5 Be grounded in a strong set of values	• Know my core values and act consistently with them even if behaviors may vary • Avoid pandering to different groups, while respecting their requirements	
6 Surround myself with people better than and different from me	• Seek colleagues and friends who differ from me • Ask opinions of people who may differ from me • Access experts who know more than me, listen to their advice, and adapt my insights	
7 Encourage divergence and convergence	• Encourage diversity of thinking if your team or organization tends to groupthink; generate options • Encourage focus if your team or organization has too much diversity and no closure; ensure actions	
8 Use a decision protocol	• Clarify the decision to be made and who is ultimately accountable for making it • Set a timeline for making decision • Gather information to make the best decision • Make decisions and build in learning processes to improve	
9 Have a growth mindset	• Take risks to experiment and try new things • Constantly learn from what worked and what did not • Be resilient when things do not work	
10 Zoom out and zoom in	• Establish a vision and overall purpose • Envision systems and how parts fit together • Focus on the details when necessary	
	TOTAL:	

Building and Practicing Paradox Navigator Skills

As with all nine HR competencies, building the skills comes primarily through experiences both at and away from work and from focused training. We have coached HR professionals to become better Paradox Navigators by asking them to engage in some of the following activities:

- Identify and list the paradoxes facing your organization. Identify key individuals representing each side of a paradox and meet with them.
- Conduct an industry analysis of the ways competitors deal with paradox in their organizations.
- Talk to ground-floor employees to find out their perspective on paradoxes they face and solutions they suggest for the company to manage them.
- Connect regularly with different departments and regions within your company to understand their outlook on business paradoxes.
- Place two table name tents in visible locations during big initiatives meetings, one labeled "client/customer" and one labeled "employee." Be sure to consider both stakeholder groups as you discuss the initiative and make decisions.
- Implement a decision protocol at your company to help individuals and teams make decisions faster.
- Appoint one individual in a meeting to make sure you aren't getting too far into the weeds of an issue while forgetting about the high-level strategic implications.
- Educate yourself:
  - Pick up a book on conflict resolution.
  - Look at leaders or others in your life who seem to manage tension well. What do they do?
  - What are the paradoxes in your business strategy? How do your competitors manage them?
- Seek out some nonprofessional life experiences that will help you better approach paradox.
  - Participate in creating a community garden in an urban center.

- Teach residents of a long-term residential living facility about recent advances in technology.
- Teach K–12 students skills from previous generations.
- Watch an hour of the most-watched YouTube channels.
- Visit a foreign country and spend time learning about their culture. Consider differences with your own and how to bridge the gap between diverse cultures.
- Make a recipe from a 1950s cookbook healthy by today's standards.

No single activity will ensure paradox navigation skills, but collectively, they will help you live in the inevitably complex and dynamic world of duality and paradox.

Conclusion

Of all nine HR competency domains in this round of our study, Paradox Navigator might be the most interesting. While rooted in old ideas and while part of everyday experience, Paradox Navigator has not been formally introduced into the HR professional skill set. Our research finds that while being a Paradox Navigator may not make many friends (personal effectiveness or stakeholder value), it is the most critical skill for business results. We believe that as HR professionals master paradox navigation skills, they will have more influence and add more value.

CHAPTER 9

STRATEGIC ENABLERS— HR COMPETENCIES THAT DELIVER STRATEGIC VALUE

9

As introduced in Chapter 2, we had identified 123 specific items that define what HR professionals should be, know, or do. Through factor analysis, we identified nine statistically distinct domains, or groupings, for HR competencies (illustrated in Figure 2.3). We then conceptually clustered these nine domains into "super-groups"—*core drivers* (three HR competencies, which delivered key outcomes and discussed in detail in the three previous chapters: Credible Activist, Strategic Positioner, Paradox Navigator), three *strategic enablers*, and three *foundation enablers*. This chapter reviews the three strategic enablers: (1) Culture and Change Champion, (2) Human Capital Curator, and (3) Total Rewards Steward. While these three did not have as much impact on the individual, stakeholder, or business outcomes as the three core drivers, they were nevertheless important descriptors of competencies required for HR professionals and predictors of each of these outcomes as was shown in Chapter 2, Tables 2.10 to 2.12.

We examine the three strategic enablers one at a time.

First Strategic Enabler: Culture and Change Champion

Since the beginning of our research on HR competencies, the management of change and of culture has been an important competency for HR professionals that impacts their perceived effectiveness. We have written extensively about both managing change and creating culture.[1]

As the external pressures on organizations have increased as discussed in Chapter 1, the need for HR professionals to manage change and create culture has also increased. In fact, we predicted that HR competencies in these areas might have been even higher predictors of individual effectiveness, stakeholder perceptions, and business results. But instead of being the number one predictor, this competency domain was the third highest predictor of individual effectiveness (14.2 percent versus Credible Activist at 19.3 percent and Strategic Positioner at 14.5 percent in Table 2.10), and the fourth highest predictor of overall business performance (10.9 percent as shown in Table 2.12). In other words, HR professionals who are Culture and Change Champions have significant impact on key individual and organizational outcomes.

The results of this current research show that culture and change are rated lower by HR professionals (self-rating) but have high scores of HR stakeholders, particularly non-HR associate raters who score designing culture very high (see Table 9.1).

Table 9.1   *Culture and change champion subdomain means by rater group*

	Culture and Change				
	All Raters[a]	Self-Ratings	Supervisor Ratings	HR Associate Ratings	Non-HR Associate Ratings
Designs culture	4.06	3.97	3.92	4.03	4.16
Manages change	4.01	3.95	3.85	4.01	4.08

Culture and Change Champion in Action at Flex

Flex CEO Mike McNamara is a firm believer that company culture is among the most important determinants for a company's success. As such, Flex is very deliberate in designing and maintaining a unified company culture, which is very difficult when you consider that Flex has 200,000 employees located throughout the globe, most of whom are not located in the United States.

In 2015, Flex began the process of rebranding itself. It changed its name from Flextronics to Flex. The company's product and service offering had evolved over the years to be more than a typical electronics manufacturing services (EMS) company to become a supply chain solutions company that designs and builds intelligent products for an increasingly connected world.

Flex began the rebranding effort by changing the mission and vision statements, which were at the core of their strategy.

- Mission statement: *To create a smarter, more connected world*
- Vision statement: *A simpler, richer life through technology*

Leaders at Flex understood that culture coexists with brand, so after identifying what they wanted to be known for, they turned their attention to designing the culture to match the rebranding agenda. The culture had historically been defined as Flex's key values and leadership traits. Flex's key values describe behaviors or the way work gets done; they help guide decision making and strategies. Flex leadership traits are meant to distinguish qualities or characteristics of an employee; they add value to work relationships. Most of the Flex key values and leadership traits did not change.

However, HR leadership asked employees for input on the new behaviors that would be required to demonstrate the key values and leadership traits according to the new brand and strategy. Figure 9.1 illustrates how the company values and leadership traits create the culture and how the culture drives the brand.

Words alone are not enough to drive change, so the HR team began integrating the values and leadership traits into HR-related practices and processes. Take talent acquisition, for example: The talent profile went from candidates who would work well in a disciplined manufacturing environment (governed by metrics and hierarchy) to candidates who were agile enough to work within multiple industries, who worked well in a small-team environment, and who had an entrepreneurial mindset.

Figure 9.1   *Flex's brand, leadership, and culture*

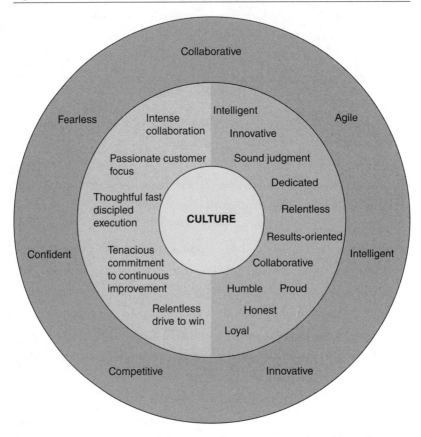

Flex also created a new Employee Value Proposition (EVP) based on surveys, interviews, and focus groups across its 200,000 employees. The new EVP
emphasized Limitless, Enriching, and Dynamic careers that include experiences across many industries, departments, and geographies. Flex had new
talent development processes in place to help facilitate this. Organizational
structure became flatter, and the physical environment changed to be more
inviting to collaboration (open office environment) to foster increased creativity and adoption of best practices.

Through these and other initiatives, Flex designed a company culture to
drive their brand identity. Internally, the culture evolution has been well-
received by employees based on results from the annual employee engagement survey.

What Are Emerging Trends Affecting the Culture and Change Champion?

Flex is an exceptional case of changing culture to match business changes. As we try to interpret these Culture and Change Champion empirical results through our personal experiences, we see four trends in recent years influencing what it means to be a Culture and Change Champion and why it matters to have one.

First, culture and change go together. In previous rounds of research, the management of change and culture has varied as an HR competence domains. Managing change encompassed culture (round 1 and round 2), culture and change statistically factored into separate domains (round 3), culture and change factored into an overall "strategic contribution" domain (round 4), and culture and change were separate factors (round 6). In this recent research, we find that culture and change statistically factor together.

HR professionals who demonstrate competence (or incompetence) in one area (culture or change) tend to do so in the other. This implies that in recent years, managing change without considering culture is an event; managing culture without the disciplines of change is a slogan. Both need to go together.

When HR professionals engage in change management activities, they need to be sensitive to the overall business culture in which the change will occur. For example, changes to HR processes such as performance management, career planning, training and development, or information management (laid out in Chapter 4) cannot likely be sustained unless and until they connect to the broader organization culture issues. Likewise, efforts to create a new culture will not likely be sustained unless and until they are institutionalized through HR processes as discussed in Chapter 3. With this logic, the efforts of the Culture and Change Champion likely enable the other eight HR competency domains.[*]

---

[*] While we do not report the specific correlations among the nine HR competency domains, the correlation between Culture and Change Champion and the other eight domains is the highest in six of the eight cases, which may confirm the enabling function of change and culture for the other competencies.

Second, change and culture have become legitimized in organization thinking and action. Flex CEO Mike McNamara continually talks about culture and how to change it to win in the marketplace. Chapter 3 lays out the case for organization capabilities in general. As noted, *culture* has more Google hits than *talent* and was the 2014 Merriam Webster word of the year. Peter Drucker was attributed to have said "culture eats strategy for lunch" and the strategic planning thought leaders are pursuing this claim.[2] Culture, as a key capability, has high business impact but low effectiveness (Figure 3.1). Many companies are working to diligently articulate and implement culture changes that help them win in the marketplace. Likewise, the management of change has become an ever more accepted part of business success, often termed *strategy execution, strategic agility, transformation,* or simply *change.* With changing technology, economic conditions, political environment, and workforce demographics (see Chapter 1), organizations have to adapt quickly or die. Many companies have enacted a company-specific "change model" that can be applied to any initiative the company launches.

These change models may vary somewhat, but they bring much-needed scientific discipline to the art of change. Much of this increased pressure for change comes from transparency where fluidity of and access to information creates public accountability. For example, in Qualtrics, the world's leading research and insights platform, all employees post their activities and goals every week for everyone to see. This completely transparent system encourages accountability and collaboration among employees because they can "observe" what everyone else is working on and see how they might work together. Many organizations host senior management off-sites. In almost all of off-sites modules on making change happen or managing culture have been included in the agenda. Culture and change are legitimate considerations for business success.

Third, culture and change are increasingly viewed from the outside-in.[3] The relative importance of navigating paradox (Chapter 8) is grounded on the increased pace of external change. Organizations respond (or do not) to their external environment. Those that do so survive and thrive; those that do not fall behind and die. Only 60 of the original Fortune 500 companies exist today, a remarkable attrition of the largest 500 companies in North America over 60 years.

Navigating the tensions inherent in paradox ensures that constructive dialogue leads to positive change. Likewise, culture is increasingly seen less as the norms, values, and behaviors inside a company and more as the value of values and the right norms and behaviors as defined from the outside in. Most have depicted culture visually as the roots of a tree, the underwater part of an iceberg, or hidden values. We believe that culture is not the roots, but the sun and rain that nourish the tree to grow. Roots are often anchored in the past; the leaves and sun are the parts of the tree that grow. The hidden part of the iceberg is unseen; the visible part is what others see and respond to.

In our view, culture is the identity of the firm in the minds of key customers, made real to employees. It is not enough to have a culture (values), but to have the *right* culture (an identity). As such culture is not only norms, behaviors, and values, but the norms, behaviors, and values *that will induce targeted customers to have a more intense relationship with the firm.*[4] This outside-in view of culture moves it from a social to an economic agenda and is part of its legitimacy in business conversations, as illustrated in the Flex example.

Fourth, HR is playing an increasing role in defining and delivering culture and change. Few would deny that the senior business leader is the primary owner of a company's culture and capacity for change. The business leader's personal behavior shapes the culture by sending signals about what matters. The business leader's encouragement to others to change and adapt also sends messages about organization flexibility and transformation. Business leaders have often turned to thought partners to help them define culture and manage change. For many firms, these thought partners have been consultants who bring legitimacy because of their analytical skills and breadth of experience.

Today, in many cases, HR professionals become the thought partners for culture and change. This means that HR professionals have to be Credible Activists (Chapter 6), Strategic Positioners (Chapter 7), and Paradox Navigators (Chapter 8) to help individual leaders change their personal behavior and create sustained organizational change. The best CHROs are essentially Culture and Change Champions who enable individual leaders and organizations to adapt to win.

We selected the term *champions* because the senior business leaders are still the owners, or those primarily responsible for culture and change, but top HR professionals champion ideas by observing what is happening, envisioning what should happen (with an outside-in lens), and proposing action steps to make the right things happen. We are often asked to identify HR professionals who play these roles. We can do so by naming those we have met, but a collection of these Culture and Change Champions can also be found among fellows of the National Academy of Human Resources. These nominated and elected fellows have passed a peer review, which often includes their ability to champion change and culture.

How Can You as an HR Professional Become a Better Culture and Change Champion?

HR professionals can be culture champions by facilitating culture dialogues, designing culture improvement processes, using HR tools to reinforce and sustain culture, and coaching leaders to reflect culture in their personal behaviors. Based on our partnerships with HR professionals in dozens of organizations engaged in culture change, we would offer the following recommendations to help HR professionals become culture champions:

1. *Think outside-in to define the right culture:* Most cultural assessments describe current culture norms or values. To define the right culture, become an anthropologist who observes events and sees patterns. In particular, understand current and future key customer demands and partner with marketing and branding experts to create a clear message about what your organization is known for by these targeted customers. Don't get locked into your historical identity. Anticipate future customers and how you want your firm to be known by them. McDonald's for decades was known for "quality, service, cleanliness, and value" and has now evolved to emphasize the customer experience. Flex was known for efficient delivery

of components but has now evolved to be known for systems solutions. Apple's evolution from computers to software to apps to music to retail shows a series of cultural transitions.

2. *Audit the extent to which there is a shared desired culture among the management team:* Find out if the management team has a common understanding of what the company wants to be known for by its best customers. Through customer dialogues, ensure that this internal identity matches customer expectations. In employee surveys, don't just look at the mean scores on cultural values, but the standard deviation to see how much the culture is shared.

3. *Translate external promises of brand identity into internal actions:* The desired culture inside a company should reflect promises outside. Be willing to experiment and try new internal practices that reflect the new culture. Communicate through customer stories of how employee behaviors met their needs. Manage the flow of talent into and through the organization based on customer expectations . . . hire people who fit culture not just technical skills; train with culture in mind. Set standards and reward behaviors that reflect customer promises and involve customers in the reward process. Link your leadership competencies to your customer promises. Create disruption teams who anticipate new customer requirements and, as American Express has done, tell these teams to "put AMEX out of business before our competitors."

4. *Raise cultural issues at key events:* Help customers see that they are not just buying a product or service, but a cultural experience (see successful firms like Disney, Facebook, Google). Help investors see that the customer-centric and unified culture will ensure long-term success. With boards of directors, make culture a continual topic of firm governance. We have argued that traditional compensation committees at the board level might be changed to become talent, leadership, and culture committees, with compensation as one of the agenda items (not the only agenda). With senior business leaders, monitor their personal behavior and communications to make sure they embody the desired culture. Observe where they spend their time, who they meet with, and what issues they talk about so

that they become cultural ambassadors. Track culture in social media sites like glassdoor.com, in employee engagement surveys (note not only the mean scores on culture questions, but the variance on all the questions), and personal observations. On a plant tour with a senior business team, an observant HR professional noted that none of the plant employees initiated conversations with any of the business leaders, which might indicate some distance between management and workers.

HR professionals can become change champions by recognizing that change is both inevitable and positive, helping define the content of change (what should be changed), and facilitating the process of making change happen (how change should occur). As discussed in the previous three chapters, some of the core competencies to change include building trust, being a Strategic Positioner, and navigating paradox. In addition, we have coached many business and HR leaders to increase their capacity to make change happen through specific skills:

- *Be aware, of yourself and of others:* Look for behavior patterns that no longer fit the requirements of the situation. The most difficult changes are often when the wrong things are done very well because of habits. Examine which habits work and which do not.
- *Be transparent:* Force a dialogue. Be able to talk about the "elephant in the room" without creating defensiveness. Help people see the need for change by sharing data on what needs to be changed and why.
- *Be able to zoom out and zoom in:* Zoom out by seeing the big picture and why change will enable future success. Zoom in by turning ideas into action and creating discipline to act.
- *Be an agile learner:* Do not hesitate to act, even if it results in failure. Have a growth mindset where you fail forward and learn from mistakes. Learn from what did or did not work, and apply that knowledge to the next opportunity.
- *Be willing to share credit* and *accept failure:* Involve the right people in making change happen. Those who are most affected by the change are likely to

have the most ideas for making the change. Be clear about how the change will benefit others; if possible make a pull (positive effect) more than a push (being forced to do it).

- *Be disciplined by having a change toolkit* that is regularly used and applied to key initiatives.
- *Be able to sequence change.* Most change efforts in organizations follow an "S-curve." This means they start small with experimentation and lots of diverse thinking. As they move up the curve, the experiments gain momentum and the changes begin to become normalize. Nearer the top of the S-curve, the change becomes a natural process inside the organization. HR change agents know how to navigate the early diverse thinking of the S-curve that leads to the focused practices further up the curve. They also know when to initiate a new S-curve (usually 60 to 70 percent up the current curve) to keep new initiatives flowing.

Finally, and consistent with our finding of being a Culture and Change Champion, make sure that individual change initiatives weave together into integrated cultural solutions.

Second Strategic Enabler: Human Capital Curator

HR's primary role for decades has been identification, assessment, and management of talent (people or workforce). While this book focuses heavily on "victory through organization" (Chapter 3), talent still matters. In the last few years the term *human capital* has received more attention as it refers to the investments that increase an individual's value to the organization.

Using this logic, we found a host of HR competencies related to improving individual contribution. We grouped these competencies into a domain referred to as Human Capital Curator.

Taking this phrase apart, *Capital* is generally considered an emotionless asset. *Curators*, on the other hand, create emotion. People today often engage in organizations to find an emotional home, not just a transient place to live. Curators pay special attention to the unique needs of those who visit the "museum" (in this case, customers and investors who engage organizations). Curators care and shape an experience more than just going through the motions and getting things done. Museum curators are charged with managing art collections, knowing which pieces to emphasize based on patrons' preferences. Curation may involve acquiring new art, deploying existing art in new ways, or selling less valuable art.

Not surprisingly, Human Capital Curator is the most important competency for creating value for line managers (14.9 percent compared to Culture and Change Champion at 13.6 percent in Table 2.11). This makes intuitive sense because line managers bear the cost of the absence of key talent and benefit directly from having high-quality human capital within their organizations. Thus to make the lives of managers better, HR can deliver on and excel at being Human Capital Curators.

Human Capital Curators offer integrated and innovative solutions in four areas: talent, leadership, performance, and technical talent (see Table 9.2).

Table 9.2 *Human capital curator subdomain means by rater group*

Human Capital Curator Domain					
	All Raters[a]	Self-Ratings	Supervisor Ratings	HR Associate Ratings	Non-HR Associate Ratings
Develops talent	4.06	3.97	3.92	4.03	4.16
Develops leaders	4.01	3.95	3.85	4.01	4.08
Drives performance	4.06	3.97	3.92	4.03	4.16
Develops technical talent	4.01	3.95	3.85	4.01	4.08

HR professionals who excel at curating human capital deploy their knowledge of individual and organizational behavior theory and of classical and cutting-edge HR research to resolve talent issues across HR practices and business units. The innovation and integration of HR practices, processes, and structure has long-run implications, but can drive business results now.

The Human Capital Curator in Action at Westinghouse

Westinghouse, an iconic U.S. brand, has been known for making a wide range of products over the last 130 years. The company, majority-owned by Toshiba Corporation since 2006, now specializes primarily in nuclear-related products and technologies. Recently, the company proposed a strategy focused on global growth. To achieve the goal, the new CEO and his CHRO knew that they needed to upgrade their technical and nontechnical talent as confirmed through the voice of their customer survey.

For Eric McAllister, the new CHRO, that meant starting with HR. The HR team in general, though very capable compliance managers, did not have strong business acumen nor could they translate the business strategy into value-add HR actions. If you want to improve your talent management practices to be in line with business strategy and expectations, you should ensure that you have HR professionals in your organizations who can think from the outside in.

The company had underinvested in talent. They were not strategic in their recruiting, solely relying on the "post and pray" approach. The company was not building nor buying talent; McAllister wondered if they really knew what good talent looked like. The company hired an external consultant to survey its employee base to see if they were meeting core expectations. What they found was interesting:

1. Managers indicated that they were fine with the level of talent and they were "meeting the bar," yet there were a multitude of different perceived levels of the bar.
2. Employees felt the bar was too low, or they did not know what was expected of them. They also felt like there were not enough development activities.

This survey solidified the assumption that the company was settling for mediocrity; the employees did not like it.

The first step for Westinghouse was to set the bar for talent, so the HR team created foundational competencies for all employees with a known minimum performance threshold. Then behaviors, actions, and results (BARs) expectations were set at each level in the organization. The HR team integrated the BARs into the HR practices and processes, including recruiting, development, and performance management. So Westinghouse now had defined the minimum performance threshold and was (and still is) now hiring, developing, and rewarding based on BARs.

With a definition for what "good" means, McAllister and his team could now pay closer attention to recruitment. They expanded the number of core schools the company recruited from. Technical recruiting was struggling, largely because none of the recruiters had a technical background, so they built a technical recruiting team.

Westinghouse is still in the beginning stages of talent improvement, but they are already seeing results. One of the key recruiting metrics, time to fill a position, has decreased from 85 days to approximately 60 days. Attrition of key talent has been cut in half, while good attrition (poor performers leaving) is increasing. This story illustrates the importance of upgrading talent to deliver a new business agenda.

What Are the Emerging Trends That Affect the Human Capital Curator?

Chapter 1 reviewed the distressing affective state of many people in general (the "Personal Context") and potential employees in particular. Chapter 5 reviewed emerging HR practices in measurement, rewards, development, and involvement to optimize people. Here we highlight high-level trends in each of the four subdomains of the Human Capital Curator.

- *Talent:* Increasingly, people's differences are being recognized and woven into talent choices. Employees differ by generation (e.g., baby boomers versus generation X versus millennials), by work orientation (e.g., full time versus part time or contingent worker), or by other diversity factors (e.g., race, gender, global background, education experience). While organizations are customizing their human capital practices to these differences, they are also discovering that employees have an almost universal need to find meaning and purpose from work. Finding such meaning goes beyond free food and worker-friendly policies (e.g., bring a pet to work) to doing work that makes a difference, involving employees in work decisions (see Chapter 5 on involvement), and creating work communities with positive relationships. HR professionals who act on these trends will increase employee productivity and contribution.

- *Leadership:* Leaders and leadership are among the most studied dimensions of the Human Capital Curator. Increasingly, the focus is shifting from the individual as a leader to the collective and distributed leadership within an organization. In addition, leadership is less about the personal qualities of a leader and more about the value that a leader (and leadership) creates for others both inside the organization (e.g., inspiring employees and delivering strategy) and outside the organization (e.g., building customer brand and shareholder value).[5] As noted in Chapter 5, developing leaders includes face-to-face and online training as well as personal experiences in new settings. HR professionals as Human Capital Curators need to build leaders and leadership through coaching, assessment, and development experiences. They also need to communicate the quality of leadership through measures such as the Leadership Capital Index to investors and customers.

- *Performance:* Chapter 5 reviews measures as part of performance and accountability and offers implications for performance management. The trend for a Human Capital Curator is to ensure that a positive conversation occurs between employees and their bosses. This positive conversation resolves the paradox of not having any accountability (which often leads to little improvement in performance) and deploying bureaucratic processes for performance reviews (which leads to cynicism).[6] We have found that a positive performance conversation focuses on three parts: help me understand (which makes a manager more a coach than controller), the data (which highlights what worked and what did not work), so we can fix the problem (which focuses on future outcomes). These conversations encourage opportunity not punishment, yet hold individuals accountable for achieving results. HR professionals as Human Capital

Curators focus less on processes and more on positive conversations to deliver performance.

- *Technical training:* It is interesting that technical training showed up as a subfactor in the Human Capital Curator domain. Traditionally in career discussions, employees move from individual contributor (stage 2) into management (stage 3) and then strategist (stage 4). We are now finding that many employees want to remain in their technical career rather than move into management positions. They move from being an individual contributor to a mentor for others to a definer of a technical field. We often asked participants in our training programs if they prefer a managerial or technical career track, and we find about a 50/50 split. Again, this career choice refers back to personal differences as part of managing talent. Human Capital Curators help employees make informed career choices and offer technical as well as managerial career tracks.

How Can You as an HR Professional Become a Better Human Capital Curator?

HR professionals as Human Capital Curators may work in centers of expertise or be embedded in a business. As evidenced in the Westinghouse story, human capital improvement often begins within the HR community. When HR professionals practice the human capital tools they propose, they are more credible. When we coach HR professionals who want to better curate human capital, we offer the following suggestions.

- *Master the science of talent:* HR is often accused of being a "soft" discipline, when in fact, there is an abundance of scientific fact and evidence within the field.[7] The science of HR is alluded to throughout this book. Chapter 4 laid out the role of information; Chapter 5 reviewed the importance of HR analytics to business success. Chapter 10 highlights the competencies of Analytics Designer and Interpreter. Evidence-based decision making on talent will inform talent choices and allow you to discern serious from faddish talent practices.

- *Discover uniqueness; don't assume others are like you.* It is so easy to judge others by our own expectations. A Human Capital Curator does not impose values, but helps others define their values and reach their goals. A talented psychologist once said that she could work with almost any client on any problem as long as she could care for the person she was counseling. Likewise, as a Human Capital Curator, you should come to care about the employees you serve. While the talent systems create organization capabilities; the people who are affected by the systems need to be at the heart of HR work.

- *Manage equality and equity at the same time:* Equality is fairness by ensuring that all employees have equal opportunity. Equity is differentiation by ensuring that those who contribute more receive more in return. Help all employees have opportunities to reach their desired potential, but treat employees differently depending on how they perform. This employee paradox is like a children's paradox where a good parent equally loves all children, but treats them differently according to their unique personalities. Help employees feel like they personally matter to you and to the organization.

- *Design and deliver integrated human capital solutions, not isolated practices:* One company found that employees were confused about what was expected of them because they hired employees with skills A, B, and C; then trained them to do D, E, and F; and then rewarded them for G, H, and I. These isolated HR practices created more confusion than clarity. In the Westinghouse case, the core competencies for leadership and technical success were the integrating mechanisms so that HR practices offer human capital solutions to business problems.

As the curators (custodians, keepers, overseers, guardians) of human capital, HR professionals ensure that employees have the right skills, engagement, and sense of purpose to be personally productive and organizationally successful.

Third Strategic Enabler: Total Rewards Steward

In our research in rounds 4 and 6 of the HR Competency Study (HRCS), when we did factor analysis of the specific knowledge and behavior items for HR professionals into domains exclusively for line managers, they included rewards in the "HR delivery domain" (round 4) and "HR innovator and integrator domain" (round 6), but the same factor analysis with HR professionals did not. Rewards are often seen by line managers as an integral part of the portfolio of HR practices, but ironically, less so by HR professionals.

Rewards, particularly compensation practices, are becoming increasingly complex and granular. Many HR generalists recognize that while compensation systems shape and reinforce employee behaviors, the complex regulatory requirements and analytical details require deep technical specialization. HR compensation specialists join WorldatWork or Center on Executive Compensation, and HR generalists are more likely to join broader HR groups (CIPD, SHRM, AHRI, ASHRM, and our other partners).

In this round, the Total Rewards Steward domain is the lowest rated of the nine competency domains by all stakeholders (Table 2.7). It also has the second lowest impact on personal effectiveness (6.2 percent in Table 2.10), relatively little personal impact on stakeholders (Table 2.11), and the second lowest impact on business performance (8.4 percent in Table 2.12). The only sizable impact of being a Total Rewards Steward is the 19 percent impact on community (which includes regulators, who intervene through compensation policies). These findings suggest that while being a Total Rewards Steward may be part of the overall HR competence portfolio, it is not a primary driver of the personal effectiveness, stakeholder value, or business results we have studied.

With these general overall results, it is fascinating to see the two subfactors in the Total Rewards Steward domain (Table 9.3). While still low compared to other HR competence domains, HR professionals are somewhat better at financial aspects of rewards (manages compensation and benefits) than the nonfinancial ones (designs meaningful work).

Our position is that rewards (both financial and nonfinancial) are an integral part of HR solutions (see the overview of rewards in Chapter 5). Rewards may not drive performance (few work over a weekend just for the increased reward), but they signal what matters (it is worth working over the weekend) and they reinforce the behaviors (it is nice that if the weekend work has positive results, employees who worked over the weekend will participate in them). We also believe that both financial and nonfinancial rewards matter and HR professionals should be proficient in using both of them.

Table 9.3   *Total Rewards Steward subdomain means by rater group*

Total Rewards Steward					
	All Raters[a]	Self- Ratings	Supervisor Ratings	HR Associate Ratings	Non-HR Associate Ratings
Designs meaningful work	3.81	3.72	3.74	3.79	3.90
Manages compensation and benefits	3.93	3.82	3.87	3.92	3.99

Total Rewards Steward in Action at Rio Tinto

Rio Tinto is one of the world's largest metals and mining companies with 47,000 employees in nearly 40 countries. Given the nature of the mining industry, Rio Tinto operates in some of the most remote locations in the world. Though the company employs 22,000 employees in Australia, the geographic and cultural differences across the group are immense with operations from Madagascar to the Subarctic. Rio Tinto's compensation and benefits teams have a very complicated job. Standardized compensation and benefits structures have limited value when universally applied; this has not been done in Rio Tinto. Instead the company has taken steps to understand the cultural context in which it operates and to tailor the compensation and benefits offer accordingly. It factors in what matters most to the local employee base, aligning meaningful offerings with employee preferences. Here are a few examples:

- *Mongolia:* The company has learned that employees in Mongolia prefer cash to more traditional company provided benefits.
- *Northwest Territories, Canada:* Bitter weather at the Diavik Diamond Mine and the Yellowknife town (where employee families are based) in the remote subarctic region of Canada can make a bad situation a deadly one,

so Rio Tinto gives all employees an automobile emergency kit to carry with them when they are not at work and covers the cost of emergency roadside assistance membership.

- *Remote Australia:* For many sites in Australia, the mine is the hub of the community for many miles around. Educational opportunities for employees' children can be limited, so Rio Tinto subsidizes boarding school education where necessary. Additionally, due to the remoteness of the location, it takes significant travel for employees to take a vacation, so Rio Tinto subsidizes the first leg of the journey.
- *Weipa, Queensland, Australia:* Rio Tinto partnered with a corporate wellness company to pilot a comprehensive wellness program at their site in Weipa, Australia. Over eight weeks, a subset of employees received coaching around nutrition, exercise, sleep, and mental health among other things to help create positive health rituals. The employee reception of the program was so positive that the company chose to roll it out to the entire Weipa community.

The company does have standardized elements of its compensation and benefits scheme. For example, the company offers employees the chance to purchase fractions of a share in its global all-employee share plan. This feature makes it easier for employees in lower-wage economies such as Madagascar to participate in the plan. Rio Tinto offers a 100 percent match on all share purchases, including fractions of a share.

Rio Tinto is a great example of a company that seeks to provide for the well-being of its global workforce through diverse employee-centric compensation and benefits offerings.

What Are the Emerging Trends That Affect the Total Rewards Steward?

Rewards, both financial and nonfinancial, send signals about what matters. A company's reward philosophy communicates if a company is focused more on revenue, profitability, customer service, social responsibility, market valuation, innovation, talent retention, or something else.[†] Financial and nonfinancial rewards also communicate the value the company has in the employee. At times it is not the actual salary an employee receives, but how that salary signals to the employee and others the worth of the employee. Because rewards communicate company and personal agendas, transparency is increasingly relevant. The following are some of the trends a Total Rewards Steward should be aware of for both financial and nonfinancial rewards.

- *Financial rewards:* As discussed in Chapter 5, monetary rewards are an excellent motivator if they meet the criteria we presented—available, linked to performance, visible, timely, and reversible. But money also enables key stakeholders to communicate core values. Regulators use compensation rules to govern executive behavior (e.g., recent U.S. legislation on say-on-pay, pay for performance, or clawbacks), to ensure pay equity (pay ratio regulation that moderates the gap between CEO and average pay), to offer a minimum wage (to send a social message), to grant paid-leave eligibility, and so forth. Companies, like Rio Tinto, also make reward choices that send signals to employees and investors. HR professionals should be particularly sensitive to compensation signals by answering three questions:
  - *First, pay for what?* Does the pay focus on individual or collective behaviors or outcomes? How does the pay balance trade-offs of short-term versus long-term results? Does the pay result in value for the company (e.g., Chipotle pays restaurant managers about $100,000 per year because they realize how much value they create for their stores)? Revenue versus cost? Innovation versus efficiency?
  - *Second, pay in what form?* Financial rewards may come in base salary, annual bonuses, or long-term incentives (performance shares, stock options). These forms of pay may vary by level and role.
  - *Third, pay compared to whom?* Most organizations benchmark pay with salary surveys to ensure external fairness as well as measures of internal equity.

[†]We are deeply indebted to Charlie Tharp for his incredible insights in this section. He has shaped our thinking on these issues.

As Total Rewards Stewards address these questions, they create a compensation philosophy and financial reward system that communicates both the strategic drivers of organization success and the basics of individual fairness. Total Rewards Stewards constantly tweak the answers to these three questions to use financial rewards to drive business and personal success.

• *Nonfinancial rewards:* While financial rewards are often visible indicators of what matters, nonfinancials[8] also send clear negative and positive signals. Negative nonfinancial rewards might include a reprimand, negative review, or being passed over or neglected on an important job opportunity or decision. Positive financial rewards include recognition (employees appreciate public acknowledgment of the work they do), work itself (employees become engaged when they find personal meaning from the work that they do and when they have the talents to do the work), and work or career opportunity (employees become more connected when they see how their work efforts will enhance their career opportunities). An employee's psychological contract at work is often as meaningful as the economic contract.

Total Rewards Stewards can help business leaders use nonfinancial levers to capture employees' passion or well-being. Sometimes the nonfinancials may be company concierge services like laundry, day care, massage rooms, and food. But the more meaningful nonfinancial rewards come when employees meld their identity to the job, find purpose from the work, build relationships, and have control over their work setting.[9]

The engagement literature shows that when employees find meaning and purpose from work, they are more engaged and productive. One critical predictor of meaning is the extent to which employees feel that they control the creation of meaning at work. Instead of asking passive questions like, "Do you find meaning at work?" a more active question would be, "Do I know what I can do (or I do my best) to find meaning at work?" By encouraging employees to take personal responsibility for meaning, Total Rewards Stewards increase well-being. In the Rio Tinto case, this meant customizing nonfinancial opportunities for employees in different roles and geographic settings. By so doing, they build nonfinancial reward systems that consistently signal what matters most to employees.

How Can You as an HR Professional Become a Better Total Rewards Steward?

HR professionals need not run and hide from the technical requirements of managing total rewards. Instead of assigning financial rewards to compensation specialists, all HR professionals can master the fundamental principles of both financial and nonfinancial rewards to better communicate a company agenda and to reinforce employee behavior. Given the lower impact of this competence domain on individual and organizational outcomes, there is clearly room for improvement.

Without becoming a rewards specialist, any HR professional could better access the power of rewards by doing the following:

- *Worrying less about being a compensation expert and more about understanding basic compensation principles:* In shaping a compensation philosophy, ask questions like, "What is the story we want to tell through our compensation system? What is our primary business agenda and how do our compensation choices reinforce that agenda? What would key investor and customer stakeholders say about our compensation choices?" Make sure that there is a line of sight between winning in the customer marketplace and investor markets and the compensation choices you make.
- *Keep compensation messages clear and understandable:* Make sure you can explain the elements of a compensation philosophy to employees at all levels so they can see a line of sight between their personal behavior and its implications for their compensation.
- *Listen to compensation experts:* They can advise the board compensation committee, senior line leaders, compensation specialists, and HR generalists on the latest trends in regulation and compensation choices. Make sure that these experts offer innovative recommendations that align financial rewards with business goals and personal behavior.

- *Use rewards to reinforce, not create, change:* When employees behave consistently with the business agenda, find ways to financially and nonfinancially reward them. This might include increases in base salary, bonuses, stock options, or spot awards. But it also might include public recognition, more control over work activities, or participation in making key work-related decisions.

- *Help employees find meaning and purpose from their work:* Like Rio Tinto, be willing to adapt nonfinancial rewards to the work setting and unique employee needs. Help employees take personal responsibility for finding meaning and purpose from work. Find out what gives an employee meaning, and build those experiences into the organization.

We believe that integrated HR solutions include HR practices in staffing, training, career development, employee involvement, organization design, work policies, and financial and nonfinancial rewards. Leaving reward choices to specialists and not integrating rewards is a bit like playing a sporting event without keeping score. The activity may be engaging, but keeping score and rewarding success encourages progress.

Conclusion: Strategic Enablers

HR professionals, to be personally effective, to serve stakeholders, and to deliver business results, need to be Culture and Change Champions, Human Capital Curators, and Total Rewards Stewards. We hope our coaching tips offered in this chapter will enable aspiring HR professionals to make progress in these competence domains.

CHAPTER 10

FOUNDATION ENABLERS— HR COMPETENCIES THAT HELP DELIVER FOUNDATIONAL VALUE

10

In Chapter 2 we highlighted that navigating paradox is the HR competency that most impacts business performance. Then in Chapter 8, we reviewed the logic and tools for navigating paradox. One of the long-standing paradoxes (or tensions) in the HR profession is strategic (long-term, transformational) versus foundational (short-term, transactional, or tactical) work. Many in HR continue to advocate that HR should move from short to long term, from transactional to transformational work. Consistent with the rationale of navigating paradox, we believe that effective HR professionals must manage both strategic *and* foundational HR work. This and/also logic has permeated our approach to HR for decades.[1] If HR professionals cannot get the basics right; they will not likely be trusted with more strategic business issues.

In the previous chapter, we discussed three strategic enablers. In this chapter we review three Foundation Enablers: (1) Compliance Manager, (2) Analytics Designer and Integrator, and (3) Technology and Media Integrator (see Figure 2.3 in Chapter 2 for a review of how these competencies fit into the overall framework of the nine HR competencies). While these three did not have as much impact on the individual, stakeholder, or business outcomes as the three core drivers, they were nevertheless important descriptors of competencies required for HR professionals and predictors of each of these outcomes as shown in Tables 2.9 through 2.12.

First Foundation Enabler: Compliance Manager

In our workshops with HR professionals, we often ask about the criteria for effective HR. The top results are often answers like support the business strategy, build capability to drive customer value, be architects of transformation, frame HR from the outside in, and so forth. We remind people that there is another, much less trendy or sexy, response, which is to make sure that the organization ensures compliance with policy.

Compliance often carries with it a negative connotation, especially when considered in the HR context. Unfortunately for many in the HR profession, they are still only known as compliance officers, or policy police. While we try to avoid that stereotype of HR, we understand that compliance is critical to long-term success because appropriate policy compliance is like making the trains run on time, picking up the phone and getting a dial tone, or turning the ignition key so the car starts. It is about protecting employee rights as required by regulation and being a liaison between employees and management.

Being a compliance manager is a highly rated competence by all raters (4.32, being nearly equal in quality to the Credible Activist competence, which is the highest of the nine competencies at 4.33; see Table 2.7), and it is high across all regions of the world (Table 2.9). Not surprisingly, it is the competence most related to individual HR professionals (Table 2.11) and HR departments (Table 2.12) serving regulators. Compliance management is the heritage of the HR profession that must be carried forward for the profession to gain legitimacy and the opportunity for more strategic work.

Organizations have a slew of compliance processes to manage. Take regulation, for example. Just as regulation can restrain business interests, it can also define what HR professionals have to know and do. Nevertheless, HR professionals must be aware of regulation and ensure that the organization follows it. HR partners with the organization to ensure that it knows of new legal guidelines and encourages and often leads compliance. At the same time, HR must protect the employees and stand up for their rights.

Table 10.1   *Compliance Manager subdomain means by rater group*

Compliance Manager				
	All Raters[a]	Self-Ratings	Supervisor Ratings	HR Associate Ratings	Non-HR Associate Ratings
Compliance Manager	4.32	4.34	4.31	4.30	4.38

[a]Columns add to 100%.

Compliance Managers in Action: The Singapore Public Service Division

It is not a surprise that an iconic case of outstanding compliance management comes from the public sector. Nor is it a surprise that Singapore's public service group offers an exceptional case study of innovative and efficient government service. Singapore is well-renowned as an iconic country where the public sector has helped the economy grow.

The Singapore Public Service Division (PSD) is a part of the prime minister's office and is the central people agency for the government of Singapore. While PSD exists to serve and develop civil servants, it acts at the behest of the prime minister and the elected officials, and it is incumbent upon PSD to ensure that the government employees help carry out the national agenda.

The national agenda is set by the elected ruling party, which is the People's Action Party for over 50 years. This government has led Singapore through a period of quick economic growth that transformed Singapore from a third-world to a first-world nation in 50 years. This has afforded citizens a high standard of living and created long-standing goodwill and trust of the government. Singapore offers a very safe, clean, and well-regulated country enjoyed by both citizens and foreigners. The government has achieved this success in large part from a democratic governance with strict rule of law. Littering can result in a fine of up to $500 and a drug trafficking offense and illegal possession of firearms can result in the death penalty.

For a country where 30 percent of the population are not citizens, maintaining a high level of governance requires cooperation from its citizens.

While the government has traditionally been able to rely on a high level of compliance from its citizens, the new generation of citizens no longer comply blindly. The government has to engage with the citizens and win the mindshare as well as the hearts of the citizens. With more than 140,000 public officers supporting the Singapore government, PSD has also seen an uptick in employees questioning and trying to get around the rules in recent years.

No longer being effective to simply dictate new policies to the public servants, PSD has focused more on co-creation of policies, whenever possible, with representatives of the 100 government agencies. For example, recently in 2012, Parliament passed a Retirement and Re-employment Act to raise the retirement age from 60 to 62. With the new law, there was a requirement that employers offer reemployment at age 62 for at least three years. The public service, being the single largest employer in Singapore, had to toe the line and lead by example to respond to the new regulation. Rather than dictate what the policy would be, PSD reached out to every agency to explain the context and intent of the new regulation, sought inputs from agencies from across different demographics, and held focus groups to ensure that everyone was on the same page and that the public servants felt empowered.

PSD has found that the employees are more inclined to believe in what they are doing when they are involved in the co-creation of policy, which in turn aligns the public servants with the national agenda.

With the passing of the act to increase the reemployment age to 67 effective July 1, 2017, the PSD has again taken a lead and started implementation from January 1, 2017, ahead of the legislation.

The mission for the HR office is, *We provide professional leadership to the HR community in the Public Service.* The Chief Human Resources Officer's Office (CHROO) provides professional leadership to the HR community in the PSD. The CHROO plans and develops the sector's and profession's manpower by doing the following:

- Building a One HR Community in the PSD
- Setting professional standards for HR officers and increasing HR capabilities through development interventions

- Being an effective change agent and strategic partner in support of Public Service transformation efforts
- Building a strong talent pipeline for the Service's HR leadership

They promote a forward-looking HR community who can ensure that the government HR work is an example of exceptional HR services.

What Are the Emerging Trends Affecting Compliance Managers?

The compliance piece of HR is about doing the day-to-day systematic stuff that is necessary to make sure the basics are done well. When that happens, HR then gains the right to play in a more strategic way. We see four general trends in compliance management that are helping HR professionals be enablers rather than blockers.

1. *Encourage collaboration of government regulation, business success, education opportunities, and labor pools:* Often we see conflict and tension between government and industry. Government becomes the parent and industry becomes the whining child; a vicious circle ensues where government proposes and industry opposes. We see positive trends in emerging markets where government, industry, education, and labor can collaborate to boost an economy. The Singapore case is a wonderful example of government and industry collaboration. In Mauritius, for example, we participated in creating a Mauritius leadership brand. This leadership brand articulated what Mauritius leaders would be known for by multiple stakeholders (citizens, investors, visitors). This brand initiative was sponsored by the government, but included a number of interviews with industry leaders. The leadership brand that was developed (see Figure 10.1) was then a guideline for leaders in government agencies to model the expected behaviors and education institutions to develop future leaders. The prime minister included this work as part of his economic reform to improve the entire country.

Figure 10.1   *Mauritius' leadership brand*

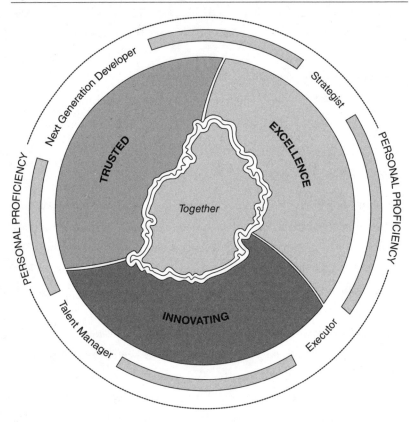

2. *Foster regulatory innovation:* Out of collaboration should come innovative regulations that set a positive context for improving work. A large financial service firm in South Africa wanted to enter an underdeveloped African market. They realized that this new market has nascent financial regulations that increased their risk in the market. So with HR's guidance, they assigned some of their regulatory experts to do a short-term work assignment in the government of the new market. Six months later, the new market produced a regulatory infrastructure that offered more stability to firms entering the market. In another case in a mature market, the CHRO realized that he was spending an inordinate amount of his time responding to regulators who did not fully appreciate his business. So he organized a forum where regulators who were setting employment standards could

meet with HR thought leaders to identity innovations in HR and to hopefully then sponsor regulation that encouraged these innovations. Finally, another pharmaceutical firm assigned one of its top HR executives for a year assignment to work with industry lobbyists to articulate and position regulation in ways that would help, not hinder, the industry. There are professional associations that encourage such collaboration (e.g., National Association of Manufacturing sponsors meetings and field trips with government and industry leaders).

3. *Regulatory compliance is best accomplished through transparency and self-accountability:* Sometimes well-intended regulation creates unintended consequences. A number of years ago, in an effort to support farmers, the government agency responsible for farm credit allowed farmers to borrow up to 90 percent of land value versus the previous 70 percent. Even as land values inflated, farmers often borrowed to the new standard. As inevitably happens, land values fell back and many farmers were deeply overextended, causing a real crisis. Government had to foreclose on many farms, to some extent, due to policy messages. Farmers, obviously, were distraught and angry at losing their farms. In one region, the CEO chose not to default on any farmer for three months. Instead, loan officers would meet weekly with the farmers who were underwater and share data with them about their loan and its performance. After 12 weeks of creative data sharing, the loan officer then asked the farmers: "What should happen next?" In most cases, farmers, while still distraught, were more able to accept the regulatory reality. Likewise in organizations, transparency of regulatory compliance without articulating formal consequences often leads to self-accountability.

4. *Focus on what* can't *be done exceeds focus on what* can *be done:* One of the authors built a house with an architect. As the architect listened to the author's desires, she did not immediately say what design codes were in place to constrain those desires. She merely said that zoning and other regulations set some basics, but that there were ways to meet the author's desires even while complying with regulation. Likewise, regulations about advertising, employment and labor, environment, privacy, and safety and

health will likely increase. In 2013, while the U.S. Congress passed fewer than 60 bills, federal regulators issued more than 3,500 new rules. Instead of obsessing about what cannot be done, thoughtful companies broaden compliance from following rules to avoid problems to creating cultures to anticipate opportunity.

These regulatory trends affect not only HR, but all aspects of the business. As compliance managers, HR professionals can model how to work with regulatory realities.

How Can You as an HR Professional Become a Better Compliance Manager?

While most do not aspire to an HR career as compliance managers, this work has to be done and done well. HR professionals should avoid two extremes of compliance management. On the one hand, they should avoid being the policy police. This means defining their primary role as ensuring that policies and regulations are maintained. They become known as paper pushers and compliance officers who control behavior by fiat and whose primary focus is on what *cannot* be done. When people write about "hating HR," these images often prevail.

On the other hand, HR professionals cannot ignore regulation and policy. Regulations are generally issued to upgrade the quality of employee life and organization work environment in areas of discrimination (policies around age, gender, disabled, race), health and safety (policies around work hours and physical setting), and fair treatment (policies around child care, minimum wage and age, and labor relations). In one case, one of the authors was invited into a company where a senior officer had a history of being a public and unrestrained racial and sexual misogynist. Eventually, employees filed a class action suit and government investigation discovered a pattern of such behavior. We asked, "Where was HR during this pattern?" The answer: "Invisible and passive." HR, and everyone else, knew of the inappropriate behaviors, but said nothing and took no action. Between policy police and inattentive observer, HR professionals can be appropriate Compliance Managers by engaging in some of the following behaviors:

- *Learn current and anticipate future regulation:* While few HR professionals are regulatory experts, they can access this expertise. Without reading and mastering pages of regulatory code, HR can be aware of current and emerging regulation and anticipate its consequences. Getting ahead of regulation avoids oversight.
- *Do regulation forums with business leaders and employees:* The purpose of these briefings is not to limit innovation, to denounce regulators, or to create fear, but to be transparent about what is happening. In one company, corruption practices were unclear in many markets. The HR professionals put together an online and in-person workshop on unacceptable corruption behaviors. This presentation informed employees before any problems arose.
- *Act quickly and fairly when inappropriate behavior occurs:* When HR professionals hear of inappropriate behavior, they should act quickly with due diligence and justice. Had HR responded sooner to the senior xenophobic leader noted earlier, an enormous amount of time and reputation could have been saved. Again, not all complaints are legitimate, but whistleblowers should be heard. HR professionals should be listening posts both by personal contact (e.g., interviewing those who leave the company) and by empirical data (e.g., a disproportionate number of employees might leave the company from one division).
- *Be a role model:* The HR department should live to a higher standard, both in legal compliance and in appropriate management practice. We have seen HR departments who encourage others to comply with regulation, but do not do so themselves. This hypocrisy limits influence.

Again, few go into HR to be regulators, and our data shows that most HR professionals are doing well as compliance managers. Getting compliance management right may not directly increase business results or stakeholder value, but it enables these conversations to be held without distraction (the dial tone works).

Second Foundation Enabler:
Analytics Designer and Integrator

Over the last decade, *analytics* has become a widespread buzzword in HR and an increasingly important concept for the HR's future. In Chapters 4 and 5 we pointed out two major challenges to HR departments using analytics to drive stakeholder and business results. First, in Chapter 4, we made the case that analytics is an outgrowth of accessing the right information. When talking about analytics, many concepts are used: scorecards, dashboards, predictive analytics, data science, evidence-based decisions, metrics, human resource accounting, cloud (or "big") data, forecasting, or workforce modeling.

The underlying agenda of all these efforts is to access and use information to make better decisions. As noted in Chapter 4, HR's role in information management should focus on HR's involvement in helping ensure the optimal flow of information, including the five steps of information management shown in Figure 4.1 (identify, import, analyze, disseminate, and utilize information). Analytics should enable improved information management, and as shown in Table 4.2, when HR departments manage information, positive stakeholder and business results follow.

A second analytics challenge is to focus less on information about HR and more on information about how HR will deliver stakeholder and business results. In Table 4.2 we reported that HR analytics (focused on assessing HR work) has only moderate impact on both stakeholder outcomes and business results. In Chapter 5 we highlighted how HR departments can pivot from HR analytics about HR to HR analytics that deliver business value.

These HR department-level findings about information and analytics also show up in the impact of analytics for HR professional effectiveness and business impact. Table 2.10 showed that knowing analytics has moderate impact (explaining 8.2 percent) of the personal effectiveness of an HR professional; Table 2.11 showed that HR analytics skills also have moderate impact on stakeholder outcomes ranging from negative 6.8 percent for employees (evidently when HR professionals focus on analytics, employee outcomes are actually reduced, which means that employees may not want to be thought of as numbers but as human beings) to positive 14.9 percent for line managers (line managers appreciate that HR professionals bring analytics discipline to their conversations).

While accessing and using information for improved business decisions matters a great deal (Chapter 4), HR professionals' competence to design and implement analytics has lagged this opportunity. Perhaps HR professionals have focused on the analytical tools and methodologies (e.g., predictive modeling, statistical insights) more than on how analytics provides information to make business decisions.

Table 10.2 reports that there are two subfactors for HR professionals as Analytics Designers and Interpreters: (1) get the data right (i.e., focus on information more than analytic tools) and (2) be a champion for standards (or make sure that information leads to appropriate actions). In both of these subdomains, HR professionals have room for improvement.

Table 10.2   *Analytics Designer and Interpreter subdomain means by rater group*

Analytics Designer and Interpreter					
	All Raters[a]	Self-Ratings	Supervisor Ratings	HR Associate Ratings	Non-HR Associate Ratings
Gets the Right Data	4.00	3.90	3.80	4.02	4.05
Champions Standards	4.02	3.89	3.77	4.05	4.07

[a]Columns add to 100%.

The Analytics Designer and Interpreter in Action at Shell

Royal Dutch Shell, more commonly known as Shell, has traditionally been among the most profitable integrated energy companies in the world. Shell has a lot of HR data ready to be dissected and used to solve key business issues, and Shell has approximately 400 employees working in analytics-related positions. The HR analytics team at Shell was formed in 2013.

With around 90,000 employees working in 70-plus countries, Shell has a diverse workforce and a wealth of employee data.

Initially the HR analytics team had to take any projects that they could get, but now they have more projects than they can handle, giving them the opportunity to select projects that will have the greatest impact on the business. The team adheres to strict internal data privacy rules and always ensures that results from analytics are presented at aggregate levels, respecting data privacy.

For example, in 2014, the HR analytics team took on a project to help improve safety. Safety has always been a priority at Shell, and the company had seen steady and consistent improvements in safety performance for many years until 2010 when year-over-year safety metrics began to plateau. In 2013, five employees lost their lives, though down from eight in 2012, the loss of employee lives was not acceptable for Shell leadership; they needed to renew their efforts to improve safety performance. Obviously, there is a business component as well, where improvements to safety lead to increased customer satisfaction, improved efficiency, and decreased costs. Certain incentives for employees to improve safety were in place. Safety metrics made up 20 percent of the company scorecard and contributed to 20 percent of an employee's bonus, but Shell struggled to break the plateau, despite having a strong safety culture (e.g., every meeting at Shell starts with a safety briefing).

With the business problem in hand, the HR analytics team worked to identify a possible solution. Supported by external research, they developed a hypothesis that improvements in engagement (i.e., motivation) would lead to improved safety performance. First, they evaluated the link between employee engagement and safety within Shell. While it had been proven outside the organization, they wanted to see if it held true for Shell and to identify the magnitude of the effect—that is, the "size of the price." They started with evaluating multiyear safety and engagement scores for a part of the business, a gas-to-liquids facility in Qatar. The hypothesis was confirmed in Qatar, so they decided to expand the study to employees in an additional 27 countries across multiple manufacturing sites and again using multiyear data.

They found that a one percentage point increase in employee engagement led to the following:

- 4 percent decrease in the total number of accidents per full-time employee (FTE)
- 4 percent decrease in loss of primary containment incidents per exposure hour
- 3 percent decrease in total recordable cases per million exposure hours

With this validation, they tackled the next question: "What drives engagement?" Again taking into account extensive external research on the topic, the team chose to focus on leadership as a key variable that influences engagement. They found that within Shell, leadership influenced 45 percent of the engagement scores, with team leadership accounting for 35 percent and top management for an additional 20 percent across Shell's businesses.

With the foundational research and the data to back it up, they came up with a simple value chain for safety performance (see Figure 10.2). They found that this simple visual helped communicate the more complex analytics.

To go further, the team turned to additional data to help take a more targeted approach to improving leadership, the first variable in the value chain. Every year, the employee survey asks employees to rate leadership in a series of questions that relates to team leaders and organization leaders. Utilizing this data, they identified those leaders who scored in the lowest quartile and clearly showed where in the organization leadership issues existed (i.e., percent of bottom quartile leaders per business, region, country, site, etc., relative to external benchmarks). The yearly survey is thus used as a diagnostic tool for the organization on leadership.

They also focused on the scores of leaders in leadership-critical and safety-critical positions. This approach allowed for intervention with specific individuals who were struggling on leadership and in safety-critical leadership roles. Once they identified the individuals, the team delivered the information to the appropriate HR leaders who worked to identify whether the leadership performance issue is motivation (will) or skill-based. At this

Figure 10.2 *Shell's analytics process for increased safety*

point, a determination was made by the line manager to either provide them the proper (re-)training they need to improve their team's engagement and safety performance or remove the leader.

They found that not only did better leadership improve safety performance, but also the increased engagement decreased absenteeism, improved sales, and increased customer satisfaction. Those benefits have been a by-product of their work. The results have been so successful that Shell has begun to deploy this project across the entire organization. It illustrates how something that can be perceived to be "an HR thing" (a yearly people survey) can turn into a powerful process for safety improvement by using analytics to clearly show the link to a key business challenge and to something everyone at Shell cares deeply about. They strive to measure and improve leadership and engagement, thus driving the desired business outcomes.

What Are the Emerging Trends for the Analytics Designer and Interpreter?

The Shell analytics case illustrates the dominant logic shift to be an effective HR analytics contributor: *focus first on the business; then use analytics to discover which HR investments will deliver business results.* Shell's analytics team started with an evident problem (safety), and then showed that safety (a legitimate outcome in and of itself) drove traditional business outcomes. Then through analytics, they discovered the antecedents of safety in a cause-and-effect logic. Their work reinforces the two subdomains of HR analytics:

- *Get the right data:* There are many types of HR data available. Drawing on work by Dick Beatty (and consistent with the Shell example), we see four phases of HR analytics, each using different data:
  - *Phase 1—HR scorecard:* Presenting basic institutional employee data (number of employees in what job and demographic categories, performance history data, etc.), HR initiative metrics (did specific assignments get done on time and within specifications—a new on-boarding program)
  - *Phase 2—HR insights:* Looking for broad insights in the volumes of existing HR data, often called cloud (or big data) analytics
  - *Phase 3—HR interventions:* Discovering the relative impact of HR practices (i.e., comparing those hired, trained, or paid in one way versus another)
  - *Phase 4—Business impact:* Determining how business challenges (financial, customer, or market results) are affected by HR practices

The emerging trend is to focus analytics at Phase 4, defining business outcomes and then showing how HR investments will impact those outcomes. In the Shell case, improved leadership increases employee sentiment, which leads to higher safety records and ultimately business performance.

Likewise, we see leading HR professionals starting analytics by clearly defining business outcomes that matter. Often these outcomes can be linked to customers (e.g., improved net promoter score or customer share), investors (cash flow or market valuation), or communities (social responsibility, community reputation). When HR professionals start with these outcomes, they can then show how HR investments will impact them. By beginning with Phase 4, HR professionals use analytics to supply information that drives business results. As Dick Beatty frequently states, the scorecard of HR is ultimately the business scorecard.

• *Be the standards champion:* Once data are collected, analyzed, and interpreted to show business impact, choices can be made to improve the results. At Shell, knowing that leaders are the lead indicator of employee engagement, then leaders (the head of the safety value chain) can be hired, trained, promoted, and incented to increase employee engagement. If data does not inform choices that set new standards, then the data are relatively useless.

Our friend Steve Kerr reminds us that not all data is useful. Without having data that leads to choices that affect business results, it is like adding up all the uniform numbers of players on a football team and claiming you have a better team because the sum of your numbers is higher. While easy to track, this sum of uniform numbers has nothing to do with playing or winning the game. Sometimes, HR analytics falls prey to the same "easy to measure" but not relevant trap. Time to hire, costs of hiring, and hours of training per employee each year are examples of HR metrics that may have little impact on business results. HR professionals use analytics to champion the right standards that shape behaviors that deliver results.

How Can You as an HR Professional Become a Better Analytics Designer and Integrator?

Becoming a better Analytics Designer and Interpreter who accesses information to make better business decisions holds enormous promise for HR professionals. Our data suggests that information management is the emerging capability HR departments should provide, but that most HR professionals as Analytics Designers and Interpreters fall short of this information opportunity. To improve as Analytics Designers and Interpreters, we suggest the following:

- *Create a line of sight between business challenges and HR investments:* This line of sight might come from a strategic map[2] or an organizational alignment process (e.g., Star Model, 7S). This line of sight from business challenge to HR helps focus what HR information can be collected to deliver business results. This line of sight also highlights business questions that HR analytics can then answer. The Shell example, where a line of sight was established between employee engagement and safety, serves well. See Figure 10.3 for the process and questions HR Analytics Designers and Interpreters should be using.
- *Learn the basics of research methodology and statistics:* Often HR work is based on conjecture rather than evidence. To evaluate reliability and validity of a proposal or practice, you need to seek evidence. You don't have to become a statistics expert or data scientist, but you do have to be comfortable talking about numbers and know the basics of statistics: means, variance, correlations, regressions, significance, and causation.
- *See patterns in data that tell a story:* Statistics and numbers are static, but they often indicate patterns that tell a compelling story. For example, we found with a number of clients in retail, financial, and lodging industries that employee engagement scores correlated over time with customer engagement, which in turn correlated with financial performance. We validated this finding with rigorous time series statistics and were able to see a relatively simple pattern (like the Shell pattern for Figure 10.2). We then were able to create a story of how financial performance increases when customers are more committed, which increases when employees are more engaged. We can then tell stories (anecdotes) of specific customer experiences that were affected by engaged employees to capture the data with a memorable illustration. How data are presented becomes an important predictor of how they are used.

- *Use data to help make and track choices:* Doing analytics is not an event that results in a presentation; rather it is about creating information that informs choices. Continually ask for evidence in public and private conversations. Use information over time to track results, and instill an ongoing learning mentality to constantly improve.

HR analytics has incredible promise to allow HR professionals to use information for improved decision making. This new domain in our 2016 HRCS research findings will likely continue to increase in personal, stakeholder, and business impact as HR professionals gain proficiency with it.

Figure 10.3   Logic and flow of connecting analytics to business

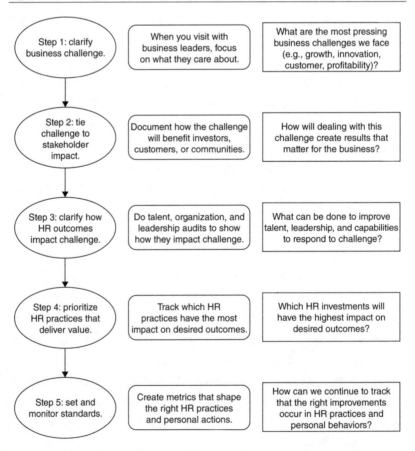

Third Foundation Enabler: The Technology and Media Integrator

As introduced in Chapter 1 and established in Chapter 4, technology is dramatically changing how people live and organizations operate. The pace of change in the information environment based on technological advances has dramatically affected business models and HR practices (see Chapter 4). Like other organization functions, HR departments have been using technology to streamline their processes, share information, and connect employees. Talent, development, rewards, employee involvement, and communication HR processes are shifting due to technology. Large global firms like Oracle (with PeopleSoft), SAP (with SuccessFactors), and Workday (with Workday Human Capital Management) offer technology platform services, engineered systems and software applications for business and HR solutions. Hundreds of smaller software and application firms offer targeted technology services on HR practices.

Social media focuses computer-related tools that allow people and companies to create, share, or exchange information inside, but even more outside, company boundaries.[3] Social media creates unlimited transparency into an organization's HR practices. Combined, the number of users of the Big Six social networks (Facebook, Twitter, LinkedIn, Instagram, Google+, and Pinterest) exceeds 2.4 billion people. Table 10.3 illustrates the focus and escalating scale of these firms. The largest, Facebook, would be the second most populous country on the planet after China. HR professionals need to leverage social media for HR practices such as staffing, training, involvement, and decision making.

Table 10.3   Social media firms[4]

Firm	Overall purpose	Focus	Size and scale
Pinterest	Social site about discovery	Focus on decor, fashion, health, cooking	70 million active users
Twitter	Micro blogging	Limit messages to 140 characters; strongest in U.S.	290 million active users; 9,100 tweets a second

(continued on next page)

Table 10.3   *Social media firms*[4] *(continued)*

Firm	Overall purpose	Focus	Size and scale
Facebook	Social sharing	Share all kinds of information; 84% of job seekers have Facebook profile	1.5 billion active monthly users; share 1 million links every 20 minutes
Instagram	Social sharing around pictures and videos	Individuals and organizations create brands	300 million active users
Google+	Brands and individual users can build circles or networks	Build user circles or networks for sharing information	300 million active users
LinkedIn	Business-oriented social network	Post on individual connection and personal/ professional brands	380 million active users; 76% of U.S. companies used LinkedIn for recruiting

Few HR professionals can stay current in all the latest technological and social media wizardry, but the advent of technology and media integration competencies (not found in earlier studies) has arrived. We found that competence in technology and social media was the second lowest overall rating of the nine competencies (next to total rewards), which may indicate the relative newness of this competency domain (see Table 2.7). This finding holds for both males and females and in all geographies (Tables 2.8 and 2.9).

Table 2.10 showed that more skilled HR technology experts were not seen as more personally effective, which may indicate a personal disconnect of HR professionals who specialize in technology. This disconnect between competence in technology and social media is most pronounced with line managers who actually see HR professionals with more technology skills in a more negative light.

These findings would be discouraging to HR professionals who wanted to improve in technology and media integration until we look again at Table 2.12. In this table, while the individual HR professional may not have much impact on key stakeholders, the collection of HR professionals in a department do.

In other words, it is important that for an HR department's practices and processes to be effective, HR professionals as a collective group need to show competence in technology and media integration, particularly when serving external customers, investors, and line managers.[5]

In addition, Table 2.12 shows that technology and media integration collective competence is the second highest (next to Paradox Navigator) in delivering business results. So an HR group should make sure that they possess technology and media competencies even if individual HR professionals do not. We also found (Table 10.4) that HR professionals are better at internal technology than at using social media outside of the organization. They really need to be doing both. As we go forward with this research, we expect the importance of this competence in delivering results will likely grow.

Table 10.4   *Technology and Media Integrator subdomain means by rater group*

Technology and Media Integrator					
	All Raters[a]	Self-Ratings	Supervisor Ratings	HR Associate Ratings	Non-HR Associate Ratings
Leverages Social Media	3.71	3.48	3.57	3.72	3.77
Integrates Technology	4.03	3.99	3.91	4.03	4.06

[a]Columns add to 100%.

The Technology and Media Integrator in Action: Unilever

In 2009, Paul Polman became the Unilever CEO. For the nearly 130-year-old company, he was a relative outsider having worked at Procter & Gamble (27 years) and Nestle (3 years). He set an aggressive goal to double the size (revenues) while halving the environmental footprint of making and using their products. The social responsibility agenda was a primary focus as captured in the Sustainable Living Plan, which affects how Unilever uses raw materials and informs how consumers use their brands. From 2009 through

2015, the business results have been very positive, particularly in an industry where competitors have posted mostly flat results.

- Revenue increase from £40 billion to £53 billion (32 percent increase)
- Operating profit increase from £5 billion to £7.5 (50 percent increase); earnings per share from 1.16 to 1.72 (48 percent increase)
- Revenue per employee (productivity) from £237/employee to £312/employee
- Employee engagement (78 percent) and pride (92–94 percent) are at high water marks
- CO_2 from energy (kg/ton of production) from 142.16 to 88.49 (38 percent decrease)
- Total waste sent for disposal (kg/ton of production) from 6.52 to 0.26
- Market capitalization from £63.4 billion to £113.4 billion (80 percent increase)

These remarkable business results are attributed to strategically focusing on four core categories (personal care, foods, home care, and refreshment), driving innovation across each category, managing capital efficiently, and creating a culture and talent pool that drive success.

HR has played a key role in this success. With Doug Baille, a seasoned business leader for 30 years and then CHRO from 2011 through 2015, Unilever HR focused first on delivering on the business agenda. He felt that his challenge was to equip the organization with the right talent, inclusive culture, and leadership strength to deliver on the CEO's responsible growth agenda. In 2016, Leena Nair became CHRO to continue to drive business results by discovering, nurturing, and inspiring talented people who could create and sustain transformational business change.

Central to these HR aspirations are both technology and social media efforts. Technology enables rapid agility both through experimentation and standardization across Unilever. As a consequence, Unilever allocates authority to local leaders to respond to local trends more quickly than local competitors.

To manage this local experimentation versus global leverage, HR has used technology to share information quickly from market to market. With Workday as their technology partner, they are using technology to do the following:

- Standardize business processes globally, streamlining operations, and reducing complexity to increase efficiencies and productivity throughout the business.
- Empower people with self-service to perform transactions, access information, and take action on any mobile device.
- Access real-time actionable analytics that can help drive hiring and sourcing decisions, such as cost, current and project capacity, and capability gaps across different geographies and business structures.
- Gain deeper insights into its workforce that will enable managers to better measure performance, recognize top talent, and align skill sets with roles.

In addition, the social responsibility agenda has become a major part of the social media efforts. Unilever has worked to shift their external branding from one focused on individual products (they have over 400 brands used by over two billion people a day) to one of "creating brands for life" marketing strategy, which then translates into an inclusive culture of concern for the individuals. Being active in social media also helps Unilever HR professionals anticipate consumer and market changes before they are required.

What Are the Emerging Trends for the Technology and Media Integrator?

The environmental context for information is laid out in Chapter 4, which shows the speed, pervasiveness, expanding scope (Internet of Things), and patterns for information. This context shapes the trends in HR technology and social media. Unilever HR adapted to these trends to help deliver financial and social results. HR professionals who recognize and adapt to technology and social media trends will increase their personal effectiveness and business impact.

Evolving Technology Trends

Human Resource Information Systems (HRIS) have been around for some time,[6] but in recent years these systems are evolving through four phases.

First, HR technology is used to design and deliver HR practices more efficiently. Through self-service portals, employees become responsible for accessing and integrating HR solutions for them. HR technologies like mobile apps and gamification also help facilitate HR innovation in staffing, development, rewards, and involvement.

In Phase 2 HR technology enables transparency and sharing of information. Through big or cloud data, employee skills are public domain and companies may approach them without their applying for work.[7] For example, technology-enabled training may expand the scale and scope of training to a large group of employees.

In Phase 3, HR technology encourages connections by involving more people in decision making and by facilitating collaboration. Nationwide Insurance, for example, now has nearly all of its 36,000 employees active on its internal social platform, making it far easier for employees to find subject experts and solve business problems in one fell swoop, rather than sending copious e-mails or searching through hard drives.[8] Some of this collaboration comes from crowdsourcing, which allows firms to hand off some tasks to workers outside the enterprise. Salesforce.com uses the LiveOps "cloud contact center" to deliver global customer support services, which involves tapping contractors who work from home and set their own hours. The platform tracks performance and rewards high performers with recognition, more work, and better pay, and allows responsiveness to demands.[9]

Finally, in Phase 4, HR technologies shift toward an experience economy where employees and customers don't just want information, but the opportunity to create emotional experiences from technology connections.[10] The experience economy is one of the trends shaping personal lifestyle and is being woven in architecture choices[11] and organization processes.[12] Employees are often looking less for a job or even a career, and more for an experience (or calling) that will increase their personal identity and well-being. Leaders learn from more experience-based training than classroom settings. Technology broadens access to experiences and magnifies the experiences through sharing them.

Evolving Social Media Trends

One of the authors is a millennial who is comfortable with social media tools. His insight is that good use of social media is not merely getting on Facebook and LinkedIn, tweeting, or sharing through Instagram. Accessing or surfing social media sites will not help HR professionals (or others) deliver more value. Applying the four-phase emerging trends logic from technology to social media offers HR professionals a glimpse into how to create value from social media work.

First, social media more efficiently connects employees inside with those outside the organization. CareerArc, a social media firm, found that 75 percent of job seekers consider an employer's brand before even applying for a job, 62 percent of job seekers visit social media channels to evaluate employer brand, and 91 percent of job seekers find poorly managed or designed online properties damaging to an employer brand.[13]

Second, social media allows for more transparency of marketplace messages. Social media sites get the right information to the right people in ways that work for them.[14] A number of firms have hired someone whose job it is to scan social media sites for comments about the firm and to respond to them. On social media sites, employees share their experiences to portray an employee value proposition to potential employees. Social media sites allow insiders to share their experience and outsiders to peek inside the firm for what is really happening. The comments on products, services, firm working conditions, and so forth, which sometimes are biased by who tends to comment, often share overall themes and how the firm is doing.

Third, social media sites build connections among many groups. Social media enables networks to quickly form focus groups who evaluate a new product or service. Immediacy of feedback from places like Glassdoor.com offer firm leaders insights into their organization. LinkedIn or Google+ groups have helped redesign products by immediate user input. Cloud data from Facebook posts on employee experiences in a company or an abundance of LinkedIn (or other job-search websites like Monster.com) posts by employees may be early warning signals of employee malaise.

Fourth, social media sites may shape an external experience, defined as reputation and brand, of the organization. As customers post their experiences with a firm's products or services on Instagram and elsewhere, the firm can recognize the experiences they are offering customers. The General Electric "getting hired by GE" social media blitz shows how GE is redefining its brand from a manufacturing to innovative technology company.

As HR professionals understand these evolving technology and social media trends, they are better able to provide insights that deliver value to key stakeholders and business results.

How Can You as an HR Professional Become a Better Technology and Media Integrator?

Improvment as a Technology and Media Integrator may come from some of the following tips:

- *Recognize and learn the essential skills for technology and social media:* These skills include accessing electronic information, filtering the onslaught of information overload, being able to search and inquire to facilitate learning (we call this fingertip learning), being open to the wisdom of crowds and commentator feedback, using information to make evidence-based decisions, visualizing information so that it tells a story, and so forth.
- *Remember that technology and social media skills (listed previously) without the softer skills that apply the technology insights will remain inert:* The World Economic Forum identified the critical 2020 employee skills to include: complex problem solving, critical thinking, and creativity, which coordinate with other softer skills, including emotional intelligence, judgment and decision making, cognitive flexibility, and so forth.[15] Coupling the two sets of skills will help you turn technology insights into impactful action.
- *Access emerging technology and social media tools:* We realize it is nearly impossible to keep up with the pace of app innovation (people post the

latest greatest social media tools such as Canva, Buffer, Brand24, Edgar, Bundle Post, and etc.).[16] These tools increasingly enable collaboration through mobile connections. At least, be aware that Outlook Express e-mail may not be one of the latest tools. One hint is to recognize technology and social media sites your employees (often younger employees) are using. Use those sites as listening posts where you can discern attitudes before they are entrenched. Try those sites out to share information—both company direction and personal successes.

- *Know the public target audiences for your social media messages (e.g., potential employees, customers, regulators, community leaders)—then shape messages for them:* Be sure to place those messages in forums where they will be seen.
- *Create a personal brand that you would like to be known for and experiment with social media sites to promote that brand:* This personal experience may then be useful as you build company brand.

As our data and experiences suggest, technology and media integration competencies will only become more important. At present, stakeholders expect that "the HR department" has these skills; over time, we believe individual HR professionals should demonstrate increased competence in these areas.

Conclusion: Foundation Enablers

HR professionals, to be personally effective, to serve stakeholders, and to deliver business results, need to be Compliance Managers, Analytics Designers and Interpreters, and Technology and Media Integrators. We hope our coaching tips offered in this chapter will enable aspiring HR professionals to make progress in these foundational competence domains.

PART IV

WHAT HAPPENS NEXT?

CHAPTER 11

NOW WHAT?

11

In summing up, we typically like to use three questions to help clients think through problems and challenges: *What's so? So what?* And *Now what?* We have already addressed two of these questions in Chapters 1 through 10; we will conclude by answering the third: Now what?

What's So and So What?—a Short Recap

Just as a quick review, we'll summarize with quick answers to our first two questions.

What's So?

The world is changing, as depicted by the Four Forces described in Chapter 1 (STEPED, VUCA, increased stakeholder expectations, and personal affect in and out of the workplace). Many recognize changing social and economic conditions (STEPED) and the pace of change (VUCA). Our stakeholder grid identifies relevant changes in stakeholder expectations (e.g., customers worried about customer share, and investors concerned about leadership capital) and our "Six I's" view of today's external factors affecting people and employees offers a disciplined view of challenges in managing human capital. As a result of the Four Forces, expectations of HR individuals and departments are increasing across three fronts: personal effectiveness, stakeholder outcomes, and business results. We believe the Four Forces capture the increased demands on and opportunities for HR.

So What?

The seventh round of our research via the Human Resources Competency Survey (HRCS) will continue to inform business and HR leaders on how to make better HR choices, transform HR departments, upgrade HR professionals, and shape the profession. In this research, and based on our experiences, we have focused on two broad categories of insights: *organization* and *individual*.

Organization Findings

Chapters 3, 4, and 5 laid out the findings and implications for why organizations matter even more than individual competencies and how to improve organization practices, particularly around information. In particular, we found the following:

- *HR departments as a whole have three to four times the impact on business results as individual HR professionals (Table 2.13):* This is a remarkable finding and shifts decades-long assumptions about "liking my HR professional, but not liking the HR department." While some have lauded the importance of organization, this research offers empirical data from over 1,200 organizations that departments matter more than people in predicting business and stakeholder results.

  More broadly, if this result is true for HR, it may also be true for organizations in general, thus the title of this book, *Victory Through Organization*. It offers an empirical rationale for the increased attention to studies of organization capabilities like external sensing, speed/agility, innovation, customer responsiveness, and accountability (see Figure 3.1). It also reinforces the increased managerial attention to culture.

  This finding evolves the "war for talent" thinking that has been an obsession for HR professionals and focal point for those using traditional HR practices. Thus our subtitle: *Why the War for Talent Is Failing Your Company and What You Can Do About It*. Our data suggest that the "war for talent" pivots to "victory through organization"; this has enormous implications for business leaders and HR professionals. Chapter 3 laid out the rationale for why organization matters and how to rethink organizations as bundles of capabilities rather than as hierarchies.

- *Effective HR departments manage information:* Our findings about the importance of information to HR success orders the array of discussions about HR analytics, scorecards, dashboards, evidence-based decisions, and so forth into a more business-oriented approach. Managing information is not about HR analytics, but about sourcing information that will help the business better compete. The five steps that describe how to bring external information into the organization offer business and HR leaders specific tools to upgrade information capabilities (see Figure 4.1).

- *Effective HR departments offer integrated HR solutions:* While information capability enables HR departments to add the most value to stakeholders, good things happen when HR work offers integrated solutions, particularly for stakeholders inside the organization. This implies that isolated and independent HR practices should evolve to integrated solutions where HR systems have more impact than HR practices. Instead of hiring for skills A, B, and C; then training for skills D, E, and F; then rewarding skills G, H, and I, integrated solutions combine hiring, training, and paying practices into a systems approach to solving problems.

Our findings indicate that as business and HR leaders consider where to invest for success, organization investments should start getting more attention.

Individual Findings

Chapters 6, 7, and 8 laid out implications for the core drivers for HR competencies (Credible Activist, Strategic Positioner, and Paradox Navigator). Chapters 9 and 10 reviewed the Strategic Enabler and Foundation Enabler competencies. Collectively these chapters offered HR professionals specific insights and tools to be more personally effective and deliver value to stakeholders and the business. In these five chapters on individual HR competencies, certain findings are worth highlighting:

- Navigating paradox is the HR competency that most influences business performance and thus lies at the center of the HR Competency Model illustrated in the all-important Figure 2.3. While the ideas of paradox have been discussed by others, this empirical finding from research in 1,200 businesses pushes paradox navigation to the center of HR (and possibly other) models of effective leadership behavior. As HR professionals navigate organizational paradoxes, they help organizations create the agility required to adapt to changing business conditions.
- The Credible Activist competency continues to give HR professionals access to business conversations. Being a Credible Activist is the ticket of admission for HR professionals, and it is particularly helpful for influencing line managers and employees.
- The Strategic Positioner competency has a major influence on customers and investors. When HR professionals seek to deliver value to these critical external stakeholders, they do so by being Strategic Positioners.
- The role of Culture and Change Champion matters, but today this competence area is particularly seen as a competence of individual HR professionals more than embedded in the HR department's HR practices.
- The Technology and Social Media competency also has business impact, but is seen less as an individual competence and more as an HR department capability.

These insights on the nine HR competence domains should help define, assess, and improve HR professionals.

Now What?

Throughout the book, we have diagnosed the opportunities presented by research and experience and have offered tools, methods, and actions. For example, the organization capability audit presented in Chapter 3 can help determine which capabilities are most critical for business success. The HR department audit in Chapter 5 can help those charged with building HR functional excellence, while the numerous action items under each of the nine HR competencies offer specifics for what HR professionals should be, know, and do to be more effective.

So now in this concluding chapter, we lay out the "Now what?" for the business leaders, senior HR leaders, aspiring HR professionals, and overall HR profession.

The "Now What?" for Business Leaders

We started the book by proposing that *HR is not about HR*. Rather—and most important—HR is about the business. Business leaders are not HR professionals, but business leaders' success requires the insights HR has to offer. We spend about 50 percent of our consulting and training time with business leaders. In these discussions, we encourage business leaders to be effective by doing the following:

- *Create victory through organization:* One of our most startling findings is that the organization is four times as important or influential to business results as the individual people within the HR organization. We believe that this finding within HR also applies to a broader organizational context. Business leaders become organization champions when they pay attention to the organization patterns by working to establish the right culture (e.g., an identity in the mind of the customer made real to employees), encouraging organization capability audits (as described in Chapter 3), talking up the importance of culture and capability, measuring and reporting culture, and helping manage the processes of turning external information into internal action. The HR individual becomes an organization champion by ensuring that the whole organization is better than the individuals within it—that is, that the whole is greater than the sum of the parts.
- *Let HR do HR:* Many business leaders have exceptional talent and organizational instincts, making them great organization champions. But good

HR is not just management by instinct, but rather is a set of research-based insights that lead to rigorously crafted HR practices. As a business leader, don't get lost in or consumed by the details of HR practices, but pay attention to the outcomes of HR: talent (competence and commitment of your workforce), leadership (leadership competencies throughout the organization that deliver value to stakeholders), and organization (capabilities and culture required to win).

- *Demand quality from your HR department:* A 100-plus-year-old company had gone 15 years without a seasoned CHRO. When the CEO recognized this professional gap, he hired an exceptional CHRO. She immediately began to build rigorous HR discipline into talent and organization practices. For example, prior to her arrival, potential leaders would self-select to attend external training programs at top universities. She implemented a talent management system that gave potential leaders an individual development plan that showed how the university program fit into an overall development agenda. She turned high-quality isolated HR practices into integrated HR solutions around talent, leadership, and a performance culture. Business leaders should expect that the HR department has clear goals and outcomes that deliver measureable business value, offer integrated HR solutions to business problems, bring information with impact to business discussions, and operate with exceptional professionalism.

- *Upgrade your HR professionals:* Legacy HR focused primarily on enforcing administrative processes, which did not require much depth and breadth of HR skills. Today, top HR professionals have much the same leadership profile as top business leaders. Business leaders should demand excellence and accountability from their HR professionals. The standards for HR have been precisely defined by this work; the nine HR competencies, and their relative importance in creating value, have become a guide for HR excellence.

- *Be a role model:* By far, the most important HR work a business leader can do is to be a role model for managing talent and organization. When we coach leaders, we remind them of the dangers of leadership hypocrisy, dangers that can create confusion and cynicism. A business leader once said, "I demand that my leaders practice participative management." No! You have to model the participation you expect and lead by example. One of our favorite quotes is from St. Francis of Medici who said: "We preach the gospel and sometimes use words." As a leader, you often judge yourself by your intent, but others judge you by your behaviors and actions. The point: Let your HR leader observe your behavior and guide you on how to lead by example. We found that top leaders in top companies known for leadership spent about 20 percent of their time building leadership (and talent and organization). In meetings and on-site visits, ask talent and organization questions, weave HR insights into your public and private communications, actively participate in HR practices (e.g., be present at training events, be the first to do a "leadership 360," and share your results).

The "Now What?" for Senior HR Leaders

Senior HR leaders become the architects of talent, leadership, and capabilities. As evidenced by our research, they add value to external and internal stakeholders and help deliver business results. We have offered a number of examples of exceptional senior HR leaders who demonstrate the nine competencies we have identified. As we coach CHROs and other senior HR leaders, we offer the following advice:

- *Lead by example*: Just as business leaders are role models, senior HR leaders have to practice what they preach, too. Instead of simply telling other leaders to build staff quality through training, to bring disciplined accountability to performance, and to set and deliver goals—senior HR leaders also have to model good HR. HR for HR increases credibility. HR departments should be iconic examples of hiring, training, rewarding, communicating, and organizing work.
- *Create a powerful HR department through information*: One mega-message of this book is that, across the enterprise, the war for talent should morph to victory through organization. HR departments should be better than the people in them. Our study reinforces the adage that information is power, but we would add that this is true only as long as the information is used

to impact business decisions. Always be ready to show the impact of HR investments on desired business outcomes.

- *Encourage collaboration within HR:* HR professionals within the HR department should learn to work together. There are centrifugal forces pulling HR into subspecialties (e.g., reward experts have their WorldatWork conferences, organization designers have their organization design forums, learning specialists have their Association for Talent Development [formerly ASTD] group, etc.). While deep expertise is helpful in discovering new insights, we found more impact in solving business problems through integrated solutions—for example, talent acquisition, training, and development, and compensation should not be done in siloed vacuums. Senior HR leaders should encourage centripetal forces that combine their specialist and unique insights into shared commitments to solve business problems. Integrated HR solutions matter more than isolated HR practices.

- *Bridge HR with other functions:* Permeable boundaries should exist not only within HR, but across business functions. HR departments need to learn to collaborate with other business groups. By collaborating with the marketing department, HR can access consumer and industry trends and make sure that customer criteria shape culture, leadership brand, and other HR investments. Marketing insights also can help HR build an HR, employer, and employee brand that distinguishes the HR department. Collaborating with the finance department can help manage cash flow (both the revenue and cost side) and creates intangibles that have market value. HR can help shape leadership capital metrics that are of interest to investors. Collaborating with the information technology (IT) department can ensure the seamless flow of external information into internal systems and hence into actions.

The "Now What?" for Aspiring HR Professionals

We have coached and trained tens of thousands of new and seasoned HR professionals. In these sessions, we've offered aspiring HR professionals specific tips that might help them be effective. These guidelines draw on the research presented in this book:

- *Know yourself*: Change and improvement ultimately comes from within. If you don't define your aspirations, someone will define them for you, probably to their advantage, not yours. Figure out your professional passions, interests, and strengths. Don't run up sand dunes by trying to do things that are not comfortable or outside your range of doability. Use the nine-competency model from Figure 2.3 to reflect on your professional identity, skills, and opportunity areas. As you discover your strengths, you will create your personal leadership brand—a brand or style you'll want to be known for by those who interact with you. In part, your brand shows how your strengths can strengthen others. You might observe your personal comfort level with each of the nine competencies; you might also get 360 feedback on how you are doing with them. The RBL group is one source for this 360 feedback.

- *Manage your career*: HR careers may take different paths. You might be an HR specialist (e.g., in compensation, learning, organization development). You might be an HR generalist (e.g., working as an embedded HR professional in business, geography, or functional units). You might move outside of HR for a stint (e.g., being line manager, moving into another function, or doing consulting outside your company). Or you might mix and match these choices. Regardless, we find that the HR competencies we have studied are key to personal effectiveness, serving stakeholders, and delivering business results. Know what you want in your career or others will define it for you.

  Have a career aspiration, but be willing to be opportunistic and flexible. Often opportunities to participate in projects, task forces, or assignments arise. Be willing to take professional risks to grow and learn new competencies, sometimes at work, sometimes outside of work. Stretch yourself to grow. You don't know your limits until you find them.

- *Invest in yourself*: Do HR for your own HR! It's ironic and sad that doctors are often their own worst patients. A lawyer who represents himself has a fool for a client. Ministers' children often lack morals. HR professionals often do not engage in their own HR. HR professionals *too* should invest in personal development. They should seek feedback on skills by doing the HR "360 audit" used to create this study (www.rbl.net). Attend the Advanced HR Executive (AHREP) program at the Michigan Ross School of Management where these ideas translate into action. Block out personal learning time and engage in learning activities that work for you (walking, reading, observing, writing, visiting new places, meditating, resting, etc.). Personal renewal sabbaticals do not have to be extensive commitments but daily routines that allow you to gain perspective and energy.

- *Cultivate networks:* Surround yourself with great people, both inside and outside of work. Networks may be for social support to form relationships, knowledge to gain insight, trust to share personal feelings, and purpose to share values. Building good networks means making and responding to bids from others, celebrating successes of others, serving others with deliberate acts of kindness, being willing and able to apologize and move on, and taking time to be with those who matter most. As they say, "You are the company you keep," these networks become important sources of connection.

  - If you hire people to work for you, seek to hire those better than you. According to multiple studies, simply being in an open network instead of a closed one is the best predictor of career success. In particular, finding networks of mentors who advise and guide you informally can be especially valuable.

- *Develop emotional reserves:* Your emotional well-being often predicts your physical energy and intellectual curiosity. Emotional well-being comes from knowing and being comfortable with who you are, from savoring joy in the daily routines of life, from focusing on what is right more than what is wrong with your life, from envisioning the future and folding it into the present, from being absorbed in the "flow" of an activity, and from living according to one's deepest values.

- *Be curious and "learning agile":* People with a growth mindset believe that they can improve with effort. They outperform those with a fixed mindset, even when they have a lower IQ, because they embrace challenges, treating them as opportunities to learn something new. There are countless successful people who would have never made it if they had succumbed to feelings of helplessness: Walt Disney was fired from the *Kansas City Star* because he "lacked imagination and had no good ideas;" Oprah Winfrey was fired from her job as a TV anchor in Baltimore for being "too emotionally invested in her stories;" Henry Ford had two failed car companies prior to succeeding with Ford; and Steven Spielberg was rejected by USC's Cinematic Arts School multiple times. Imagine what would have happened if any of these people had a fixed mindset. They would have succumbed to the rejection and given up hope. People with a growth mindset don't feel helpless; they know that in order to succeed, they need to be willing to fail hard and then bounce right back.

Your author team has a personal rule of thumb: We should have about 20 to 25 percent new material in our teaching every two and half to three years. This is a high standard for learning agility. As an HR professional this means working outside your comfort zone by taking on assignments that stretch you, observing new ways of doing things, experimenting, continuously improving on what works and does not work, and simply having a mindset for learning.

The "Now What?" for the HR Profession

The HR profession is vibrant and evolving. There are over 1.5 million HR professionals worldwide. The World Federation of People Management Association (WFPMA) has outposts in over 90 countries representing over 600,000 HR professionals. HR leaders are sought after to be on boards of directors. HR compensation often matches and exceeds other staff functions. HR no longer advocates just to "be at the table" of business dialogue, but now delivers real value to these discussions. We hope our research has added to this professionalization of the HR profession.

Principles of Professional Excellence

Our approach to this HR competency research has modeled professional excellence by following four principles that embody the development of the HR profession.

- *Collaboration:* In this round of our research, we partnered with 22 leading HR associations. Through such partnerships we believe we make the overall HR profession better. Many of these associations are building their own HR competency models, but they have now been willing to come together for this foundational research that informs the entire profession.
- *Innovation:* As we have done seven rounds of such HR competency work, we are reminded that we must continue to focus on the future. The future of the HR profession is stronger when we focus less on information that solves puzzles (traditional predictive analytics) than on ideas that shape mysteries (seeking answers to new questions) of what can be done. By aspiring to what *can be*, HR will continue to be vibrant rather than getting mired in tiresome and endless debates about what has been done.
- *Application:* The gap between theory, research, and practice is reduced when the focus is application. Application means that theory starts with a phenomenon and works to find a theoretically robust and replicable solution.[1] Research is not just about statistical elegance, but about getting data that leads to ideas with impact. Practice is not just solving a particular case study or situation, but building principles (theories) that endure. We hope to model this virtuous cycle in our work.
- *Globalization:* We are very pleased to have data from countries around the world (Africa, Asia, Australia, China, India, Japan, Latin America, the Middle East, and North and South America). While generic principles of HR may traverse the globe, HR insights from around the world should be shared. The field of HR is far past the imperialistic days when ideas from one market were imposed on others. As we share globally, we will learn that good HR ideas and practices exist throughout the world that can be shared and replicated.

We hope that our work continues to create an HR profession where personal agendas are put aside for a broader good. Synergies and interdependencies occur as people with differences work together. We envision a profession where new ideas are generated, experiments ensue, and debates occur, but in a broader context of looking forward to make progress. We hope that the HR profession can evolve to a transcendent state so that employees inside an organization and customers, investors, and communities outside are blessed by—and benefit from—good HR work.

A Word About Certification

Professions have standards that typically show up in certifications. Competencies enable certification. Certification has clearly become a major topic for HR associations around the world.

Clearly, certification has different meanings based on career stage. For early HR entrants, certification is like a license validating their ability to practice the craft (like an attorney passing the bar or psychologist being licensed). But the licensing does not ensure quality of the practicing profession. This proficiency certification indicates the quality of HR professionals in being able to do the jobs they are assigned. This certification is being proposed by the Society of Human Resource Managers (SHRM) through situational judgment tests.[*]

Proficiency is also assessed for the professional through granular assessments of which HR competencies apply in which setting (size of company, level of HR, role of HR, experience in HR, business strategy, organization culture, etc.). National Human Resource Development Network (NHRDN) in India has developed competency work that will lead to an Indian national

---

[*] Situational judgment tests are elegantly summarized as a way to ascribe confidence in individuals being able to do specific jobs: Michael Campion, Robert Ployhart, and William MacKenzie, Jr., "The State of Research on Situational Judgment Tests: A Content Analysis and Directions for Future Research," *Human Performance* 27, no. 4, 283–310. SHRM is adapting the situational judgment methodology from selecting someone for a job to defining someone's overall competence.

HR competency model (HRSCAPE) with eight functional competencies at four levels (basic, competent, advanced, expert). At the mastery level, HR competencies define someone who is a "Fellow" or truly advanced in his or her career. Australian Human Resources Institute's (AHRI) work differentiates competencies by career level and validates competency master for very seasoned and senior HR leaders.

The answer to the appropriate question, "What do I have to be, know, and do to be an effective HR professional?" is much more than asking HR professionals what they think. It requires partnership of HR professional associations around the world, focusing on outcomes of HR skills, aligning competencies to current and future business conditions, tailoring competencies to specific situations, and identifying the competencies that matter most for stakeholder and business performance.

Now What? The Conclusion

In 1987 when we started our HR competency research, we envisioned a single cross-sectional study of what makes HR professionals effective. Seven rounds and 30 years later we realize that our aspiration to help HR add value is not an event, but a long-term process.

This seventh round of data collection is by far the most complex to date. In *Victory Through Organization*, we have touched on about 30 to 40 percent of what this current research shows. We have much more refined data on how HR organizations are effective based on organization capabilities, business strategy, organization culture, and skills of HR professionals. In the ensuing months, we hope to ferret out this more granular data to further inform on how HR delivers value.

But our aspiration remains the same. We want to inform and inspire HR professionals and HR departments to live up to their potential. Never forget that HR is not about HR, but about delivering real value to the business.

NOTES

Chapter 2

1. The following books report on our prior studies:

   Dave Ulrich, Bill Schiemann, and Libby Sartain (editors). 2015. *The Rise of HR: Wisdom from 73 Thought Leaders*. E-book distributed by Human Resource Certification Institute (HRCI).

   Dave Ulrich, Jon Younger, Wayne Brockbank, and Michael Ulrich. 2012. *HR from the Outside In: Six Competencies for the Future of Human Resources*. McGraw-Hill Publishing Company.

   Dave Ulrich, Wayne Brockbank, Jon Younger, and Michael Ulrich. 2012. *Global HR Competencies: Mastering Competitive Value from the Outside In*. McGraw-Hill Publishing Company.

   Dave Ulrich, Justin Allen, Wayne Brockbank, Jon Younger, and Mark Nyman. 2009. *HR Transformation: Building Human Resources from the Outside In*. McGraw-Hill Publishing Company.

   Dave Ulrich, Wayne Brockbank, Dani Johnson, Kurt Sandholtz, and Jon Younger. 2008. *HR Competencies: Mastery at the Intersection of People and Business*. Society for Human Resource Management (SHRM).

   Dave Ulrich and Wayne Brockbank. 2005. *The HR Value Proposition*. McGraw-Hill Publishing Company.

2. The following books outline our prior work in this area:

   Patrick Wright, Dave Ulrich, Elizabeth Sartain, Richard Antoine (editors). 2016. *View from the Top: Leveraging Human and Organization Capital to Deliver Value*. Washington, DC: SHRM.

   Dave Ulrich, Jon Younger, Wayne Brockbank, and Michael Ulrich. 2012. *HR from the Outside In: Six Competencies for the Future of Human Resources*. McGraw-Hill Publishing Company.

   Dave Ulrich, Wayne Brockbank, Jon Younger, and Michael Ulrich. 2012. *Global HR Competencies: Mastering Competitive Value from the Outside In*. McGraw-Hill Publishing Company.

   Dave Ulrich, Justin Allen, Wayne Brockbank, Jon Younger, and Mark Nyman. 2009. *HR Transformation: Building Human Resources from the Outside In*. McGraw-Hill Publishing Company.

Dave Ulrich, Wayne Brockbank, Dani Johnson, Kurt Sandholtz, and Jon Younger. 2008. *HR Competencies: Mastery at the Intersection of People and Business.* SHRM.

John Storey, Patrick Wright, and Dave Ulrich. 2008. *The Routledge Companion to Strategic Human Resource Management.* Routledge.

Dave Ulrich and Wayne Brockbank. 2005. *The HR Value Proposition.* McGraw-Hill Publishing Company.

Mike Losey, Sue Meisinger, and Dave Ulrich. 2005. *The Future of Human Resource Management: 64 Thought Leaders Explore the Critical HR Issues for Today and Tomorrow.* New York: Wiley.

Edward Lawler, Dave Ulrich, Jac Fitzenz, James Madden, and Regina Marcua. 2004. *Human Resources Business Process Outsourcing: Transforming How HR Work Gets Done.* San Francisco: Jossey-Bass.

Brian Becker, Mark Huselid, and Dave Ulrich. 2001. *The HR Scorecard: Linking People, Strategy, and Performance.* Boston: Harvard Business Press.

Dave Ulrich. 1998. *Delivering Results: A New Mandate for Human Resources Professionals.* Boston: Harvard Business Press.

Dave Ulrich. 1997. *Human Resource Champions: The Next Agenda for Adding Value and Delivering Results.* Cambridge, MA: Harvard Business Press.

3. The summary of HR competencies is in Dave Ulrich, Wayne Brockbank, Mike Ulrich, and Dave Kryscynski, 2015, "Toward a Synthesis of HR Competency Models: The Common HR 'Food Groups' or Domains," *People and Strategy,* Fall, Vol. 4, 56–65.

4. For more information about the same, contact the authors.

5. We want to make a brief comment on the statistics we use for these (and other) allocated points. We did correlations among the nine HR competence domains and personal effectiveness and among the nine domains. These correlations were all highly correlated (0.63 to 0.83). We also did regression of the nine domains on the performance outcome, which showed that whichever domain was entered first into the equation predicted much of the outcome. To solve this statistics problem (all nine domains matter and whichever is considered first matters most), we discovered and used regression decomposition techniques as advocated by leading statisticians. These techniques partition the percent of the outcome explained by each of the independent variables. We used this decomposition methodology in all of our regressions to accurately reflect the relevant impact of independent variables (HR competence domains

and HR work activities) on outcomes (individual performance, stakeholders, and business outcomes).

Genizi, A. 1993. "Decomposition of R^2 in Multiple Regression with Correlated Regressors," *Statistica Sinica* Vol. 3, 407–420.

K. F. Nimon, and F. L. Oswald. 2013. "Understanding the Results of Multiple Linear Regression Beyond Standardized Regression Coefficients," *Organizational Research Methods.*

Chapter 3

1. N. Smallwood and D. Ulrich. (2004). "Capitalizing on Capabilities." *Harvard Business Review.* June. Accessed from https://hbr.org/2004/06/capitalizing-on-capabilities on August 27, 2016.

2. http://grantspace.org/tools/knowledge-base/Funding-Research/Statistics/number-of-nonprofits-in-the-u.s. Accessed May 21, 2016.

3. "Religion: Gallup Historical Trends." www.gallup.com. Gallup, Inc. Accessed August 25, 2015.

4. N. Houthoofd and J. Hendrick. (2012). Industry Segment Effects and Firm Effects on Firm Performance in Single Industry Firms. HUB research paper 2012/17. Maart.

5. G. S. Hansen and B. Wernerfelt. (1989). "Determinants of Firm Performance: The Relative Importance of Economic and Organizational Factors," *Strategic Management Journal*, Vol. 10, No. 5, 399–411.

6. Adam Smith. *An Inquiry into the Nature and Causes of the Wealth of Nations.* Edwin Cannan, ed. (1904.) Library of Economics and Liberty. Retrieved May 21, 2016, from the World Wide Web: www.econlib.org/library/Smith/smWN.html.

7. E. W. Oliver. (1981). "The Economics of Organization: The Transaction Cost Approach." *The American Journal of Sociology,* vol. 87, no. 3, 548–577.

8. E. Ennen and A. Richter. (2010). "The Whole Is More Than the Sum of Its Parts—Or Is It? A Review of the Empirical Literature on Complementarities in Organizations." *Journal of Management*, vol. 36, no. 1, 207–233.

9. N. Jerome (2013). "Application of Maslow's Hierarchy of Needs Theory: Impact and Implications for Organizational Culture, Human Resource, and Employee Performance," *International Journal of Business and Management Invention*, Vol. 2, no. 31, 39–45.

10. D. Ulrich and W. Ulrich (2010). *The Why of Work*. New York: McGraw-Hill Publishing Company.

11. M. Gladwell (2008). *Outliers*. New York: Little, Brown and Company.

12. E. Michaels, H. Handfield-Jones, and B. Axelrod. (2001). *The War for Talent*. Boston: Harvard Business Press.

13. T. Chamorro-Premuzic (November 16, 2012). "Dark Side of Charisma," Boston: *Harvard Business Review*.

14. M. Gladwell (2009). *What the Dog Saw*. New York: Little, Brown, and Company.

15. G. S. Becker (1994). *Human Capital: A Theoretical and Empirical Analysis with Special Reference to Education*, 3d edition. Chicago: The University of Chicago Press.

16. B. Groysberg, L. Lee and A. Nanda (2008). "Can They Take It with Them? The Portability of Star Knowledge Workers' Performance," *Management Science*, Vol. 54, No. 7, 1213–1230.

17. B. Groysberg (2010). *Chasing Stars: The Myth of Talent and the Portability of Performance*. Princeton, NJ: Princeton University Press.

18. D. Ulrich and W. Ulrich (2010). Talent requires teamwork. Accessed from RBL.net.

19. P. R. Lawrence and J. W. Lorsch (1967). *Organization and Environment*. Boston: Harvard Business School, Division of Research.

20. J. R. Galbraith (1977). *Organization Design*. Reading, MA: Addison-Wesley.

21. M. E. Porter (1985). *Competitive Advantage*. New York: Free Press.

22. E. Schein (1992). *Organizational Culture and Leadership: A Dynamic View*. San Francisco: Jossey-Bass.

23. T. J. Peters and R. H. Waterman (1982). *In Search of Excellence*. New York: Harper Collins.

24. L. Gryger, R. Saar and P. Schaar (2010). Building Organizational Capabilities. Accessed May 14, 2016. http://www.mckinsey.com/business-functions/organization/our-insights/building-organizational-capabilities-mckinsey-global-survey-results.

25. C. K. Prahalad and G. Hamel (1990). "The Core Competence of the Corporation," *Harvard Business Review*. May-June.

26. G. Saloner, A. Shepard and J. Podolny (2005). *Strategic Management*. New York: John Wiley & Sons.

27. N. Smallwood and D. Ulrich (2004). "Capitalizing on Capabilities," *Harvard Business Review.* June.

28. C. A. Hartnell, A. Y. Ou and A. Kinicki (2011). "Organizational Culture and Organizational Effectiveness: A Meta-Analytical Investigation of the Competing Values Framework's Theoretical Suppositions," *Journal of Applied Psychology*, Vol. 96, No. 4, 677–694.

29. C. A. O'Reilly, D. F. Caldwell, J. A. Chatman and B. Doerr (2014). "The Promise and Problems of Organizational Culture: CEO Personality, Culture, and Firm Performance," *Group & Organization Management*, Vol. 39, no. 6, 595–625.

30. A. L. Kroeber and C. Kluckhohn (1952). *Culture: A Critical Review of Concepts and Definitions.* New York: Vintage Books.

31. L. Richardson (2016). Customer complaints and increasing business: How Disney World hugged this hater. *Influitive.* Accessed May 30 from http://influitive.com/blog/customer-complaints-and-increasing-business-how-disney-world-hugged-this-hater/.

32. D. Ulrich and W. Brockbank (2005). *The HR Value Proposition.* Boston Harvard Business Press.

33. M. A. Huselid (1995). "The Impact of Human Resource Management Practices on Turnover, Productivity, and Corporate Financial Performance," *Academy of Management Journal*, Vol. 38, no. 3, 635–672.

34. The content audit is informed by the Organization Capability Audit from the RBL Group. Accessed from http://rbl.net/index.php/products/product/organizational-capabilities-audit on June 2, 2017.

Chapter 4

1. These four categories were constructed based on factor analysis. The full description of these factor analyses are available from the authors. The items that constitute each factor were then averaged to generate the scores for each HR Department Activity. The full list of items that comprise each HR department activity are provided in subsequent sections of this chapter and in Chapter 5.

2. D. Tapscott and A. Williams. (2008). *Wikinomics: How Mass Collaboration Changes Everything.* London: Penguin.

3. K. Leboeuf (2016). 2016 Updated: What Happens in One Internet Minute. Excelacom. Accessed on June 18, 2016, at http://www.excelacom.com/resources/blog/2016-update-what-happens-in-one-internet-minute.

4. www.internetlivestats.com/internet-users. Accessed June 14, 2016.

5. D. Castro and A. McQuinn. (2015). Cross-Border Data Flows Enable Growth in All Industries. Information Technology and Innovation Foundation. February.

6. McKinsey, 2016.

7. http://www.businessinsider.com/uber-doubles-its-drivers-in-2015-2015-10. Accessed June 15, 2016.

8. http://www.linuxmovies.org/2011/06/linux-movies-hollywood-loves-linux/ Accessed June 12, 2016.

9. http://www.koreaninsight.com/tag/ok-cashbag/ Accessed June 13, 2016.

10. Mckinsey, 2016.

11. A. Gildman (2014). The World's Top eBay Sellers. Web retailer.

12. https://www.tripadvisor.com/PressCenter-c4-Fact_Sheet.html. Accessed June 20, 2016.

13. https://issuu.com/eas-estonia/docs/lie_spring_2016_issuu/36. Accessed June 22, 2016.

14. Mckinsey, 2015.

15. *The Economists* (2016). June 18. p. 38.

16. Accenture & GE. (2014). Industrial Internet Insights Reports for 2015. Accessed on June 26, 2016, https://www.accenture.com/ae-en/_acnmedia/ Accenture/next-gen/reassembling-industry/pdf/Accenture-Industrial-Internet-Changing-Competitive-Landscape-Industries.pdf.

17. M. Gladwell (2009). *What the Dog Saw*. New York: Little, Brown and Company.

18. J. Younger and N. Smallwood. (2016). *Agile Talent: How to Source and Manage Outside Experts*. Boston, MA: Harvard Business Press.

19. W. G. Castellano (2014). *Practices for Engaging the 21st Century Workforce*. Upper Saddle River, New Jersey: Pearson Education.

20. J. J. Foss, T. Pedersen, M. R. Fosgaard, and D. Stea. (2015). "Why Complementary HRM Practices Impact Performance: The Case of Rewards, Job Design, and Work Climate in a Knowledge-Sharing Context," *Human Resource Management*, Vol. 54, No. 6, 955–976.

21. A. A. Katou, P. S. Budhwar, and C. Patel. (2014). "Content vs. Process in the HRM-Performance Relationship: An Empirical Examination," *Human Resource Management*, Vol. 53, No. 4, 527, 544.

22. K. Sanders, H. Shipton, and J. F. S. Gomes. (2014). "Is the HRM Process Important? Past, Current, and Future Challenges," *Human Resource Management*, Vol. 53, No. 4, 489–503.

23. B. S. Klass, M. Semadeni, M. Klimchak, and A. Ward. (2012). "High-Performance Work System Implementation in Small and Medium Enterprises: A Knowledge-Creation Perspective," *Human Resource Management*, Vol. 51, No. 4, 487–510.

24. T. R. Brook, S.Y. Todd, J. G. Combs, D. J. Woehr, and D. J. Detchen. (2011). "Does Human Capital Matter? A Meta-Analysis of the Relationship Between Human Capital and Firm Performance," *Journal of Applied Psychology*, Vol. 96, No. 3, 443–456.

25. J. G. Messersmith, P. D. Patel, D. P. Lepak, and J. S. Gould-Williams. (2011). "Unlocking the Black Box: Exploring the Link Between High-Performance Work Systems and Performance," *Journal of Applied Psychology*, Vol. 6, No. 6, 1105–1118.

26. R. Schmelter, R. Mauer, C. Börsch, and M. Brettel (2010). "Boosting Corporate Entrepreneurship Through HRM Practices, Evidence from German SMEs," *Human Resource Management*, Vol. 49, No. 4., 715–741.

27. J. Kaifeng, D. P. Lepak, J. Jia, and J. C. Baer. (2012). "How Does Human Resource Management Influence Organizational Outcomes? A Meta-Analytical Investigation of Mediating Mechanisms," *Academy of Management Journal*, Vol. 55, No. 6, 1264–1294.

28. C. Chuang, and H. Liao (2010). "Strategic Human Resource Management in Service Context: Taking Care of Business by Taking Care of Employees and Customers," *Personnel Psychology*, Vol. 63, 153–196.

29. M. A. Huselid (1995). "The Impact of Human Resource Management Practices on Turnover, Productivity, and Corporate Financial Performance," *Academy of Management Journal*, Vol. 38, 635–672.

30. P. Tamkin, M. Cowling, and W. Hunt. (2008). "People and the Bottom Line," Institute for Employment Studies. University of Sussex, Brighton.

Chapter 5

1. E. O'Boyle Jr., and H. Aguinis, "The Best and the Rest: Revisiting the Norm of Normality of Individual Performance," *Personnel Psychology* 65, no. 1 (2012): 79–119.

2. H. Aguinis and E. Boyle Jr., "Star Performers in the Twenty-First Century Organization," *Personnel Psychology* 67, no. 2 (2014): 313–350.

3. R. R. Kehoe, D. P. Lepak, and F. S. Bentley, "Let's Call a Star a Star: Task Performance, External Status and Exceptional Contributors in Organizations," *Journal of Management* (2016), accessed on June 27, 2016, at http://jom.sagepub.com/content/early/2016/02/01/0149206316628644 .abstract.

4. S. E. Scullen, M. K. Mount, and M. Goff, "Understanding the Latent Structure of Job Performance Ratings," *Journal of Applied Psychology* 85, no. 6 (2000): 956–970.

5. J. Pfeffer, "Low Grades for Performance Reviews," *BusinessWeek* (August 3, 2009): 68.

6. W. Woodward, Annual Performance Reviews: Lose–Lose? (2016), accessed June 23, 2016 http://www.foxbusiness.com/features/2016/02/11/annual-performance-reviews-lose-lose.html.

7. M. Buckingham and A. Goodall, "Reinventing Performance Management," *Harvard Business Review* (April 2016): 40–48.

8. Steve Kerr, *Reward Systems. Does Yours Measure Up?* (Boston, MA: Harvard Business Press, 2009).

9. B. Bill, "Neither Rigged nor Fair," *The Economist* (June 25, 2016): 16–18.

10. W. J. Rothwell and H. C. Kazanas, *Improving On-the-Job Training*, 2d edition (Hoboken, NJ: John Wiley & Sons, 2004).
    M. Alipour, M. Salehi, and A. Shahnavaz, "A Study of On-the-Job Training Effectiveness," *International Journal of Business and Management* 4, no. 11 (2009): 63–68.

11. D. Bean, R. Musson, and C. Li, "WeOrg: the freedom to choose," last modified 2011, accessed June 30, 2016, http://www.managementexchange.com/story/we-org.

12. Eddy, James, Hall, Stephen J. D., Robinson, Stephen R., "How global organizations develop local talent," *McKinsey Quarterly* (April 8, 2012).

13. J. Fitz-enz and J. R. Mattox, *Predictive Analytics for Human Resources* (Hoboken, NJ: John Wiley & Sons, 2014). J. Fitz-enz, G. Pease, and B. Byerly, *Human Capital Analytics* (Hoboken, NJ: John Wiley & Sons, 2012).

14. E. E. Lawler and J. W. Boudreau, *Global Trends in Human Resource Management: A Twenty-Year Analysis* (Stanford, CA: Stanford Business Books, 2015).

15. D. Ulrich, "Measuring Human Resources: An Overview of Practices and Prescription for Results," *Human Resource Management* 36, (1997): 303–320.

16. B. E. Becker, M. A. Huselid, and D. Ulrich, *The HR Scorecard: Linking People, Strategy and Performance* (Boston, MA: Harvard Business School Press, 2001).

17. M. A. Huselid, R. W. Beatty, and B. E. Becker, "'A Players' or 'A Positions'? The Strategic Logic of Workforce Management," *Harvard*

Business Review (December 2005), accessed on July 3, 2016, https://hbr.org/2005/12/a-players-or-a-positions-the-strategic-logic-of-work-force-management.

18. R. W. Beatty, "HR Analytics and Metrics: Scoring on the Business Scorecard," in *The Rise of HR*, edited by D. Ulrich, W. A. Schiemann, and L. Sartain (Alexandria, VA: HR Certification Institute, 2015).

19. T. Davenport, J. Harris, and J. Shapiro, "Competing on Talent Analytics," *Harvard Business Review* (October 2010), accessed on July 3, 2016, http://www.harvardbusiness.org/sites/default/files/HBR_Competing_on_Talent_Analytics.pdf.

20. D. Ulrich, N. Smallwood, and K. Sweetman, *The Leadership Code: Five Rules to Lead By* (Boston, MA: Harvard Business Press, 2008).

Chapter 7

1. D. Ulrich, *The leadership capital index: Realizing the market value of leadership* (2015), accessed February 3, 2017. https://books.google.com/books?hl=en&lr=&id=6ZBzCQAAQBAJ&oi=fnd&pg=PP1&dq=leadership+capital+index&ots=-saaWbynga&sig=c5s-XadfyKTRXz1WAE9Mrt_jRtM.

2. D. Ulrich and N. Smallwood, *Why the bottom line isn't!: How to build value through people and organization* (2003), accessed December 28, 2016. https://books.google.com/books?hl=en&lr=&id=hL69unT1EZkC&oi=fnd&pg=PR7&dq=why+the+bottom+line+isn%27t&ots=akdATIR2h_&sig=Uu8Qdk9D53mq7MKX1Luv6HAZESI.

3. Many frameworks exist for assessing risk. An alternative framework to that proposed by COSO comes from work by Bob Kaplan and his colleagues around the balanced scorecard. They propose three types of risk: employee, strategy, and external. The same logic we apply to the COSO framework could be applied to these risk types.

   Robert. S. Kaplan, "Risk Management and the Strategy Execution System," *Balanced Scorecard Report* (November–December 2009).

   Robert S. Kaplan and Anette Mikes, "Managing the Multiple Dimensions of Risk," *Balanced Scorecard Report* (July–August 2011).

   Robert S. Kaplan and Anette Mikes, "Managing the Multiple Dimensions of Risk, *Balanced Scorecard Report* (September–October 2011).

   Ulrich, D., & Smallwood, N. 2003. *Why the bottom line isn't!: How to build value through people and organization.* https://books.google.com/books?

hl=en&lr=&id=hL69unT1EZkC&oi=fnd&pg=PR7&dq=why+the+botto
m+line+isn%27t&ots=akdATIR2h_&sig=Uu8Qdk9D53mq7MKX1Luv6
HAZESI, December 28, 2016.

Chapter 8

1. Yan Zhang, David Waldman, Yu-Lan Han, and Xiao–Bei Li,
   "Paradoxical Leader Behaviors in People Management: Antecedents
   and Consequences," *Academic of Management Journal* 58, no. 2 (2015):
   538–566.

   T. Fang, "Asian Management Research Needs More Self-Confidence:
   Reflection on Hofstede (2007) and Beyond," *Asia Pacific Journal of
   Management* 27 (2010): 155–170.

   T. Fang, "Yin Yang: A New Perspective on Culture," *Management and
   Organization Review* 8 (2010): 25–50.

2. Howard V. Hong and Edna H. Hong, eds., *Kierkegaard's Writings, VII:
   Philosophical Fragments* (Princeton, NJ: Princeton University Press,
   1985): 37.

3. There is a great summary of paradox literature in:
   Nathalie Guilmot and Ina Ehnert, *27 Years of Research on Organization
   Paradox and Coping Strategies: A Review* (Association of International
   Management Strategy (AIMS) conference).

   Some of the management thinkers about paradox include:

   S. R. Clegg, J. V. Cuhna, and M. P. Cuhna, "Management Paradoxes:
   A Relational View, *Human Relations* 55 (2002): 483–503.

   P. A. L. Evans, "The Dualistic Leader: Thriving on Paradox," in S.
   Chowdhury (ed.), *Management 21C: New Visions for the New Millennium*
   (NewYork, NY/London, UK: Prentice Hall/Financial Times, 2000):
   66–82.

   A. H. Van de Ven and M. S. Poole, "Paradoxical Requirements for a
   Theory of Organizational Change," in R. Quinn and K. Cameron (eds.),
   *Paradox and Transformation: Toward a Theory of Change in Organization
   and Management* (New York: HarperCollins, 1988): 19–80.

   R. E. Quinn and K. S. Cameron, *Paradox and Transformation: Toward
   a Theory of Change in Organization and Management* (Cambridge, MA:
   Ballinger, 1998).

   M.-J. Chen, "Transcending Paradox: The Chinese Middle Way
   Perspective," *Asia Pacific Journal of Management,* 19 (2002): 179–199.

4. Barry Johnson, *A Perspective on Paradox and Its Application to Modern Management.* Polarity Partnerships, LLC, 2109 J Street, Suite 301, Sacramento, CA 95816, USA. E-mail: barry@polaritypartnerships.com.

5. Kim Cameron, "Effectiveness as Paradox: Consensus and Conflict in Conceptions of Organizational Effectiveness," *Management Science* 32 (1986), 539–553.

   Robert E. Quinn and Kim S. Cameron, *Paradox and Transformation: Toward a Theory of Change in Organization and Management* (Cambridge, MA: Ballinger, 1988).

   Robert E. Quinn, *Deep Change—Discovering the Leader Within.* San Francisco: Jossey Bass, 1996.

6. Marianne Lewis, "Exploring Paradox: Toward a More Comprehensive Guide," *Academy of Management Review* 25 (2000): 760–776.

7. Wendy Smith and M. Lewis, "Toward a Theory of Paradox: A Dynamic Equilibrium Model of Organizations," *Academy of Management Review* 36 (2011): 381–403.

   Wendy K. Smith, "Dynamic Decision Making: A Model of Senior Leaders Managing Strategic Paradoxes," *Academy of Management Journal,* 57, no. 4 (2014): 1592–1623.

8. Yan Zhang, David Waldman, Yu-Lan Han, and Xiao-Bei Li, "Paradoxical Leader Behaviors in People Management: Antecedents and Consequences," *Academic of Management Journal* 58, no. 2 (2015): 538–566.

9. Jean Britton Leslie, Peter Ping Li, and Sophia Zhao, *Managing Paradox: Blending East and West Philosophies to Unlock Its Advantages and Disadvantages* (white paper, Center for Creating Leadership), sourced at: http://insights.ccl.org/articles/leading-effectively-articles/manage-paradox-for-better-performance/.

10. O. Gottschalg and Z Ollo, "Interest Alignment and Competitive Advantage", *Academy of Management Review,* (2007): Vol 32 (2), pp. 418–437.

Chapter 9

1. Dave Ulrich and Wayne Brockbank, "Creating a Winning Culture from the Outside In," *HBR Blog* (2016).

   Dave Ulrich and Wayne Brockbank, "Take Culture to New Heights," *Workforce Magazine* (May–June 2016): 26–29.

Wayne Brockbank and Dave Ulrich, "The Why, What, and How of Culture: Replacing the War for Talent with Victory Through Organization," *Talent Quarterly* (2016).

Dave Ulrich, Dale Lake, Jon Younger, and Wayne Brockbank, "Change Insights and HR Implications," *NHRD Publication* (2012).

Dave Ulrich, Todd Jick, and Steve Kerr, *The GE Workout: How to Implement GE's Revolutionary Method for Busting Bureaucracy and Attacking Organization Problems* (New York: McGraw-Hill Publishing Company, 2002).

2. For a summary of strategic planning thought leaders and their approach to strategy and culture see

    Dave Ulrich, *Leadership Capital Index: Realizing the Market Value of Leadership* (San Francisco: Berrett Kohler, 2015).

3. Dave Ulrich, Jon Younger, Wayne Brockbank, and Michael Ulrich, *HR from the Outside In: Six Competencies for the Future of Human Resources* (McGraw-Hill Publishing Company, 2012).

4. Dave Ulrich, "The Value of Values," *Your Workplace* 16, no. 5 (2014): 30–31.

5. Dave Ulrich, *Leadership Capital: Realizing the Market Value of Leadership* (Oakland, CA: Berrett Kohler, 2015).

6. Dave Ulrich, "Resolving Performance Management Paradox Through Positive Performance Accountabilty," *Talent Quarterly* (2016).

7. William Schiemann and Dave Ulrich, "Rise of HR—New Mandates for I/O Psychology," *Industrial and Organizational Psychology: Perspectives on Science and Practice* 10, no. 1 (2016).

8. There are wonderful lists of nonfinancial rewards.

    Bob Nelson, *1501 Ways to Reward Employees* (Workman Publishing Company, 2012).

    Bob Nelson and Barton Morris, *1001 Ways to Energize Employees* (Workman Publishing Company, 1997).

9. D. Ulrich and W. Ulrich, *The Why of Work* (McGraw-Hill Publishing Company, 2011).

Chapter 10

1. Dave Ulrich, *Human Resource Champions* (Boston: Harvard Business Press, 1996).

2. Robert S. Kaplan and David P. Norton, *The Balanced Scorecard, Translating Strategy into Action* (Harvard Business Press, 1996): 30–32, 148–150.

   Robert Kaplan and David P. Norton, *Strategy Maps, Converting Intangible Assets into Tangible Outcomes* (Harvard Business School Publishing, 2004).

3. A. M. Kaplan and M. Haenlein, "Users of the World, Unite! The Challenges and Opportunities of Social Media," *Business Horizons* 53, no.1 (2010): 59–68.

4. https://leveragenewagemedia.com/blog/social-media-infographic/.

5. Maxim Wolf, Julian Sims, and Huadong Yang, "The Role of Social Media in Human Resource Management," UK Academy for Information Systems Conference Proceedings 2014, Paper 30, http://aisel.aisnet.org/ukais2014/3.

6. Alfred Walker, *Human Resources Information Systems* (Van Nostrand Reinhold Company, 1982).

   Alfred Walker, *Handbook of Human Resource Information Systems: Reshaping the Human Resource Function with Technology* (New York: McGraw-Hill Publishing Company, 1992).

   Alfred Walker (ed.), *Web-Based Human Resources* (New York: McGraw-Hill Publishing Company, 2001).

7. http://www.forbes.com/sites/jeannemeister/2014/01/06/2014-the-year-social-hr-matters/#335c4c9a62dc.

8. http://www.forbes.com/sites/jeannemeister/2014/01/06/2014-the-year-social-hr-matters/2/#7bf009a02a6d.

9. https://www.accenture.com/us-en/insight-outlook-how-collaboration-technologies-are-improving-process-workforce-business.

10. Brian Lonsway, *Making Leisure Work: Architecture and the Experience Economy* (London: Routledge, 2009).

11. http://www.gensler.com/2016-design-forecast-lifestyle.

12. Joseph Pine and James Gilmore, *The Experience Economy* (Boston: Harvard Business School Press, 1999).

13. http://www.careerarc.com/blog/2015/06/38-percent-of-employees-who-were-let-go-share-negative-views-of-employers-new-careerarc-employer-branding-study/.

14. http://www.cipd.co.uk/binaries/social-technology-social-business_2013.pdf.

15. https://www.weforum.org/reports/the-future-of-jobs.

16. See article Peter Daisyme, "Top 20 Social-Media Tools to Add to Your Arsenal in 2016," Entrepreneur.com, sourced at https://www.entrepreneur .com/article/254712.

Chapter 11

1. David Kryscynski and Dave Ulrich, "Making Strategic Human Capital Relevant: A Time-Sensitive Opportunity," *Academy of Management Perspective* 29, no. 3 (2015): 357–369. Awarded best article of the year by Academy of Management.

INDEX

Note: An *f* follows page numbers referencing figures; a *t*, tables; an *n*, footnotes.